Nimo's War, Emma's War

Nimo's War, Emma's War

Making Feminist Sense of the Iraq War

Cynthia Enloe

UNIVERSITY OF CALIFORNIA PRESS

Berkeley   Los Angeles   London

University of California Press, one of the most distinguished
university presses in the United States, enriches lives around
the world by advancing scholarship in the humanities, social
sciences, and natural sciences. Its activities are supported by
the UC Press Foundation and by philanthropic contributions
from individuals and institutions. For more information, visit
www.ucpress.edu.

University of California Press
Berkeley and Los Angeles, California

University of California Press, Ltd.
London, England

Library of Congress Cataloging-in-Publication Data

Enloe, Cynthia H., 1938–
   Nimo's war, Emma's war : making feminist sense of the Iraq
War / Cynthia Enloe.
      p.   cm.
   Includes bibliographical references and index.
   ISBN 978-0-520-26077-1 (cloth : alk. paper)
   ISBN 978-0-520-26078-8 (pbk. : alk. paper)
   1. Women and war—Iraq.   2. Women soldiers—Iraq.
3. Women—Iraq.   4. Iraq War, 2003–   I. Title.

HQ1233.E553   2010
956.7044'3082—dc22   2010001809

Manufactured in the United States of America

19   18   17   16   15   14   13   12   11   10
10   9   8   7   6   5   4   3   2   1

This book is printed on Cascades Enviro 100, a 100% post
consumer waste, recycled, de-inked fiber. FSC recycled
certified and processed chlorine free. It is acid free, Ecologo
certified, and manufactured by BioGas energy.

In memory of
Judy Wachs
1938–2008

CONTENTS

about how crafting a feminist curiosity might make the Iraq War—its causes, its twists and turns, and its consequences—more understandable. Having a feminist curiosity entails questioning allegedly "natural" dynamics between women and men, as well as delving into what women do and what they think.

In Maryland, a woman in her thirties came up after a talk, waited until most people had left, and then whispered her story. She told of having been abused by her soldier/husband and then, when she reported the abuse, having been brushed off by his commander. He had warned her that if she brought charges against her husband, she would likely lose her military base housing. At another event, this time in Boston, no one in the audience knew anyone deployed to Iraq. Still, one young woman made the connection between Iraqi women's experiences of war and the experiences of women in northern Uganda with whom she had worked. At another Boston college, students and faculty listened carefully as an older male student, a military veteran, described how, while he was stationed in South Korea, he had seen the workings of racially stratified prostitution around a U.S. military base.

In Kentucky, a young woman told all of us in the crowded room that her younger brother, soon to be deployed on his first tour to Iraq, enlisted largely because he so admired their grandfather, who for years had told heartening stories of his own wartime soldiering. In Montana, a young woman lined up at the microphone in the aisle in order to voice her anger—"and my mom would be furious too if she were here"—at what she heard as the implication that any American soldier who had died in the Iraq War had died for anything less than a worthy cause. "My brother died in Iraq." All of us, her hundreds of listeners, stayed very still.

This book began as talks to diverse audiences. In fact, I didn't think I was writing a book. I was just trying to find a way to make the complex wartime lives of Iraqi women as real as those of American women. Narratives—telling stories—seemed to help. It made it harder for listeners to deny that Iraqi women had their own histories, their own feelings and dilemmas, their own organizing strategies. Stories made it somewhat more comprehensible that there was no such thing as monolithic "Muslim women" or "Middle Eastern women." I began with Nimo in her Baghdad beauty parlor. Nimo's story—or

PREFACE

I keep thinking about the young woman in the bright pink cap. A young African American woman, she was about my height, five feet two, wearing jeans and a spangly T-shirt. She was sitting in the front row. During the event's discussion time she spoke up. She had a good, strong voice. People in the back of the college's large auditorium said they could hear her clearly. They were listening attentively as she described the pressure put on soldiers in her unit when they returned from their duty in Iraq, pressure to absorb privately whatever lingering questions or disturbing memories they had brought home with them. She said that perhaps especially the men in her group internalized their superiors' expectation that they would not admit to needing mental health counseling. After the event, she lingered and we continued our conversation. She would be graduating from the college that spring. With only one more year left on her army contract, she was looking forward to getting out of the military. She was worried, though, that she soon might be sent overseas again, maybe this time to Afghanistan. "I know they need me. I'm a sniper."

This exchange was in South Carolina in March 2009. It was another in what had become an ongoing series of mind-opening conversations I had had ever since I began being invited to speak to college and community groups

ILLUSTRATIONS

the little of it that I knew—underscored for me the feminist discovery that paying serious attention to any woman's life can make us smarter about war and about militarism.

Nimo's wartime story could also remind us that women live their lives in particular spaces, and that one has to go to surprising places—for instance, a beauty parlor—to investigate any war's gendered dynamics. Initially, I teamed up Nimo with Kim. She was the young American woman in San Francisco married to a National Guard soldier. Paying attention to Kim could reveal how much strategists in this war—and any war—depended on certain women to play certain roles in order to carry out their state's war-waging operations. Still, I didn't want Kim to feel any more "real" to audiences than Nimo. This proved a challenge in early twenty-first-century America.

As the talks continued—and the Iraq War stretched on year after excruciating year—I had the chance to refine and revise them, incorporating insights garnered from members of audiences in Illinois, Missouri, Idaho, California, and Ohio but also in Turkey, Korea, Canada, Ireland, Israel, the United Kingdom, and Norway. Sometimes Maha replaced Nimo. Emma often took the place of Kim. More and more, listeners became contributors. Each taught me to pay fresh attention to puzzles, connections and implications, I earlier had missed.

I am indebted first, then, to all the generous students—many of whom were "required" to come hear a lecture by an out-of-town feminist—and to the hardworking faculty, risk-taking deans, and committed community members who came to these talks over the last six years. They all taught me so much. Together, they reconfirmed my conviction that teaching—in all its myriad forms—nurtures writing.

One of the reasons I was so reluctant to imagine that these narratives and the analytical thoughts they provoked might add up to a book is that I am not an Iraq specialist. I don't read or speak Arabic or Kurdish. Only when my friend and feminist colleague Nadje Al-Ali said it might be of use, did I plunge into the writing. And it is because of Nadje's own splendid research into, and writing about the history and contemporary politics of Iraqi women that this small book has any legs to stand on. In fact, my own measure of this book's success is if its readers go immediately to their local libraries or independent bookstores and order Nadje Al-Ali's deeply informed books.

So many scholars and activists have shared their work with me. The notes at the end really are an extended thank-you. In addition to Nadje Al-Ali, among those who have most personally influenced my thinking about the Iraq War's gendered dynamics have been Carol Cohn, Vron Ware, Teresia Teiawa, Seira Tamang, Ailbhe Smyth, Rela Mazali, Sharon Krefetz, Ann Wright, Terrell Carver, Lory Manning, Aaron Belkin, Catherine Lutz, David Vine, Joseph Gerson, Jana Lipman, Bob Benewick, Keith Severin, Debbie Licorish, Ozgur Heval Cinar, Ayse Gul Altinay, and Cynthia Cockburn. The University of California Press's two external reviewers provided both heartening encouragement and on-the-mark suggestions, which were of enormous help as I revised the manuscript.

A special thank you to Julie Clayton and to Gyoung Sun Jang, each of whom contributed her distinctive and remarkable professional skills in this book at strategic stages of its completion. Kate Warne, the press production editor, and copyeditor Edith Gladstone turned this manuscript into a readable, handsome book.

Gilda Bruckman, co-founder of New Words, the Boston feminist bookstore, is family. She also has continued to be a savvy sounding board for this and all my feminist writing efforts. My dear friend Serena Hilsinger, novelist and poet, was the manuscript's first reader. Laura Zimmerman, a longtime pal and writing mentor to an eclectic circle of feminists, also was a generous early reader. Gilda, Serena, and Laura are avid and wide-ranging readers. Each, in her own particularly insightful way, went to the heart of the book, offering support, caveats, and solutions derived from her own deep commitments to the disparate ways stories can be effectively told in print. I am truly grateful.

This is Naomi Schneider's and my fifth book together. As senior editor for the University of California Press, Naomi has nurtured scores of social science authors, encouraging them—us—to do research and to write books that contribute to the pursuit of justice in all its subtle manifestations. Knowing, as I wrote, that I was writing a book that would be one of Naomi's constantly reminded me that books matter, ideas matter, and readers matter.

Over our twenty-six years together, Joni Seager has taught me how vital environmental responsibility is in our lives, from creating compost bins in the backyard to taking steps to slow the melting of ice floes in her beloved Canadian North. She has revealed in her research how militaries, whether on local bases or wartime maneuvers, jeopardize the environment. Joni published the fourth edition of her amazing world atlas of women while I was just beginning to wonder if the talks on the Iraq War might gel into a book. Watching Joni make such cogent feminist sense of women's lives in scores of societies gave me heart to try to make sense of women's lives in just two.

Writing about women's experiences of war makes one acutely conscious of how precious each life is. In the midst of writing this book, one of my dearest friends died. Judy Wachs was so full of joie de vivre. Judy cofounded Voice of the Turtle, a lively group of talented musicians who sought, through their revival of Sephardic folk music from Morocco and Bulgaria to Turkey and Spain, to build bridges between people who are taught too often to fear one another. All of us who were warmed by Judy's effervescence learned that it takes actions both dramatic and mundane to undo those too-easy narratives that serve as platforms for launching future violence. This book is dedicated to Judy. Nimo and Judy, I have a hunch, would have had good laughs together.

CHAPTER ONE

Eight Women, One War

Nimo, Maha, Safah, Shatha, Emma, Danielle, Kim, and Charlene. Four Iraqi women, four American women. I have never met any of these women. But I feel as though I have been living with them for the past six years. They have changed my mind. My mind slips into a particular mood when I think of each of these women. My thoughts orient themselves differently when I give them over to any one of them, while walking to the subway, or standing in line at the post office. Nimo takes me to a small beauty salon where women chat easily, the lights flicker and the water sputters out of the faucet; Kim makes me feel what it is like to be awoken in the middle of the night by a phone call from an anxious military wife. The sputtering water, the night-time phone call—these are among women's lived realities during the long Iraq War.

Nimo, Maha, Safah, Shatha, Emma, Danielle, Kim, and Charlene. I am deeply indebted to each one of them. They have taught me anew that there are always fresh questions to ask about what it takes to wage wars—about all the efforts to manipulate disparate ideas about femininity, about the attempts to mobilize particular groups of women, about the pressures on certain women to remain loyal and silent. There are more efforts to control women and to squeeze standards for femininity and manliness into narrow molds than most war wagers will admit. There are far more efforts than most analysts care to acknowledge.

Together, these eight women also have taught me that in the midst of warfare the politics of marriage, the politics of femininities, the genderings of racial and ethnic identities, and the workings of misogyny each continue. Warfare does not stop the gendered clock. Sometimes, it sets the hands of the clock back.

These eight women have taught me, too, to be a lot more curious about what skills and resources it takes for a woman to survive a war: persuading an uncle to take you and your children into his small apartment after militiamen have murdered your husband and destroyed your home; having workmates who will cover for you when you have to travel across the country to your wounded son's bedside; mustering the gumption to confront the strangers who have occupied your house; creating new goals for yourself after losing an arm; returning to school after seeing your aunt shot point-blank.

Nimo, Maha, Safah, Shatha, Emma, Danielle, Kim, and Charlene. I don't think any of these eight women ever have met, though perhaps in prewar days Maha walked by Nimo's Baghdad beauty salon or Kim saw Danielle on ESPN as she smoothly outmaneuvered other players on the basketball court.

The Iraq War started when the U.S.-led coalition invaded Iraq in March 2003 and then was fought on many fronts for months and years afterward. We can draw new understandings of warfare and wartimes by paying close attention to these eight women without turning any one of them into merely the iconic "working woman," " wife," "widow," "mother," or "woman soldier." Nor do we need to succumb to the temptation to treat each of these eight women as so distinctive in her experiences and personality that she stands alone, outside history. To be curious about a particular woman's experiences and ideas, to respect her individuality, is not to say that she is unable to shed light on larger canvases of warfare and wartime.

This double-claim—that each of these eight women is neither unique nor universal—is easier to assert, of course, than it is to demonstrate. Readers, I think, will see me tussling here with the dynamic relationship between generality and particularity as I try to understand each woman's experience for its own sake, while simultaneously seeking to tease out from her life the wider implications of those experiences.

My own inclination is toward comparison and generalization, to delve into one to shed light on the other, to use the particular to reveal the general. That's the teacher in me. At the same time, though, more perhaps than in any of my previous writings, I have worried about doing justice to each woman individually. Emma is more than a Latina, more than an American mother of a teenage son. Safah is more than an Iraqi teenage girl, more than a massacre survivor. I realize now that I scarcely know how much more.

As the scores of notes in the following chapters will attest, there have been dozens of books, reports, and articles about Iraqi women's and American women's experiences of the Iraq War. I have learned from them all. What I am suggesting in this modest book is that we have something important to discover by thinking of Iraqi and American women together—not because they have known each other (though a few have), not because they have made common alliance (though some have), but, rather, because thinking about women on several "sides" in the same war might make starkly visible how wars and their prolonged aftermaths depend both on particular ideas about and practices of femininity and masculinity, and on women in warring states *not* discovering their connections with one another.

By taking each of these eight women seriously and exploring their varied wartime experiences together, I have been led toward two new fundamental understandings about war. First, these eight women, considered together, have underscored for me how every war takes place—is waged, is coped with, is assessed—at a particular moment in ongoing gendered histories, national gendered histories, and international gendered history. Shatha, for instance, competed for a seat in the wartime Iraqi parliament at a time when women's rights activists internationally were successfully pressing governments to establish legislative quotas for women. Danielle enlisted in the U.S. Army at a time in U.S. history when government officials no longer could enjoy the masculinized luxury of filling its ranks with male conscripts. That is, the early 2000s activists' push for establishing parliamentary quotas for women helped shape the Iraq War. So did U.S. male war strategists' reluctant postconscription acceptance of women recruits.

In military academies, civilian classrooms, and on blogs and editorial pages all over the world, commentators compare wars—the Vietnam War with the Chechen War, the Yugoslav War with the Congo War. So what is new here is not that wartime observers chart similarities and differences between wars. Rather, what paying close attention to these eight women newly reveals is that any given war takes place not simply at a particular moment in the history of weapons technology (was the stirrup invented yet? Which side had access to remote-controlled drones?). Nor has any given war taken place just at a particular moment in the evolution of the nation-state (did the warring state have effective tax collectors? Could the state's war strategists call on a widely felt national identity strong enough to trump communal loyalties?). Not even awareness of the evolution of political economies is sufficient (would Western state elites have fought over Iraq if petroleum-dependent industrialization had not been then in full bloom?).

Those conventional historicized investigations alone, I've found, are not enough to make adequate sense of a given war or to compare wars reliably. Any war takes place at a particular moment in the history of gender—that is, in the history of women's organizing, in the history of women's relationships to the state, in the history of contested masculinities, in the history of patriarchy's rationalization and reach. The Iraq War is better understood if we ask how its occurring at a distinctive point in the national and international histories of women and of patriarchy has shaped its causes, its winding course, and its aftermath.

Taking on board this deeper understanding of the historicity of warfare would alter the required reading lists at West Point and Sandhurst, but also at Oxford, Berkeley, and Tokyo University. Professors teaching courses on military history and national security doctrines would have to start assigning books on the history of marriage. They would have to require their students to delve into historicized investigations of wartime prostitution. They themselves—as historians and analysts of war and national security—would have to become familiar with the rich primary sources on women's movements in 1890s Russia, 1910s Britain, 1920s Korea, 1930s Japan, 1960s Iran, 1970s United States, 1980s Yugoslavia, 1980s Iraq, 1990s Rwanda, 2000s Congo, and 2000s Pakistan.

A second new idea started to take shape as I spent more and more time in my head with Nimo, Maha, Safah, Shatha, Emma, Danielle, Kim, and Charlene. I gradually began to see war's distinct phases, gendered phases. The politics of any war is unlikely to be the same at its start, its middle, and its end. Think of 1940 Britain compared with 1942 and 1945 Britain. Furthermore, the differences between any war's own time periods are likely to be marked by distinctly different gender dynamics and preoccupations. Feminist historians of World Wars I and II have discovered this. Feminist historians of the Crimean, Boer, and Iran-Iraq wars have confirmed this. The politics of marriage, of property, of sexuality, of women's paid work, of parenting—each changed in the midst of each war.

Each of those gendered political changes altered the dynamics of war—who were the key players, what were their resources and their rationalizations. We ignore the wartime transformations of marriage politics at our own analytical risk.

Gendered wartime phases marked the Iraq War as well. For instance, Iraqi women's beauty salons did not become the target of bomb-throwing militiamen at the outset of the Iraq War. They were set afire in its second gendered phase, when some men organized into militarized groups had convinced themselves that a certain practice of feminized beauty was subverting the country's wartime civic order. Similarly, Charlene's maternal work to heal a shattered young American male veteran didn't attract much congressional attention until later in the Iraq War, when her government's inadequate care of returning soldiers became the focus of press reports.

This is not to argue that all wars proceed lockstep through identical gendered phases. The gendered phases of the Iraq War may be quite different than those of, say, the 1990s Yugoslav wars or World War I. In fact, the gendered wartime and postwar phases may turn out to be quite different in their timing and their patterns in the several societies engaged in the *same* war. Thus while feminized beauty was politicized in 2005 Iraq and the United

States, the wartime politics of beauty in both countries were not identical. Yet these eight women have taught me to be alert to gendered phases within any war, thus to stay focused month by month, year by year to often subtle changes: which masculinities were privileged early in the war versus two years later; which women became the objects of political elites' anxiety as the death rates rose, which as they fell; what issues were prioritized by politically engaged women initially, though later strategically downgraded. Paying attention to these eight particular women over time throughout this one war has taught me to cultivate a long attention span, to eschew analytical laziness, to avoid referring simplistically to "the war."

I began to notice each of these eight women one by one during the early phase of the Iraq War. At that point, in 2003 and 2004, I was not intent upon collecting eight women's wartime stories. I was just seeking to gain a more subtle understanding of this war by listening to the voices of particular women. This is an enterprise feminists have taught us is always analytically rewarding.

I was freshly reminded of this reward when, in the later phases of the Iraq War, I began reading a new book published by the feminists of the anti-militarism group Women in Black, Belgrade. To help readers comprehend not only the war at its outset and at its peak, but also the war in its ongoing aftermath, the editors had decided to present women's own firsthand accounts of the 1990s war that tore apart the former Yugoslavia. They called their book *Women's Side of War.*[1] The Belgrade Women in Black editors were committed to letting women speak for themselves about what they each did in this war, what the war did to them, and how, a decade later, they continued to think about both. Readers can hear one hundred and ten women's voices between this book's covers. Much of what they say is surprising, a lot of it is discomforting. Some women never before had spoken about these experiences. Other women had been writing since the war began but continued to reassess their earlier thoughts. Perhaps one day Iraqi and American (and British, Georgian, Korean, Fijian, Spanish, Polish, and Australian) feminist activist editors will collect in one place diverse women's voices telling of their experiences in the Iraq War.

To hope for such an ambitious volume of women's firsthand recollections is not to say that there is no place for analysis. Instead, what feminists from many countries have taught us is that reflective thinking requires a perpetual return to women's own voices. That is what some thoughtful journalists offered us in the midst of the Iraq War.

The journalists whose profiles of individual Iraqi and American women I have relied upon here did not select women who were making wartime headlines. Lynndie England, Jessica Lynch, and Condoleezza Rice are not here. Nor did these innovative journalists treat the women they featured as mere symbols or abstractions or widgets. Each woman was portrayed with her own voice, her own neighbors, relatives, and allies, with her own resources, calculations, and worries. At this time in American media history, when money-strapped newspapers are closing their overseas bureaus and some cities' daily papers are disappearing altogether, I found myself more indebted than ever to the women and men working as professional journalists—and to those editors who provided them with the discretion, resources, and time to do this sort of painstaking reporting.

I am not sanguine about the press. Its flaws are multiple and run deep: coziness with governmental sources, nervousness about advertisers' sensibilities, vulnerability to publishers' ideological interventions, and preoccupation with corporate profits. I value commentators. I read and listen to a lot of them, benefiting from their insights. Yet their commentaries necessarily rely on the expanded, not shrunken, existence of careful, detailed, ethical, energetic, and sometimes risky reporting done by on-the-ground journalists. Sabrina Tavernise's decision to treat a small Baghdad beauty parlor as a site for gathering wartime news, Damien Cave's decision to pay attention to a Texas high school in order to reveal how a government acquires its soldiers—these journalistic decisions (and their editors' support for these decisions) make it possible for citizens to begin to make sense of the gendered politics of wars.

As will become obvious in the chapters that follow, however, we acquire the means for crafting a full and nuanced analysis of any war when we place the highest quality journalism in an enriched context that researchers can provide. Thus the work of researchers within the World Health Organization, Oxfam, the United Nations High Commission for Refugees, Refugees International, the International Committee of the Red Cross, UNICEF, Small Arms Survey, Amnesty International, and Human Rights Watch, many of them in partnership with Iraqi researchers, has clarified the patterns, the preconditions, and consequences to which the journalists' accounts first gave substance.

Distinctive to the Iraq War (and the contemporaneous conflicts in Afghanistan, Pakistan, Congo, Sudan, Sri Lanka, and Somalia) is the prominence of researchers trained in gendered analysis who are working inside these organizations. Employing these gender analytical skills made their reports on the Iraq War more realistic and thus more useful. Feminist-informed gender analysis is not a luxury; it is a necessity. Consequently, we know a lot more about the interactions in this war, for instance, between men as refugees, women as refugees, men in relief agencies, and women in relief agencies than we did about those crucial relationships during World War II or the Pakistan-Bangladesh War.

Wartime research also has its own gendered history. That gendered history of research—what is deemed worth asking, what is never asked, who is considered worth interviewing, who is considered too marginal to interview—shapes how we see any war; it determines what lessons we take away from any war. Why did it take until the 1990s for the Japanese Imperial government's 1930s–40s program of sex slavery to come to light? Why did the U.S. occupation authorities' racialized dating policies in postwar Germany only surface fifty years later? The answer in part is that in each instance powerful state actors had a stake in suppressing knowledge about these policies. But these silences also reflect the absence of systematic gender analysis in the tool kits of the hundreds of researchers who investigated, allegedly, every conceivable dimension of World War II. The full dimensions and multiple processes of the Iraq War are far more exposed because this war broke out when gender analysis was having an impact on at least some researchers' curiosities. We all are the beneficiaries of that gendered exposure.

Individual academic scholars often lack the funds, the protection, and the staffs to conduct long-term research in violence-riddled war zones. They are excluded, intimidated, and poor. Yet, against formidable odds, some do. I have tried to make their work visible in the notes at the end of this book. Including citations and bibliographies is not merely an academic ritual. It can help readers appreciate all the physical and mental work done by other investigators that has made this small book possible. These scholars' work has been invaluable in revealing the wartime patterns of violence, silence, displacement, strategizing, and mobilization that often have limited, but occasionally have widened each of these eight women's outlook and actions.

Other university-based scholars have conducted careful research not during the shooting and killing, but just before a society plunges into armed conflict. The Iraq War began when Iraqis were still trying to put their lives together in the decade-long aftermath of the 1990–91 Gulf War. For Americans, by contrast, the Iraq War began when their country already was at war in Afghanistan. Scholars' work on prewar gender dynamics is essential to our understanding of the gendered processes of wartime because no armed conflict erupts on a blank slate. Armed conflict occurs among people who already have been—or have not been—encouraging girls to stay in school. War occurs among people who already have been—or have not been—electing women to the post of commander in chief. A war occurs among people who already have been—or have not been—ensuring that divorced women don't descend into poverty, among people who already have—or have not—held accountable the male perpetrators of "peacetime" sexual violence. These prewar (or "between-wars") prior gendered beliefs, structures, and practices will have major impacts not only on how the given war will be justified, but on how that war will be waged and on how it will be remembered by the next generation.

Once again, the Iraq War occurred when academic scholarship—the questions asked, the methodologies employed—was more informed by explicitly feminist intellectual skills and feminist intellectual exchanges than ever before in history. During the years of the Iraq War there were scholars earning doctorates in women's studies in Ireland, Japan, Israel, Canada, and the United States. New master's degree programs in women's and gender studies were being launched in a dozen countries around the world. Many of these young scholars chose as their theses topics questions about the gender dynamics of specific wars.

The Iraq War was being waged when universities were appointing feminist-informed scholars to academic posts in Namibia, South Africa, Barbados, Mexico, Chile, Hungary, Serbia, Israel, Turkey, Jordan, Tunisia, Indonesia, Thailand, Malaysia, Bangladesh, India, and scores of other countries. These faculty members were being permitted to design new courses for students that explored the militarizations of femininities and masculinities. The National Women's Studies Association was convening large conferences every year in wartime United States. The International Congress of Women's Studies drew hundreds of feminist scholars to Seoul and then Madrid in the midst of the Iraq War.

Publishers in the early 2000s were contracting authors to write books on women and war, gender and war, women and militarization, gender and militarization. Most scholars interested in women's and gender studies could barely keep up with the outpouring of scholarly books. Journals such as the *International Feminist Journal of Politics, Politics and Gender,* the *European Journal of Women's Studies, Security Dialogue, Journal of Peacekeeping, Men and Masculinities, Feminist Economics, Signs, Feminist Review, Women's Studies International Forum, International Migration Review, Minerva Journal of Women and War, Gender, Place and Culture, Hypatia, Middle East Journal of Women's Studies, The Asian Journal of Women's Studies,* and many more (not all in English), were providing outlets for the latest gender-conscious scholarship, much of it shedding light on the gendered causes, processes, and consequences of militarization and wars.

Virtually none of these scholarly forums existed during World War II or the Korean War. Some of them did not exist even in the 1990s during the Gulf War or Rwandan and Yugoslav wars. The more scholarly forums there are, each promoting serious attention to the workings of masculinities and femininities, each providing models for rigorous (that is, reliable) feminist scholarship, the more likely it is that accounts of any given armed conflict will take note of women's experiences, ideas, and actions. Once again, the Iraq War was likely therefore to prompt more research than ever before that would not take masculinized cultures and patriarchal structures for granted.

All the information presented in these chapters is available in the public domain. I have not been privy to confidential or classified sources. This means that any attentive person could acquire an understanding of this war that flows from taking seriously women's lives. In an important sense, though, sticking to what is available in the public domain has been a limitation. Unlike the wonderful Iraqi British scholar Yasmin Husein Al-Jawaheri, who spent months during the post–Gulf War 1990s interviewing women in several Baghdad neighborhoods, and on whose rich research I have drawn, I have not spoken to any of these eight women whose wartime lives I've sought to understand. I did enjoy one brief e-mail exchange with Emma, who lives in Texas. At times, I thought I should make more of an effort to track down the four American women, to have phone or in-person interviews with them. But that, I was afraid, might tilt the whole book toward the four American women. They would have become more engaging for readers, maybe even for me. That would have subverted one of the principal aims of this book: to create for readers a sense of balance, of equal engagement with all eight of these diverse women.

Nonetheless, there are inequalities of public information about these eight women, even among each country's four women. Thus, because over the course of the Iraq War Emma took on increasingly public responsibilities, local press mentions of her activities were easier to find. By contrast, Charlene largely dropped off the public stage. Likewise, by deciding to run for elected office, Shatha attracted ongoing media attention, while Maha seemed to disappear from view.

Nor is there a neat symmetry between the four Iraqi and four American women. There is no American teenage girl in these pages to match and compare with thirteen-year-old Safah. There is no Iraqi military wife here to match and compare with Kim, the American wife of Mike, the National Guard soldier. If not comparably symmetrical, then what is the value of including these eight women here between the same bindings? Rather than comparing the proverbial "apples and oranges," I have found that thinking about Iraqi and American women together has opened intellectual windows. By considering the experiences and ideas of all eight women, I have discovered I could look into the Iraq War from several new perspectives.

In particular, together, these eight women have made me rethink the meanings of, and evidence for, "the cost of war" and "security." There is a great deal of fresh thinking nowadays about security, especially efforts to de-center the preoccupation with a militarized "national security." Taking seriously individual Iraqi and American women can further those useful efforts—to establish new, more realistic measurements, to go to new sites to explore trends in security and insecurity. Moreover, considering the four Iraqi and four American women together I have become more realistic about how the "costs" of any war should be tallied. Mothers' and wives' silences can have costly postwar consequences. Girls' lost schooling carries a price both for each girl and for her entire society. Wartime reversion to patriarchal marriage codes is costly. Official denials of soldiers' and civilian survivors' mental health problems need to have a price tag affixed to them. All these costs are too rarely entered into the war wagers' ledgers.

In a way, I hope readers will feel rather frustrated. I hope they, like I, will want to know more. Did Maha ever feel privileged when she was married to a policeman? Does Kim ever ask her husband to describe what he saw in Iraq?

I have kept a tight rein on my imagination, however. I have not drifted into fictionalizing. Thus I have made no attempts here to tease out psychological inner voices, to attribute emotions beyond what each woman herself has described.

These eight women, as different as their wartime experiences and their wartime thoughts have been, also do not capture the full range of women who have lived through the Iraq War and who were counted upon by governments to absorb the costs of this war. Most dramatically absent from these pages are women in those countries whose governments decided to support the U.S. government's military invasion and postinvasion occupation of Iraq. Many people may not be able to name any of those "coalition" countries, beyond perhaps Britain. Yet women in Honduras, Australia, Georgia, South

Korea, Japan, Ukraine, Spain, Italy, and Poland also had to make up their minds about what they thought about their own government's support of the Iraq War; many became mothers of deployed soldiers and returning soldiers. Some women in each of these countries were military wives who were expected by their governments to merge their loyalties to their husbands with a loyalty to their husband's governmental superiors. If we ever are to have a realistically complete gendered understanding of this hydra-headed experience we call the Iraq War, we will need to listen to women from all these countries.

Missing too are the women in the lives of the men from Pakistan, India, Fiji, the United States, South Africa, and other countries, men who were hired by the dozens of private contractors who played such a significant role in determining how the Iraq War was waged. Some of these contracted men worked as armed security personnel in Iraq. Others drove trucks along dangerous Iraqi highways, delivering pizzas, DVDs, and fuel to American bases. These men's mothers, wives, girlfriends, and sisters had their own thoughts about their sons and husbands taking these jobs. These women's assessments of security and cost will need analyzing. And we will need a gender analysis of each of the private contractors. Executives of these contracting companies were themselves adopting certain modes of masculinity at the same time as they were honing company policies that were based on gendered assumptions both about the men they hired and about the women in their employees' lives. We need to know more. What would a feminist analysis of Kellogg Brown and Root (KBR) look like? What would we learn about the Iraq War by taking seriously the experiences and actions of the wife of a Blackwater male security guard?

Then there is the risk that by devoting attention to Charlene, as the mother of a military man, one unconsciously will slip into imagining that only American women have been the mothers of soldiers in the Iraq War. In reality, of course, Iraq's own post-Saddam Hussein military could not have been recruited and sustained unless thousands of Iraqi women, as mothers of sons, had been persuaded that their sons' joining the new American-sponsored military was safe enough, rewarding enough, and reputable enough to deserve their maternal support. So far, we know all too little about what the mothers of Iraqi soldiers thought of their sons' enlistment or about any efforts they might have exerted to influence their sons' decisions. Even lacking their American military counterparts' expensive and elaborate media recruiting campaigns, did the Iraqi men at the top of the new military's hierarchy take any steps to win over the mothers of young men?

Likewise, as the numbers of Iraqi men as soldiers—and police—who have been severely injured climbed sharply upward, and as more and more Iraqi male soldiers and police engaged in combat and took part in nighttime raids on civilian homes, how have their Iraqi wives coped with the burden of picking up the wartime pieces of these veterans' lives? "Military wives" is not a uniquely American category. We will not be able to make full and reliable sense of the Iraq War until we know how these Iraqi women assess the war and deal with the physical and emotional burdens imposed on them in the name of waging and recovering from this war.

"Military wife" may not be the appropriate term to use for women married to men in militias, but their lives too call for future consideration. Where are the women in the personal lives of those Iraqi men who joined the armed insurgency, the party-affiliated sectarian militias, and the U.S.-sponsored Sunni Awakening Councils? We need to know how pressured these Iraqi women were to accept their husbands' decisions to take up arms. How much did their own household economies come to depend on the salaries paid by militia leaders to their rank and file men? We need, too, to discover how marital relationships between civilian women and their militiamen/husbands were affected by there being a loaded gun in their home. Just to note that each of these armed groups, such significant players determining the course of the Iraq War, has been profoundly masculinized is useful, but it is not enough.

While the four American women featured here come from four different states—Texas, Illinois, California, and Wisconsin—three of the four Iraqi women come from one city, Baghdad. Where are Iraq's rural women? In the years just before the war, Nimo, Maha, and Shatha did live in quite different neighborhoods in the capital, but they shared the urbanized modernity of life in the country's largest city. And even Safah, while living outside Baghdad, also lived in a sizable town. Iraqi women living rural lives deserve more attention by analysts of the Iraq War. These Iraqi women were experiencing the evolving gendered phases of the war while living in villages where tribal affiliations carried more weight, where schooling was harder to gain, where disruptions in long-distance transport did particular damage to agricultural livelihoods, where it was a greater challenge to create women's organizations, and where a suspicion of middle-class educated urban women's activism could be shared by both women and men. Feminists have warned us not to conflate rural and urban women, even if superficially they seem to share class or ethnic affiliations. Much of the Iraq War was fought in Baghdad, Falluja, Mosul, and Basra city block by city block. But if taking seriously Charlene's life in small town America can shed light on the genderings of the Iraq War, so too can taking seriously the lives and ideas of rural Iraqi women.

None of these eight women have become—at least as far as I could trace their lives—self-identified feminists or anti-war activists. Still, as readers will discover, both Iraqi and American feminists and critics of militarism are visible here in these pages. Furthermore, those women who did develop feminist critiques and strategies regarding the war and the foreign occupation had their own ideas about women as widows, as soldiers, as wives, and as daughters, and as prostitutes. Those Iraqi and American women's lives—even if seemingly carried on outside the networks of feminist activism—would be affected by how successful or thwarted these feminists and anti-war activist women were in their political campaigns.

Only as the war dragged on did I understand that there is a risk—a valuable risk—in selecting a person early in an armed conflict and then in committing oneself to stick with that person as she (or he) developed, and as circumstances around her changed over the next several years. Often we as researchers select people as subjects of analysis in the latter stages of their experiences or even after they have died, at a point when we can see at least superficially what they have tried to make of themselves, after they have experienced most of what we are eager to understand. In that sense, we maximize our sense of control over what we will be attempting to understand.

We choose Alexandra Kollontai long after the Russian Revolution or Fannie Lou Hamer years after the peak of the American civil rights movement.

By choosing Nimo, Maha, Safah, Shatha, Emma, Danielle, Kim, and Charlene during the earlier stages of the Iraq War—during the period of mid-2003 to late 2004—and deciding to stick with them, I felt a bit like a novelist who explains how her fictional characters start to have wills of their own, taking paths that the novelist who created them initially had no idea they would take, maybe didn't even want them to take. The eight women featured here, of course, are not figments of a novelist's imagination. Each of them, moreover, has not thought and acted just at the moment when an enterprising journalist discovered them and offered the rest of us a snapshot of their lives. Each woman has continued to sort out her ideas, her relationships to friends, communities, and weapons-wielding men. Each woman here has continued to refine and revise her opinions about work and politics. She has gone on making decisions about how to use her limited resources to fashion a life in wartime and afterward.

This research strategy has had consequences. Several of the eight women have made choices that surprised me. I didn't anticipate that Emma's public life would take the turn it did. Danielle's assessment of her military experience in the years shortly after her medical discharge was not according to some preordained script. Similarly, I couldn't have forecast how the Iraqi provincial elections would affect Shatha's political party. Back in 2003, I didn't know where in Iraq Kim's husband's unit would be stationed. When I first read about Nimo, I had no inkling that Iraqi beauty parlors would become a battleground.

It has been beneficially humbling to be so surprised along this journey. It has reminded me that most women in wartime, while acting under severe constraints, do go on thinking and rethinking. The rest of us just have to try to keep up with them.

The Iraqi Women

CHAPTER TWO

Nimo

Wartime Politics in a Beauty Parlor

Nimo uses just her first name for her business. Nimo's Beauty Salon, her Baghdad shop sign reads in Arabic. Her full name is Nimo Din'Kha Skander. Though small, Nimo's shop once attracted Saddam Hussein's wife as a customer. One of the president's several palatial compounds was nearby. In late spring 2003 the area was becoming better known as "the Green Zone," the heavily fortified 5.6-square-mile area that the American authorities had commandeered as their headquarters.

In May 2003, just two months after the U.S.-led military invasion of Iraq and the fall of the twenty-four-year-long regime of Saddam Hussein, an American journalist, Sabrina Tavernise, decided to visit Nimo's one-room beauty salon, tucked into a small street in this busy central Baghdad neighborhood of Karada. She was there to get a better sense of how Iraqi women were weighing the dramatic political changes reshaping their lives and the entire country's political landscape. She found women talking with Nimo and each other in the small shop as they were getting facials and having their hair cut and washed.[1]

Some women came into Nimo's beauty salon wearing hijabs to cover their hair, others entered bare-headed. They mixed easily. Although the Karada neighborhood had a large Shiite population, sectarian religious or ethnic identities didn't seem to play a role within the shop. Each woman

FIGURE I. Nimo in her Baghdad beauty salon in May 2003 giving a pedicure and talking with her customers. (Photo: Farah Nosh)

had survived the tumultuous last twenty years, coping first with the prolonged Iraq-Iran War, then the war against Iraq's Kurdish community in the north, the regime's invasion of Kuwait and the subsequent intense U.S. aerial bombardment, followed by the 1991–2003 devastating international economic sanctions—and their government's increasingly authoritarian and zigzagging gendered responses to each. A woman endured only if she tried to adapt. Just because on this day in May 2003 she was in a beauty parlor didn't mean that she hadn't been thinking seriously about politics.

The conversations among the women in Nimo's beauty parlor were taking place during the early weeks of the U.S. military occupation. Saddam Hussein and his senior officials had gone into hiding. The regime's army had virtually melted away as the U.S. troops, supported by impressive air power overhead, advanced from Kuwait toward Baghdad. In the Karada neighborhood, known among Iraqis as a commercially vibrant and socially liberal area of Baghdad, the coming of the Americans generally had been greeted with optimism. Many of Nimo's neighbors had gone out on Karada's wide main thoroughfare to welcome the American soldiers in April 2003, as they had rolled into the capital in their armored vehicles.[2] This optimistic local assessment would soon change. Already there had been looting here in the city center, as the Iraqi police dissolved and the Americans mysteriously refused to intervene. Yet in May 2003, when Nimo spoke to the American reporter, she and her customers still were seeing the recently arrived American occupiers as a source of hope.[3]

One of Nimo's customers, Hanah Radhi, while getting a facial, expressed skepticism about any post-Saddam Iraqi man who might eventually succeed the American occupiers in power. She predicted: "When an Iraqi comes to rule, after two years he turns on us—he becomes a dragon."[4] Nimo listened as she worked and her customers exchanged news and opinions. One woman mentioned that she had heard that a conservative religious leader was using his mosque position to call for all women to wear the hijab. Over the years, Nimo had honed her own political philosophy. She had come to believe that religious affiliation was a "private thing." She elaborated: "I want to move freely, live a joyful life out in the open.... I don't want a government of religion."[5]

Nimo's Beauty Salon thus was, among other things, a political space. It was a space where women felt comfortable expressing their own, and listening to other women's ideas about the most important political events and uncertainties of the day. Feminists have taught us to look and listen for politics outside the conventional venues of polling booths and the corridors of power, in arenas that often are dismissed as "private" or "domestic" or "feminine." So it took a feminist imagination for a reporter to choose this beauty salon as a place in which to investigate Iraq's wartime politics. It might well have been, too, that some of these women, who, as in so many societies, had been deemed nonpolitical or prepolitical—"naive," "emotional," "parochial"— would not have seen themselves as conducting politics when they assessed a military occupation or its likely successor while getting a facial. Had these same Iraqi women, who clearly had fashioned political ideas of their own, been interviewed in some less hospitable, more masculinized space, they might not have felt as free or confident to spell out their political analyses.

Many more local and foreign journalists covering the war in Iraq presumed they should pay attention to what was being said in the mosques, in the tea houses, inside the Green Zone, those masculinized spaces where men felt at ease with other men, licensed to spell out their own political calculations. Most societies and local communities have similarly spatialized. gender divisions of labor (if you have spent time in the United States, think of the weights room at the local gym, hardware stores, basketball courts, taverns, video game arcades, or fire stations, compared to, say, secretaries' lunch rooms, nursing stations, thrift shops, nail salons, or playgrounds at midday).[6]

Those wartime journalists, policy makers, or researchers who make no conscious gender assessment of their choices of venue when trying to chart the political tides are likely to draw distorted, masculinized conclusions. For instance, observers' understandings of any wartime politics are likely to be masculinized when they fail to question whether they are spending most of their time in the village's or the city's most masculinized places. In particular, if they spend their time in coffeehouses and war council rooms rather than in kitchens and beauty parlors, analysts are likely to shrink unrealistically the parameters of "politics." They are also likely to underestimate the true costs of the war and to select unrealistic criteria for measuring "security."

Despite such analytical risks, especially in the midst of a war, beauty parlors are notoriously trivialized sites. Women looking at themselves in the mirror as tanks roll up their streets. Women thinking about the curl of their hair while their country is occupied by foreigners. Women spending money on their looks while their husbands and children lack sufficient food. Women gossiping about marriages gone sour when serious people are struggling for power. Such trivializing dismissive images grow out of unexamined presumptions: that femininity itself is not a battleground; that anxieties about women's beauty are prepolitical; that marriage is not about power; and that the same men who are immersed in national politics do not try to control women's bodies. Nimo and her customers, surrounded by sinks, hair blowers, creams, and rollers, seemed to reject all four of these common presumptions as politically naive. Instead, they implied that women's bodies, femininity, and marriages already had been politicized; and that this newest wartime was likely to be just the next phase in that ongoing politicization. Within the next few years, as the war's terrain shifted, this understanding, grasped early by Nimo and her customers, would become clearer to more observers.

Nimo, her small business, and her customers were playing their parts in Iraq's complex history. Nimo's Beauty Salon, the modest shop on a side street off Karada's broad commercial avenue, provides a window into Iraqi women's roller-coaster ride of paid employment and unemployment. Nimo herself was, in 2003, an entrepreneur. She owned a small retail establishment catering only to women, relatively well-off urban women. At this point, Nimo had a job, earned an income, even if modest. While in fashionable cities such as Cairo and Paris, many hairdressers fashioning the hair of their female clientele were men, in Baghdad, while there were Iraqi male hairdressers, it appeared that the overwhelming majority of hairdressers were women.[7]

Unemployment among Iraqis had been rising steadily and the salaries paid to those still with jobs had been falling since the imposition of the international economic sanctions in 1991. Two months into the U.S.-led invasion, many more Iraqi men and women were losing jobs. In May 2003, Nimo was swimming against the gendered economic tide.

Most observers of the U.S.-led invasion and occupation aimed their sights on unemployed male ex-soldiers. Visions of unemployed former soldiers always send shivers up and down the spines of political observers: demobilized male soldiers are young, they may feel entitled, and, if ignored, thus be resentful; they may come disproportionately from one politically salient ethnic or sectarian group; they are skilled in the wielding of violence; they probably have held on to their government-issued guns. By contrast, women losing their jobs are taken less seriously.[8]

Unemployed Iraqi women were not the cause for elite's political worry in the spring of 2003. Consequently, trends in women's access to paid work were less noted. What incites anxiety is deemed worth tracking. What does not provoke anxiety can be allowed to happen in the shadows, uncounted, uncharted. Women's fertility rates, by contrast, do make policy makers in most countries worry; they are carefully monitored. Women's loss of paid employment—who needs to invest resources in tracking that?

In fact, since the late 1960s, Iraqi women had gained a significant foothold in their country's paid workforce, especially in the cities, Mosul, Basra, Kirkuk, and Baghdad. This was due in part to Iraqi women's own decades of organized campaigning to open up women's access to both formal education and economic opportunities. Women had become active in the Iraq Communist Party, in the nationalist movement, in the Baath Party, as well as in autonomous women's groups. University of London's Nadje Al-Ali discovered that some of the older Iraqi women activists had been inspired by Egyptian feminists. The Egyptian Feminist Union's activists had argued throughout the 1920s, 1930s, and 1940s that women's access to schooling, to paid work in the professions, and to political participation were necessarily tied together and, together, imperative for achieving genuine nation building.[9]

These local activist women's goals had been evolving since the 1920s, inspiring Iraqis to talk of the Iraqi "New Woman." There were debates about the emergent New Woman—urban, urbane, autonomous, employed, publicly outspoken—in countries as disparate as Japan, Turkey, Korea, Germany, the United States, China, and Egypt.[10] It was at this historical juncture, in the years after World War I, that cinema's images of women became influential in many Middle Eastern societies. As women appeared on the silver screen with coiffed hair and in urban fashions, moviegoers' own notions of feminine beauty began to change. There was a new demand on the part of women, many with new sources of discretionary income, to emulate what they saw on the big screen. Not coincidentally, this was the time when beauty parlors began to open up not only in Paris, but in Cairo and Casablanca.[11]

It would be another generation, however, before ideas about respectable women as able to work for pay outside their homes would jibe with the modernizing objectives of the Baath Party's male leadership. The Baathists were secular nationalists who, after they came to power in 1968, sought to put into practice their vision of the modernization of the Iraqi economy as a primary bastion against British imperial domination. The Baathists became the chief—though, as we will see, certainly not the only—political influence in Iraqi from the 1970s until the U.S.-led invasion.

As so often happens when women's own objectives serve a male political elite's agenda, later commentators would imagine that men's analysis, men's strategizing, and men's wielding of power alone prompted the influx of women into the paid labor force. In this process of misremembering, earlier women activists' subtle thinking and their organized political campaigning for widening women's economic opportunities are overshadowed or completely forgotten. In industrial revolution Britain, Meiji era Japan, Stalinist Russia, industrializing cold war South Korea, and contemporary "Emerald Tiger" Ireland, there have existed women's political movements with explicit proposals for women's education and economic advancement. Yet much of the scholarly attention has been devoted to the male modernizing elites who envisioned drawing women into paid employment as good for the whole nation's economic growth and for their own regime's political security.[12] The women working for pay, these elite men calculated, would help enrich the country, promote its modernization, fend off imperialist intrusion, and keep them in power.

It wasn't the Nimos of Iraq who the late twentieth-century Baathist male planners had in mind. Iraqi male nationalist policy makers weren't thinking of women becoming small shop owners, retailer workers, or entrepreneurs. They were intent, instead, upon women becoming employees of a vastly expanded Iraqi state. They wanted women to work as teachers, doctors, engineers, civil servants. For a woman to work for the nationalized electricity company, to teach in the expanding state school system, or to do accounting for one of the many government ministries, she would have to be educated and to be seen as autonomous enough from her family to be paid her own wage.

Sexism did not evaporate simply at the wave of the state's wand, however. Looking back at that era, a woman named Zeynab recalls in a conversation with Nadje Al-Ali the attitudes she confronted as a science student at university in the 1970s:

I was working as a lab assistant. Most of the people in the college were men. People in the top positions were men. I worked there for fifteen years and they never allowed me to go to graduate school. They all focused on men. . . . The male students looked at women as second-class citizens. They thought we were not capable. It always bothered me.[13]

From the 1970s through the mid-1980s, in the deceptive language of economists, Iraqi women were increasingly likely to be "in the labor force" or "economically active." What economists mean by these two misleading phrases is that Iraqi women were more likely to be *paid* for their labor— and paid for their labor in ways that economists could count, not "informally," not "under the table," not "off the record." Feminist economists in recent years have given us a far more realistic understanding of women's economic roles and thus of entire economies because they have devised more subtle labor-counting systems. For instance, they have taken account of women's significant labor contributions to agricultural production, even though women may not be paid for their weeding, their poultry raising, or their subsistence gardening. Feminist economists also have treated women's street vending of vegetables and handicrafts, their domestic work as maids, and their long-distance trading of everything from bolts of cloth to boxes of ammunition—together conceptualized as forming the economy's "informal sector"—as the labor and economic activity it is.[14]

The U.S.-led military invasion, which Nimo and her customers were assessing that day in May, was the fourth war Iraqis had experienced in just two decades. Each war and its aftermath—its "postwar" years—had had a distinct impact on Iraqi women's ability to gain and keep paid employment. By 1980, on the eve of the Iraq-Iran War, while many Iraqi women still were expected to perform labor as unpaid agricultural and household workers, women's presence as trained workers in the expansive state job sector had become common. By the 1990s, there were two hundred Iraq state companies.[15] In the early years of the eight-year war between neighbors, as the Iraqi military mobilized hundreds of thousands of men to fight, the government did what so many modern war-waging governments have done: it hired more women to work in state and state-supported agencies and industries, to "free men to fight."

However, those eight years of war with Iran (during which the U.S. government had backed Iraq) drained the public sector of its resources and set off an Iraqi economic crisis. The regime was losing its legitimacy in the eyes of many Iraqis. Saddam Hussein, by this time unchallenged leader of a centralized Baathist Party and head of the increasingly authoritarian Iraqi government, responded to this postwar loss of political legitimacy by seeking new allies and retooling his agenda for Iraqi women. First, he courted as political allies traditional male tribal leaders, the mainly rural men he and other Baathist men previously had dismissively scorned as "backward." Second, he cut back on what had become a public welfare and health system that was one of the most admired in the Middle East. Third, starting in 1986, even before the Iraq-Iran war was over, he turned the tables on Iraqi women, calling on them to prioritize maternity over careers and paid work.[16] Remasculinization and deepening patriarchy often mark a country's postwar era's political economy. It is one of the reasons that feminist researchers and activists stay alert even after the guns are silenced.

Many Iraqi women, nonetheless, still managed to hold on to their state jobs into the early 1990s. By 1987, according to the Iraqi government's figures, more women were joining the country's paid workforce, but women were declining as a proportion of the total. Whereas in 1977, women comprised a record 17.5 percent of all Iraqis working for pay, by 1987, that proportion had slipped to just 11.7 percent.[17]

There was soon to come yet another blow to Iraqi women's paid work. It would be even harsher and would leave self-employed Nimo looking even luckier—at least for the moment. In 1991, as punishment for the Saddam Hussein regime's August 1990 military invasion of Kuwait, the governments represented on the United Nations Security Council imposed sweeping economic sanctions on Iraq, prohibiting UN member states from purchasing Iraq's oil and from engaging with it in any commercial trade. As Iraqi British researcher Yasmin Husein Al-Jawaheri has revealed, these sanctions had profoundly gendered impacts, impacts that the American and other Security Council architects of the punitive sanctions appeared not to have considered at all.[18]

From the 1960s to the 1990s, the state sector of the Iraqi economy had expanded to become the workplace of a great many employed women. Consequently, when the international sanctions compelled the Saddam Hussein regime to shrink the state-funded sector even more drastically, it was women who disproportionately lost their jobs and had their salaries drastically reduced. Fewer schools, fewer hospitals, fewer museums, smaller ministry staffs, and power utilities damaged by the U.S. bombing during the Gulf War in 1990–91—each translated into Iraqi women losing jobs and enduring pay cuts.

During the twelve years of international sanctions, 1991–2003, several trends in Iraqi women's employment became visible. First, women's unemployment rose. Second, those women with university educations who were able to find jobs saw their salaries drop. Third, many educated women became discouraged and either tried to emigrate, took menial jobs or dropped out of the paid labor force.[19] One young woman, Huda, a university student majoring in psychology, described to Yasmin Husein Al-Jawaheri her sense of shrinking opportunities for university student women like herself as the postwar 1990s Iraqi economy spiraled downward:

> It is a lost time in my life. I seriously doubt that it will be better for me after graduation. I wonder about my future. I know it is very difficult to find a job. However, why should I bother? The salary wouldn't even pay for my daily transport expenses. I think it is better to be a housewife and forget about psychology—however, marriage is another hopeless issue![20]

For Iraqi women, as for women in most societies, past and present, prospects for marriage and for coping with a sexist and/or shrinking job market are tightly intertwined. Marriage, for many women, is assessed not just as an emotional choice, but as an economic prospect. Marriage to a man with a job is deemed to provide the man's wife with economic security. Many mothers and fathers urge a daughter to marry, even if the husband is not an appealing choice, because they think that only by marrying will their daughter secure her long-term economic well-being. Thus access to a good paying job of one's own allows a woman not only to put off marriage until a compatible prospective husband comes along but allows her to withstand the shock of divorce if the marriage fails. Thus under the pressures of the 1990s postwar U.S.-backed international sanctions, not only did Iraqi women's education-job calculus change, their strategic weighing of marriage and economic security became more complex.

As unemployment soared in the 1990s, many Iraqi men and women turned to the private sector. Men were more likely to find jobs there. Women ran into a gender barrier: the widespread notion that a woman's feminine respectability would be compromised if she worked in the private sector. Since the 1970s, there had developed among Iraqis, especially among urban residents, a popular acceptance of an educated woman being able to work in government offices alongside men and interacting with men as clients without losing her status as a "respectable woman." Somehow, both their own educational credentials and the state as their employer provided women who were nurses, secretaries, biologists, physicians, engineers, architects, curators, teachers, and bank officers with a layer of status protection. By contrast, a woman working in the private sector, especially in a retail business serving a male as well as female clientele, was seen by her family, her neighbors, perhaps even herself, as more at risk of losing this important status of a "respectable woman."

In any society, feminine respectability is a currency that no woman surrenders lightly. A woman who jeopardizes her status of respectability becomes vulnerable, insecure.

In the mid-1990s, Zahra was a thirty-year-old Iraqi woman, a public bank employee. Zahra detailed to Yasmin Husein Al-Jawaheri what happened to her when she had the chance to get what seemed to her a better banking job in the private sector. Zahra's mother objected; she worried that it would be "shameful to work for strangers." The state had not qualified as a "stranger." Zahra's brother, by then having emigrated and working in Sweden, exerted long-distance pressure. He saw himself as having a stake in his sister's feminine respectability. Zahra recalled, "He was phoning every day from Sweden to make sure that I refused the new job offer." Despite the economically hard times, Zahra ended up turning down the better job and staying at the state bank.[21]

Other women told Al-Jawaheri that they felt they had no choice; they knew that taking a retail job jeopardized their hard-won feminine respectability—as judged by both women and men—but in the wake of 1990s postwar, sanctions-driven state cutbacks, they had to take that risk. This was the eyes-wide-open calculation that Sana made. In the late 1990s, Sana was thirty-eight, a university graduate, and a divorced mother of three children:

> I am a graduate of the Academy of Art. Before the sanctions I had a well-paid job in the National Theater, but the theater was financially affected and many employees had to leave. . . . Everything was turned upside down. My husband left. . . . My family is still blaming me. . . . I was left alone to face the insecurity. I know that working in a shop is not approved of by society or by my family. But it provides me with an income, which eventually I could not manage without. Honestly, I don't really care whether people accept me as I am or not.[22]

Let's return now to Nimo, working in her one-room beauty parlor in May 2003. She didn't have a prestigious job, yet she wasn't unemployed. She was her own boss. She was working in the private sector, in retail, but she had no male employees and no male customers. Despite the postinvasion looting and growing lawlessness, Nimo still was able to open her shop and attract customers. In May 2003, enough women still felt free to leave their homes, though paying to get one's hair washed was a luxury that required extra income. Nimo was maintaining her own feminine respectability, providing a safe space for women to talk and gaining for herself a modicum of economic security. It was, however, fragile.

By July 2003, Human Rights Watch was publishing its careful study, conducted by a woman researcher, which showed that sexual assaults against Iraqi women and girls were increasing in Baghdad. Kidnapping of women was becoming more prevalent, the city's shrinking, distracted all-male police force was doing little to prevent violence against women or to arrest the male perpetrators. Moreover, the American occupation authorities did not have prevention of violence against women high on their own agenda.[23]

At this same time, American occupation officials were launching their plan to privatize most of the Iraqi state companies. If this plan were implemented, enterprises for which it was deemed respectable for Iraqi women to work would no longer be under the state umbrella. They would either disappear altogether because of competition from foreign imports (also promoted by the U.S. occupation authorities) or be bought up by private—most likely foreign—investors. For instance, six hundred women working as sewers at Baghdad's Agras garment factory lost their jobs in 2005 as the Iraqi managers began to import clothing from China.[24]

Under the American economic reconstruction plan, even if violence did not escalate or overseas imports did not force Iraqi companies to close, fewer women would have those state paid jobs considered respectable for even an educated woman, and thus fewer urban women would have money to support their families, much less discretionary income to spend on their own appearance.[25]

By year three of the Iraq war, more and more women with professional degrees—lawyers, engineers, biologists, doctors, dentists—were seeking work in the private sector as maids. Najila Muhammad was thirty-four in 2006, the mother of three and caretaker of her mother. A graduate of an Iraqi university, she had been employed as a biologist. Now her husband was unemployed and her own scientific laboratory's managers were no longer able to pay their employees. To make the family's ends meet, Najila obtained a housekeeper's job, earning $100 per month. Another woman, trained as an engineer, lost her job in 2003, and after searching for a professional post for three years, gave up, and became a domestic worker: "Since then, I've been cleaning houses and washing clothes—even though I studied for four years to become an engineer. But I had to support my children after I became widowed."[26] Jenan Mubarak, director general of an Iraqi independent organization, the Iraqi Centre for Women's Rehabilitation and Employment, explained that not only were these professionally trained women becoming impoverished, they were also having to cope with the discrimination and harassment that are often experienced by domestic servants.[27]

All these trends began to converge in late 2003: women's unemployment was rising, middle-class professional women were becoming impoverished, women were taking on more and more responsibility for the care of husbands and children, kidnappings and assaults were increasing, conservative ideas about women's public behavior were spreading. Together, by two years into the war, they dried up Nimo's business.

Wars have phases. They evolve over months, even years. Each phase is likely to have its own gendered dynamic. Relations between husbands and wives, daughters and fathers, women and the wartime state, women and the foreign military forces, or women and rival male-led political groups—none of them stand still. Nor do ideals of and anxieties over models of masculinity and femininity. Taking seriously Nimo and other Iraqi employed women enables us to chart those gendered wartime phases and their implications.

Already, in the early weeks of the U.S. invasion and occupation, the ability to keep a small beauty parlor running was becoming a challenge. Flows of water and electricity, necessities for any beauty parlor, were becoming more and more erratic. The 1991 U.S.-led bombings of Baghdad had targeted public power utilities. The postwar 1991–2003 international sanctions had made repairs to Iraq's infrastructure difficult. The American bombings of March–April 2003 had damaged those power stations that had been recently repaired.

That April another American woman reporter, Farnaz Fassihi, covering the preinvasion and invasion experiences of Iraqis, took a rare break from her strenuous journalist's daily work to go with a friend to another modest woman-owned Baghdad beauty salon. She was there less to gather women's political views than to relax for an hour with a pedicure. "Catherine and I settle onto stiff chairs and two young women squat before us. We dip our toes into red plastic bowls." You can almost hear the two women journalists let out sighs of relief. Then, "Halfway through the pedicure with one foot to go, electricity cuts off. It's over 110 degrees outside and within a few short minutes the heat becomes unbearable." The beauty parlor owner is reassuring: "'Normal, normal,' says the owner, waving her hands dismissively. 'We have two hours of electricity and six hours of blackout every day.'"[28]

There is more than electricity at issue here in the beauty parlor in April 2003. Unbidden, the owner offered Fassihi and her colleague their own political analysis: "What is taking the Americans so long to fix it? After the last war, Saddam fixed our electricity in one month. One month! America, with all its engineers and top technology, can't fix our electricity? They are doing this on purpose. They want us to suffer."[29] Fassihi and her colleague soon left the beauty parlor, with their toenails half-painted.

For the women like Nimo who, against the odds, had created their own sources of income as workers in or owners of beauty parlors, the foreign occupiers' failure to ensure reliable flows of water and electricity pushed them even closer to the economic brink.

Um Mustapha, a worker in another Baghdad beauty parlor, was married, but by the second year of the war her husband was unemployed. She described the relationship between her hairdressing job, electricity, water, marriage, and her economic security this way:

> I work in a salon for the ladies. There is no electricity, no water, the heat
> is killing us. Customers, when they peer in, see only darkness. They shy
> away, and this is where we are supposed to make a living. And what's the
> quintessential thing for a hairdresser? Electricity.... Thank god, our
> salon has not been targeted—but ... what would it cost to throw a bomb
> in our direction? It is a risk we have to take. It is our livelihood. Most of
> our men are sitting at home.[30]

Months later, in early 2004, Fassihi, still covering the war as the *Wall Street Journal's* Baghdad bureau chief, described ordinary Iraqis' access to electricity: "A ration of two hours of electricity and four off has been instituted, but it's random and month after month the ratio decreases."[31] Even in late 2007, almost three years after the start of the U.S. occupation, according to the International Committee of the Red Cross, water treatment plants were "completely shut down or operating at reduced capacity," and parts of Baghdad and neighboring Anbar province "often have only one hour of electricity per day." The failure of water and electricity infrastructure was, the ICRC concluded, causing a "humanitarian crisis."[32] Even as late as 2008, during year six of the war, Baghdad's population was judged to be struggling "with a shortage of clean drinking water."[33]

Electricity and water. Each became for many Iraqis a measure of political good faith. Each also became a measure of security—and insecurity. Water and electricity, like security itself, are gendered.[34] The failures at the start of the U.S.-led invasion and in the early weeks of the occupation might have been taken by Iraqis as an annoyance, something temporary to be coped with. But as the war evolved and as these basic public utilities continued to be erratic or nonexistent, women's lives changed. Failing electricity and intermittent water added immeasurably to the household workload of women as mothers, wives, and daughters. It is women who are expected to clean their homes' curtains, rugs, and surfaces after Iraq's famous dust storms, *ajaja*. Unclean water also meant more sick children for resource-strapped mothers to care for. One young Iraqi English-speaking woman blogger, who adopted for herself the Internet name Riverbend, described her family's daily wartime effort to sustain some minimal source of water: "The water flow is so weak, it takes about 17 minutes to fill up a 10 liter plastic pail (I was timing it). We've carried up about 10 buckets now. The water still doesn't reach the kitchen faucets so we've managed to move the dirty dishes to the bathroom and wash them there."[35] This was January 2005. The war had been going on for almost two years.

The American promises of restoring public utilities were beginning to sound hollow to many Iraqis. As the war in Iraq evolved, as law enforcement deteriorated, as kidnappings escalated, and as new masculinized political groups assumed for themselves responsibility for policing women's behavior and appearance in public, women and girls were more and more confined to their homes, their darkened homes, hot in 100-degree long summers, cold in Iraq's raw winters. Electricity and water were no mere amenities.

In December 2008, an official U.S. government history of the failed American Iraq reconstruction effort became public. *The New York Times* and the nonprofit investigative Web site ProPublica obtained a draft of the report compiled by the special inspector general for Iraq reconstruction entitled "Hard Lessons: The Iraq Reconstruction Experience."[36] The history detailed the U.S. government's unpreparedness, bureaucratic fragmentation, and contradictory priorities, which together resulted in Nimo and other hairdressers, as well as ordinary households such as Riverbend's, continuing to struggle with sporadic and unreliable sources of electricity and water. In the conclusion to his report, Stewart W. Bowen Jr., the special inspector general, chose to quote Charles Dickens: "We spent as much money as we could, and got as little for it as people could make up their minds to give us."[37]

At the same time as unreliable water and electricity flows jeopardized hairdressers' modest livelihoods and vastly increased women's household burdens, the Iraq War moved into its next phase: women's bodies became common targets of more violently politicized competition. In particular, controlling beauty—women's physical beauty—became an object of war.[38]

In the political vacuum created by the fall of the Baathist regime, new Sunni and Shiite insurgent groups mobilized and wielded violence. Each was masculinized in its social agenda, its membership, and its leadership. Women working for pay, a source of nationalist pride in earlier years, now became an object of scorn in the eyes of many newly politicized and armed men in this latest wartime phase. Standards of feminine respectability became ever more confining. Responsibilities of men, not only inside the family, but publicly as surrogate fathers and brothers, became ever more politicized.

As this phase developed, according to Jordanian feminist researcher Salam Al-Mahadin, two not unrelated regionwide phenomena were galloping ahead: first, Muslim intellectuals and clerics were mobilizing thousands of new adherents to an especially patriarchal version of Islam; second, Middle Eastern media companies were spawning scores of new Arab-language satellite television channels featuring sexualized representations of women's bodies.[39]

In other words, the militarization of women's beauty in wartime Iraq wasn't occurring in a vacuum. It was occurring in an environment where the contest was escalating between a patriarchially mobilized version of religion, on the one side, and, on the other, media companies that were further sexualizing and commercializing women's bodies.

Riverbend, the Iraqi woman blogger, had been one of the rare Iraqi women who had been hired to work in the private sector in a mixed male-female workplace and had kept her job throughout the 1990s. Riverbend was a graduate in computer science who worked in a small start-up company as a programmer/network administrator. Her work, she remembers, was "tedious, it was back-breaking, it was geeky and it was . . . wonderful." She lived with her parents but moved around the city freely. She described her workday routine: "At 8 am I'd walk in lugging a backpack filled with enough CDs, floppies, notebooks, chewed-on pens, paperclips and screwdrivers to make Bill Gates proud." Her salary was equal to that of her male officemates.[40]

In June 2003, once the first months of postinvasion confusion seemed to have passed, Riverbend tried to return to her beloved computer job. But the gendered politics of security, respectability, and employment in U.S.-occupied Iraq had shifted. Her own family now was nervous about her going out in public, much less returning to work. They insisted that two male relatives accompany her to provide protection. She arrived at her office to find mostly men, only one other woman; several of the men were unfamiliar, apparently affiliated with the recently empowered Shiite conservative political parties. The desks were gone. Papers were strewn everywhere. Riverbend was happy to see at least one of the male former employees she recognized, until he told her "things had changed," he was quitting the company and going to leave the country. Finally, she found one of the company's directors. He told her that "females weren't welcome right now." The message was that women could no longer be protected. Women should go home. It was the end of Riverbend's paid employment.[41]

Iraqi women began to need protection—or to be seen as needing protection—both because women were increasingly being imagined by many fathers, brothers, and husbands and by Iraqi public spokesmen as vulnerable, and because violence against women was escalating in this new phase of the Iraq War.

The U.S. occupiers dismantled the former state bureaucracy, failed to repair the water and electricity infrastructure, inspired an armed Sunni male-led insurgency, and empowered Shiite-identified political parties, each of which mobilized its own masculinized armed militia. Each of these wartime developments had particular implications for women. Women not only lost their physical security, their expressions of femininity became the battleground for the new political actors, Iraqi and American. It was in this phase of the war that beauty parlors such as Nimo's took on increasing, unwanted political significance. Beauty parlors went from providing feminized secure spaces, where women could relax and informally exchange neighborhood news mixed with political ideas, to being imagined by the men with guns to be symbols of Iraqi women's decadence and the nation's disgrace.

Halla Muhammed Maarouf had been working in a beauty parlor since she was fifteen. She had married young, to Walid, who worked as a security guard. They both kept working after their marriage. They enjoyed small city pleasures such as buying ice cream and eating it together outside on a warm Baghdad evening. At the time of the U.S.-led invasion, Halla was working as an assistant in her mother's Baghdad beauty salon. A year later, beauty parlors were being firebombed. "Shards of glass and bottles leaking sweet-smelling liquid were all that was left." The remains littered one city street that had housed several salons. Halla's mother was forced to close down her salon.[42]

As so often happens in wars, as more and more men were killed by wartime violence, women of all ages, classes, and ethnicities had had to try to become the principal income earners for their extended households. Halla, now twenty-three, was among them. By mid-2004, Halla had lost both her husband, Walid, and her brother. She had become a war widow and an unemployed beauty salon worker. She had two children of her own to care for at the same time as she was helping to support her extended family. She calculated that she could not earn the money she needed to support her own children and her two younger brothers since her mother's parlor was closed down. Anyway, the wages she could earn as a beauty parlor assistant were too meager now to meet her growing wartime household demands. She dreamed of working in a large hotel, or maybe even being able to open her own boutique. But in 2004, Halla had to do what she could to adapt to the gendered realities of this war: she decided that selling her sexual services was her best economic alternative.[43]

In the years of hardships and economic sanctions after the Gulf War, prostitution had expanded. As the Saddam Hussein regime became increas-

ingly insecure and more reliant on patriarchal male allies, prostitution had
become more and more politicized. In 2000, the regime rounded up and
executed more than 200 Iraqi women whom its officials accused of engaging
in prostitution.[44] Now, as the newest war evolved in distinctive gendered
phases, prostitution and women seeking to earn badly needed income by
working as prostitutes again were becoming politically salient. Halla was
keenly aware of the risks. She tried to be discreet in soliciting male customers, Iraqi men. In 2004, she wasn't afraid of the Iraqi police; they tended
to treat prostitution as a minor offense now, compared with their other
concerns. She was, however, on the look out for male vigilantes. The same
men who were burning down beauty parlors were hunting for prostitutes.
Prostitutes and beauty parlors: both were, in these men's eyes, violating
their notions of religious propriety as well as dishonoring the Iraqi society.
Collective honor and religious propriety are virtually always gendered, and
usually sexualized. Both commonly become more intensely politicized as a
war progresses. As wartime strains the social order and more women from
many walks of life decide to take unorthodox steps to sustain their own and
their families' material survival, violence against women is adopted by some
men as the means to restore the gendered order.

Halla, the widowed former beauty salon assistant and daughter of a beauty
salon owner, had to decipher the confused political trends. "Maybe there is
an order to kill all prostitutes," she speculated. Nor did she draw much dis-
tinction between the armed militias and the emergent political parties with
whom the armed men were affiliated. "If the Islamic parties arrive to power,"
Halla told an American woman reporter, "maybe even the Americans can't
stop them."[45]

It is not clear what was happening to Nimo or her shop by this time.
Karada, Nimo's once thriving commercial district, was becoming a magnet
for bombers. Two years after Nimo and her customers speculated about the
American and Iraqi politicians' goals, and a year after Halla's mother lost her
shop and Halla herself started supporting her extended family by working as
a prostitute, "the lights of Karada were dimmer."[46] The women whom Nimo
had counted on as customers were becoming house-bound, as kidnappings

and killings rose sharply. Between spring and late September 2005, more than 3,000 people had been killed in Baghdad alone.[47]

Kareema was just such a woman who in earlier years might have patronized Nimo's beauty parlor. In 2003 she had been an engineering student. She came from a family of professional women; all of her four sisters and sisters-in-law were doctors and engineers. When the war began in March 2003, they had expected that it would take only several weeks before they could resume their studies and their professional jobs. But now, two and a half years later, as the masculinization of public spaces had become extreme, Kareema and her sisters remained indoors most of the day. When they did go out, according to a neighbor, who had known them as urbane, confident women, they now donned long black cloaks and gloves.[48] Spending time and money at a beauty parlor no longer seemed safe, even feasible.

Several months after Halla was interviewed, the radio journalist Lourdes Garcia-Navarro, National Public Radio's reporter in Baghdad, decided to stop into one of the still-operating beauty parlors in the Karada neighborhood to take the political pulse. At Dena and Mena's Hair Salon she found the business slow, but the customers and owner were willing to talk about the upcoming Iraqi election.[49] Despite the rising ethnic and sectarian violence, this beauty parlor had managed to continue to attract a small mixed clientele. One customer, Nasrin Misir, identified as Shiite, was there to get her hair done in preparation to attend a Christian friend's wedding.

The women in this beauty parlor talked politics. They were pessimistic about what the January 2005 national elections could accomplish. The American occupation authorities hoped that the elections would mark a new phase in the conflict. But the women in this beauty parlor assessed the war's different phases in their own terms. Their chief criterion was women's security. They told Garcia-Navarro that women's insecurity appeared in late 2004 to be far from the Iraqi officials' power to control. "We are walking the street," the hairdresser explained, "and we are worried. We don't know if when we walk out the door we'll make it back. Explosions are everywhere. The Americans are everywhere. Terrorists are everywhere."[50] This was a year and a half after the conversation at Nimo's, in which women expressed modest optimism in the Americans' ability and willingness to increase Iraqi women's security. Now the beauty parlor consensus had become one in which Americans were listed along with explosives and terrorists.

Nor was the targeting of women and of women's public spaces happening only in Baghdad. In the largely Shiite southern city of Basra, too, beauty parlors had become the targets of masculinized violence. Once again Lourdes Garcia-Navarro, the National Public Radio journalist, decided that talking with women in a beauty parlor would give her a sense of how women's security was faring. Since the 2003 invasion, Basra had been under British military authority but, in reality, increasingly had come under the control of conservative Shiite-identified political parties and their all-male armed militias.[51] The hairdresser "with arched brows and a dimpled smile" talked as she continued to pluck a client's eyebrows. She recently had returned from six months of exile in Iran and Syria after her salon had been attacked in 2007:

> It was Thursday at 3:30 in the afternoon. They stormed my salon, but I had run away seconds before because the neighborhood kids had warned me that the militiamen were pointing at my store. They shot up the building, destroying everything.[52]

Earlier she had heard that these armed men, who had gained so much power in Basra, considered women's beauty salons to be *haraam*, forbidden. She knew it was nothing personal. It was ideas about all women and about femininity that fueled these men's anger. At first she was defiant. "They threatened all of us female hairdressers. Some of those girls fled. Others had their salons burned, but I was among those who stayed." Then she and her salon became the target. She went into exile. She was not alone. In December 2007, a hairdresser was murdered in the northern city of Mosul.[53] Some beauty salon owners and their staff fled to the Kurdish-controlled region of the north.[54] Other former hairdressers also had been forced to become refugees in Syria and Jordan.[55]

Then in spring 2008, in what appeared to be yet another new phase in the drawn-out conflict, news came that the Iraqi government of Prime Minister

Nuri Kamal al-Maliki had decided to pour more soldiers into a military (and perhaps partisan) campaign to oust his Shiite rivals and gain more effective control over the Basra. The exiled Basra hairdresser decided to take the risk and return to the country. She reopened her salon in Basra. More women were feeling secure enough to leave their homes, even to come to a beauty salon in 2008. But, talking to journalist Garcia-Navarro and among themselves, the owner and her customers were withholding judgment. They were not yet convinced that the Iraqi military or the local police would invest their political and military resources in women's security.[56]

In certain neighborhoods of Baghdad—the wealthier neighborhoods, the areas with the best police protection—some beauty salon owners were also reopening their shops in the summer of 2008. Murina Saad, for instance, had closed her salon in 2007 in the face of escalating threats. She had resorted to making house calls, hiding her supplies under her cloak.[57] A year later she judged that the police were taking women's security, at least in the more affluent parts of the city, seriously enough that she could risk reopening her business. Her customers returned, though in smaller numbers. One woman, daring to come out to another reopened salon, said she was conscious of the continuing threats to women, but she wanted to look "neat and elegant" for her cousin's wedding and she believed that all her women relatives were asserting their own notion of femininity to celebrate in solidarity.[58]

Unbeknownst to Murina, Halla, and Nimo, women activists in several Middle Eastern countries were seeing beauty salons as providing women with more secure livelihoods and safe spaces for building community. Palestinian activists working with wartime refugee women in the West Bank in the early 1990s, for instance, gained funding from a Swedish nongovernmental organization to create a beauty parlor for working-class Palestinian women. Its organizers designed the beauty parlor so that it would be a training ground for women interested in learning cosmetology and small business management. They also expanded the conventional concept of feminine beauty so that the beauty parlor could assist badly wounded women to care for themselves and regain their own sense of self-esteem.[59] A decade later in 2004 Afghanistan, in the wake of its own U.S.-led military invasion, a small group of overseas women tried to launch and sustain a school to teach Afghan women the techniques, styles, and managerial skills to open their own beauty parlors. They too imagined that beauty parlors could provide a niche in a patriarchal wartime economy in which women could maintain their status as respectable women by working solely with women and, nonetheless, develop their income stream, and, with it, growing self-confidence.[60] Afghanistan had not experienced the Iraqi combination of such a sustained women's movement and masculinized state-building strategy to draw so many women into public sector employment during its recent decades. Still, Afghan women's appearance, their economic livelihoods, and thus beauty parlors took on a new political salience not only in the years of the Taliban rule, but also in the more recent period of foreign invasion, economic dislocation, local state's reconstruction, and the Taliban's resurgence.[61]

The point here is not to romanticize beauty parlors or, for that matter, any other feminized spaces. Beauty parlors are not universally inclusive. They can seem to thousands of rural women a world away from their own confined, hardscrabble lives. Moreover, any given beauty parlor may feel inhospitable to some women because of their perceived class, ethnic, or racial identities. Beauty parlors also can be places not of economic opportunity, but of dead-end employment in any society that pushes women into low-paid service jobs. And, while a beauty parlor may provide a safe, relaxed place in which women can trade news and opinions away from the scrutiny of husbands, fathers and brothers, it simultaneously can reinforce the already potent assumption that a woman's physical appearance is her most valuable asset (or liability).

All these caveats notwithstanding, to ignore Iraqi beauty parlors, their owners, and patrons risks misunderstanding the Iraq War. Casually dismissing beauty parlors and the women in them as trivial, removed from the "serious business" of war waging, risks imagining the political arena as being much smaller than in reality it is. Such an uncurious dismissal of beauty parlors also risks underestimating what becomes more intensely politicized in the course of any war: for instance, the further politicization of women's paid work, standards of feminized respectability, and masculinized fears of national degeneracy.

Failing to listen closely to what Nimo and other women say to each other when they are free momentarily from masculinized surveillance is likely to lead an observer to make unreliable conclusions about the sorts of security and insecurity that shape people's actions and assessments during each of the gendered phases of wartime.

In late September 2008, Iraqis were preparing to celebrate as the Muslim holy month of Ramadan was coming to an end. Nimo's Karada neighborhood once again was bustling, seeming to confirm some American officials' claim that security was returning to the capital. Baghdadis had come out of their homes on this Sunday evening as daytime fasting ended. People were out shopping for new clothes and for gifts for children. In Karada "vendors were selling shoes, clothes, watches and perfume."[62] On Karada's Abbar Street shoppers stopped at a café famous for its pomegranate and raisin juice. City life seemed to be just secure enough to take part in some of the less expensive joys of urban living. Electricity and water still might be erratic, the male-led political parties might be jostling for power, the Americans in their armored vehicles might still be cruising up and down the streets, but at least women and men could come out to Karada to enjoy an evening of strolling among their neighbors. Then, at 7:00, in the midst of the shoppers, strollers, and café patrons, two bombs were set off in Karada, killing and wounding dozens of people. At the same time, bombers set off deadly explosives in Shurta and Mansour, two other Baghdad neighborhoods. A local resident who witnessed the Shurta explosion seemed to express many people's fear and confusion when he spoke to a reporter: "The situation is turning worse again, I do not know why."[63]

Four months later, on January 1, 2009, political control of the Green Zone passed from the hands of American occupation authorities to those of elected Iraqi government officials. There was speculation that perhaps some of the checkpoints would be dismantled. Maybe even ordinary Iraqis—not just Iraqi legislators and those working for the Americans—would be able to pass through this sprawling 5.6-square-mile area of Baghdad.[64] Despite ongoing violence in and around Karada, opening up the Green Zone might help revive small businesses in nearby Karada. Perhaps Iraqi women fortunate to have paying jobs, such as those working inside the Green Zone, would even feel secure enough to venture out to have their hair done, to get a facial, to compare with each other their assessments of marriage and security. Perhaps.

CHAPTER THREE

Maha

A Widow Returns to Baghdad

"I loved Saydia but I can never go back; it broke my heart." Maha Hashim was explaining to a reporter why she and her four children had been forced out of their home in the Baghdad neighborhood of Saydia and currently were squeezed into her uncle's small high-rise apartment in another part of the capital. It was December 2007. The Iraq war seemed to be entering yet another new phase. Two years of intense sectarian violence combined with ongoing U.S. military operations had forced many Iraqis, Maha among them, to flee across international borders. Now the newly confident governing elite, headed by Prime Minister Nuri Kamal al-Maliki, was urging Maha and her overseas compatriots to return home. It remained unclear, however, where the returnees would live and how they would make a living.[1]

Earlier, back home in Saydia, Maha Hashim had been a wife and mother. She had enjoyed a recognized status and adequate resources to carry out her responsibilities. By the fifth year of the Iraq War, however, Maha had become a displaced widow, a household head, a supporter of four children, and unemployed. Her husband, a policeman, had been killed in 2006 in the escalating sectarian violence that marked the second phase of the war, the sort of violence the U.S. military and Washington civilian policy makers had been unprepared for and had helped fuel. Maha's house in this once-peaceful southern Baghdad neighborhood had been destroyed when a driver drove a truck bomb into it.[2]

Maha's neighborhood of Saydia, in the Baghdad district of West Rasheed, was on the other side of the Tigris River from Nimo's Karada neighborhood. Saydia had been a prosperous, secular, mixed neighborhood when Maha and her husband lived there with their children in the 1990s and early 2000s. It was an area where people commonly identified families by what the adult man of the household did for a living. Saydia was one of the capital's neighborhoods in which the Saddam Hussein regime had given houses to favored male officials and senior military officers. The area's local dynamics weren't particularly sectarian, however. Businessmen, government officials, and their families, of various ethnic and religious affiliations, lived up and down Saydia's streets. In the Saydia of the 1990s and early 2000s what had seemed to matter more than ethnic or religious identity was a family's loyalty to the regime.[3] Maha herself was Sunni, but it was her husband's job in the police force that had allowed the whole family to fit in and feel secure in Saydia. Even in the wake of the previous twenty years' back-to-back wars and the subsequent international economic sanctions, Maha could enjoy Saydia's lively street life. Men and women would relax outdoors in the evenings, socializing along the main shopping street.

In late 2006, three years and another wartime later, two reporters pieced together a map that showed what sectarian violence had done to just one block of Maha's once-comfortable Saydia neighborhood:[4]

House 1: Occupied by a Sunni three-generation family of seven, headed by a businessman. In 2006, a grandson in the household was abducted and held for $20,000 ransom. Upon receiving the money, the kidnappers returned the boy along with a note, apologizing for their act but explaining that they needed the ransom money in order to leave Iraq.

House 2: Formerly the residence of a Sunni businessman who ran his mineral water business out of his home, this house was vacant by late 2006. The family's twenty-three-year-old son had been kidnapped; despite the family paying the $70,000 ransom, he was killed by the kidnappers. After another son was threatened, the businessman and his family members abandoned the house.

House 3: By the end of 2006, this house was rented and occupied by members of a Shiite family. They moved in after the former owner, a minister in the Saddam Hussein government, abandoned the house and fled to Jordan following the attempted assassination of a son and rumors that the former minister himself was on the target list of a Shiite militia.

House 4: Vacant in late 2006, this house had been abandoned by its former owner, a Sunni man who had been a brigadier general in the Saddam Hussein army; he left Iraq to live with his son in London.

House 5: This house was occupied and guarded by two relatives of the Sunni family who had fled to Syria in the wake of the abduction of a son and the attempted abduction of the mother by Shiite armed groups.

House 6: Occupied by a Sunni family with nine children, this household was headed by a successful businessman. One of the children had been kidnapped and ransomed for $100,000 by a Shiite militia. In 2006, the house was surrounded by private security guards, while the businessman simultaneously paid monthly "protection" payments to the same militia.

House 7: By late 2006, this house was vacant. After the husband, a contractor for the U.S. government, received death threats, accusing him of being a collaborator with the foreign occupiers, he moved into the Green Zone. The rest of his family left Iraq for Jordan.

House 8: This house stood vacant in 2006, after the male head of the family, a Sunni, a distant cousin of Saddam Hussein and an officer in the regime's Republican Guard, had received death threats from the Shiite Mahdi Army and one of his sons had survived an ambush. The family left for Dubai.

House 9: Vacant in late 2006, this house was abandoned after the male owner, a Yemeni diplomat, was asked by his Saydia neighbors to leave when they began to fear that his presence in the neighborhood would attract violent assaults by members of the Iraqi members of the group calling itself Al Qaeda in Mesopotamia (also known as Al Qaeda in Iraq).

House 10: Vacant, this house was left empty by a Lebanese family whose members fled in the wake of an attack on the house by police commandos and the arrest of two of the family's sons, on accusations of being members of Al Qaeda in Mesopotamia; they were later released.

House 11: This house was confiscated by the U.S.-backed Iraqi government after it was abandoned by a Sunni family; the family had fled to Syria in response to death threats delivered to the husband, formerly a high-ranking official in the Baathist Party.

An American army officer, Captain Michael Comstock, tried to describe the steps by which this ethnic cleansing of Saydia was accomplished during 2006. He was writing for other American military strategists, seeking to spell out the strategic lessons for U.S. counterinsurgency forces that could be drawn from carefully dissecting the ethnic cleansing of one urban neighborhood during this phase of the Iraq War.[5] The principal militia that had targeted Saydia for ethnic cleansing and subsequent control, according to Comstock, was the Jaysh al'Mahdi. Sometimes called in English the Mahdi Army, it was an armed branch of the Shiite movement led by the Shiite cleric Moqtada al-Sadr. According to reports submitted by U.S. military officers on the ground in Saydia—officers whose units failed to stop the Mahdi Army's takeover of the neighborhood—the militiamen worked methodically.

The militiamen not only used intimidation and violence to force Maha, her children and other families to leave Saydia, they made life for the remaining residents unbearable by cutting off their already-meager supplies of electricity and water. Soon after the owners left, the militias brought Shiite families into the area to occupy some of the abandoned houses. Many of these men and women felt entitled and grateful, even though the Mahdi Army charged them rent, since they had been driven out of their own homes in other parts of Iraq by men they identified as being Sunni militiamen. The Shiite militiamen did not act alone in their Saydia campaign. They often had the support of the men recruited into the new post-Saddam Hussein Iraqi police force, a security force designed and trained by the United States and its contractors. The new police force was formally now under the authority of the highly politicized and increasingly corrupt Ministry of Interior. The U.S. military and the Shiite militias often competed with each other for the loyalties of the men in the new police force.[6]

Once Saydia was transformed into a more ethnically homogeneous, Shiite-dominated armed neighborhood, the Mahdi Army proceeded to alter the visual landscape of Saydia: "Propaganda spread throughout Saydia and [quoting a U.S. military officer's report] 'Banners (were) strewn across the muhallas, as well as flags and graffiti to designate which neighborhoods were Sunni or Shi'a.'"[7] Beyond acting as propagandists, the militiamen became entrepreneurs.[8] In addition to charging the new occupants rent, they took control of public utilities and billed the newly installed residents for the services. Their entrepreneurial efforts in Saydia went further. Again, quoting observations made by a U.S. military officer describing the next stage of the militiamen's takeover of Saydia, Comstock tells us: "The Shi'a affiliated gangs/militias operating in Saydia traffic and sell weapons, [they are] involved in the operation of whore houses, murder, [they] intimidate and extort [residents] for support and money, steal, kidnap, torture, extort store owners for money, make explosives, and have successfully corrupted INP [Iraqi National Police] so that they provide active and passive support to their operations."[9]

A brothel in ethnically reconfigured Saydia, noted the American military observer, was one militia enterprise this group of militiamen managed, along with the sale of weapons and the extortion of shop owners. Is the organizing of prostitution usually part of an ethnic cleansing campaign? Of course, anyone with the least bit of feminist curiosity would want to know more about the women inside the brothel and the men who were their paying clients. Perhaps there was an unemployed hairdresser or a displaced widow among the women inside. Did the male clients—men from the militias, policemen, shopkeepers, new male residents?—care about the sectarian identities of the prostituted women? There are no answers even hinted at in this stark military report of the ethnic cleansing of Saydia.

Yet prostitution in the era during and in the years following any war is always worth investigating. Watching prostitution over time enables us to gain a clearer picture of what causes its increases, its declines. Does prostitution reach its peak when masculinized violence is at its height? Or does the trend in the impoverishment and widowhood of women most closely match the rises and falls in prostitution? Furthermore, one should not assume that the same political dynamics shape all sites of prostitution in even a single war. Following Maha as she copes with being driven out of her home in Saydia will underscore this complex equation. Saydia, Karada, Iraqi Kurdistan, refugee neighborhoods of Damascus and Amman—women's disempowerment and men's attempts to control women's bodies may be common in all five sites, but the particular mix of ethnic identities, militarism, multidimensional masculinized violence against women, state recognition, and feminist intervention may be quite distinct in each.[10]

One is left to imagine, therefore, not only what the dynamics were inside the militia-run brothel, but inside each of these Saydia homes before and after their earlier residents fled. From the bare house-by-house details offered by the reporters, one might presume that none of the adult women in the original families had paid jobs, but that might not be so. Daughters are also made invisible here; we don't know if they were in school, perhaps enrolled in university, training for careers. Nor do we know if any of the marriages were "mixed," one spouse Shiite, the other Sunni, and how that might have affected the intensity of intimidation aimed at them by militiamen. How the worried family members worked out among themselves the excruciating calculus of money, affection, aspiration, social roots, property titles, fear and physical safety is also left offstage by gender-uncurious observers.

The unexamined scenario these journalists and military commentators offered to describe and, implicitly, to explain the early stages of Saydia's ethnic cleansing is this: the husband acted as the head of each Saydia household. His job, his partisan loyalties, and his income were what allowed the family to live in this once-pleasant urban neighborhood. The adult woman of the household had no property, no loyalties or career of her own; in prewar Saydia she was merely a dependent, even if a rather comfortable dependent. One further unspoken assumption is that all members of each Saydia household were of identical religious and ethnic backgrounds and found those identities salient. As the death threats and kidnappings mounted, and as sectarian identities became ever more politicized, so this scenario seems to assume, it was left to the adult employed husband alone to weigh the pros and cons of staying or leaving Saydia, and, if the decision was to leave, to determine the family's destination. There were, presumably, no debates or internal conflicts within any of these families about who would stay, who would leave, and with whom the children would go. All the violence and intimidation, it is further imagined, were occurring outside the household, none within.

"Ethnic cleansing" has become, since the 1990s war in the former Yugoslavia, the term widely used to name the wielding of violence and intimidation for the sake of driving people of one ethnic or sectarian community out of a region—a province, a village, a neighborhood—for the sake of securing that space for members of another ethnic or sectarian community. Ethnic cleansing is an Orwellian phrase, its antiseptic connotation making it all the more frightening. By December 2007, officials estimated that in Baghdad alone, 300,000 city residents had left one neighborhood for another, seeking a modicum of security and shelter.[11]

As a step-by-step process, ethnic cleansing in practice is not as simple as the imagined scenario implies. It is a process that is complicated by the workings of, and wartime challenges to, gender ideologies and traditions, by the accepted standards of "manliness," by expectations of a "good mother," a "dutiful daughter," or "responsible son."

And what about those wielders of violence who are relied upon to drive women and men of one group out of a neighborhood or town? These are the people who send death threats, ransack houses, arrest family members, murder family members, shut off electricity, run a brothel and, sometimes, rape mothers or daughters. The gender-*un*conscious portrayal of ethnic cleansing refers to these actors as members of militias or as the personnel of biased government security forces. The unspoken assumption is that they are men. But there is too often little exploration of this assumption. For instance, we know little about how these men's understandings of, perhaps anxieties about, their own masculinities have been mobilized to serve this violent ethnicized or sectarian purpose.[12]

What did the men who killed Maha's policeman husband think they were doing? And how was the driver who drove the truck bomb into Maha's house recruited and convinced that here was a worthy cause? Perhaps these men imagined that in acting as intimidators and in wielding this violence against their fellow Baghdadis they were acting as manly fathers or as responsible sons. Even raising this possibility leads one to wonder how the kidnappers', killers', or truck driver's mothers, aunts, wives, and daughters assessed these men's violent actions.

Often the responsibility for carrying out revenge for the killing of a family member is presumed by both women and men in that extended family to fall on the shoulders of the men of the household. Added to that masculinization of revenge is the masculinized expectation of earning income. Though so many Iraqi women had entered the paid workforce since the 1970s, there remained a widespread assumption that it was male family members—as fathers, uncles, husbands, or sons—who should be the principal economic providers. Thus when some of the Iraqi insurgent and sectarian militias began to offer money to local men who joined their ranks—perhaps $50 a month—some mothers, aunts, and daughters saw it as a chance for men, regardless of their own attitudes toward violence or ethnic cleansing, to bring home money to support their households.[13] Moreover, sectarian militias and armed insurgent groups offered men who had been floundering, after they themselves had been displaced from their home neighborhoods by ethnic cleansing violence, a new community, a new sense of masculinized belonging.[14]

Marital relationships within households targeted for ethnic or sectarian cleansing have their own complex dynamics. In pre-2003 Iraq, as in pre-1992 Bosnia, pre-1994 Rwanda, and pre-2008 Georgia, men and women of different ethnic or sectarian affiliations intermarried. Some political leaders even saw these "mixed marriages" as a sign of growing national unity and of the country's modernization. Furthermore, in modernizing societies, such as Iraq under Baathist rule, social class and partisan compatibility often trumped religious affiliation. As Nadje Al-Ali notes, "Baghdadi families have frequently been multi-religious and multi-ethnic, and mixed marriages amongst urban Baghdadi middle classes were quite common."[15] Wars, in other words, are waged not just in the streets, on rooftops, and from the skies; wars are fought inside marriages. The escalation of violence depends on shredding existing marriages and redefining who can acceptably marry whom.

By early 2006, as the militarized occupation, insurgency, and sectarian battles all converged, mixed marriages were unraveling. According to a specialist in Iraqi family law, Shatha al-Quraishi, parents in mixed marriages began, often for the first time, to weigh the benefits and costs of assigning their sons and daughters one sectarian public identity or another: "For a parent, the first question now is going to be: Sunni or Shiite? . . . People are starting to talk about it. I can feel it. I can touch that something has changed."[16] This was new.

For several decades many Iraqis, especially those in middle-class urban families, had considered intermarriages part of modernization. As one Iraqi woman, a psychological counselor, explained, "We used to dismiss such instances [of parents rejecting intermarriages]. . . . They were old-fashioned. They were not civilized. They were just holding to a tradition that was meaningless."[17] But the ways in which the Iraq War was being waged—who was considering whom an enemy, which bonds of trust were being dissolved, who was being armed to combat whom, which spoils were being distributed by the foreign occupiers to whom—were reviving these seemingly outdated patterns. Wars—even those waged with the latest high-tech weaponry—can revive the "old-fashioned" ways. Wars can make "uncivilized" relationships between women and men seem reasonable. Rejected marriage proposals, rising divorce rates, new patterns of domestic violence within marriages—by 2006, all were becoming part and parcel of this war. Moreover, each was more than just a consequence of war; together, they served to perpetuate the armed conflict.

One family court judge in Baghdad told a reporter that, before this latest war, about half of all the marriage contracts he had signed were for wives and husbands coming from different Muslim sects, Shiites marrying Sunnis. But by the fourth year of the Iraq War, a mere 5 percent of those marriage contracts he was signing were for mixed marriages.[18] Haifa Zangana, an Iraqi critical of the Americans' presence, noting the previously widespread practice of intermarriage, not only among Shiite and Sunni women and men, but also among Iraqi Kurds and Arabs, asked a Kurdish friend married to an Iraqi Arab man how feasible she thought was the frequently suggested wartime proposal for a ethnically mapped, federally divided Iraq. Her friend's reply, "Well, first of all they would have to divide our bed in two."[19]

These "mixed" families' internal complexities—and the hybrid identities of their children—had to be denied if the ethnic cleansers were to conduct their intimidating, dislocating operations. Even within marriages of seemingly similar ethnic or sectarian affiliations, one spouse might have felt much more strongly about that identity than did the other. It is by no means certain, for instance, that Maha had the same attitude toward the predominance of Sunnis in the Saddam Hussein regime as did her policeman husband since he, not she, depended in part on this affiliation for employment. In other words, to fully appreciate how intimidation and violence work to destroy trust among neighbors and to replace heterogeneity with (presumed) homogeneity, we need to newly scrutinize the simplistic gender-uncurious scenario. Instead, we need to cross the threshold, go inside households, and take account of the often complex always-evolving relationships between wives and husbands, between boys, girls, and parents, and between women and men of different generations.

As the Iraq War evolved, Iraqi widowed women had been joined by divorced women as the chief caretakers of and breadwinners for their children. Divorces had multiplied in Iraq during the post–Gulf War's decade of international economic sanctions. Material hardships had translated into untenable domestic tensions.[20] Moreover, after the U.S. invasion set off sectarian conflicts, more marriages came apart as sectarian militiamen tried to impose their own ideas of who should be married to whom. In 1990s Bosnia and Rwanda pressures were imposed on women and men to avoid marriage between people of different ethnicities or religious traditions. So too in Iraq. While under the secularist Baathist regime Shiite and Sunni women and men were free to intermarry, after 2003, Iraqi women activists reported harmoniously married men and women of different sects being compelled to dissolve their marriages in order to comply with the militiamen's imagined new social order. This too raised the number of divorced Iraqi women fending for themselves and for their children in the midst of war.[21]

Marriage never becomes irrelevant simply because "there's a war on." In

the midst of this war, the newly emergent political parties and nongovernmental groups competed with each other to repeal or sustain the Baathist
era's personal status laws, which would determine the rights of women in
marriage. As we will see in chapter five, these political struggles over the
rules for women in marriage were as intense as those over oil.[22]

Following Maha on her wartime journey reveals the salience of marriage—and thus widowhood—as a cause for social anxiety and for women's
organizing amid wartime politics. Taking seriously the unfolding experiences of women displaced by wartime violence, moreover, draws our attention to the deeply gendered politics of wartime prostitution. Watching
women as refugees and displaced persons confirms feminists' growing conviction that any humanitarian relief organization will be of genuine use to
women in war zones only if it confronts the intertwined trends in domestic
violence, sexual violence, and sexual exploitation of women.

In the middle of the Iraq War, from 2006 to early 2007, the World Health
Organization teamed up with the Iraqi Ministry of Health to conduct an
ambitious survey of 9,345 Iraqi households spread over all the country's
regions.[23] Testifying to the rise in both gender consciousness and gender
analytical skills within the international health community, the researchers for the first time included in an Iraq health survey women's experiences
of domestic violence. They explored Iraqi women's experiences not only of
physical, but of what they termed emotional violence—acts of humiliation
by husbands in front of others, insulting behavior, and threats of divorce.[24]
Moreover, they crafted a methodology that took account of the social pressures that lead many women to remain silent about domestic abuse: researchers only asked about these experiences if they were assured that the woman
interviewed was alone; they did not ask these questions if a male relative was
present in the room.[25]

The researchers found that during 2005–7 Iraqi women's experiences of
emotional violence in their homes declined as their education levels rose,
but that the differences between highly educated and less educated women
were small.[26] Overall, 21.2 percent of Iraqi married women had experienced
domestic physical violence during this midwar period. Nor did researchers

find that women of different ages or education levels varied significantly in their having been physically abused within the last twelve months.[27]

These Iraqi findings should prompt us to pose deeper questions about the interplay of multiple forms of masculinized wartime violence. Masculinized militarized violence, which people working with the United Nations have begun to talk about as one form of "gender-based violence," itself can intrude into any woman's life at quite specific times. For instance, what are the consequences for any woman's confidence, mental health, and ability to cope with the stresses of war if she has been first abused by a husband within her own home and then been driven out of that home by soldiers or militiamen? What we think of as militarized violence may be only one of several forms of masculinized violence that many women experience in the midst of war. For any woman, each sort of violence may have an exacerbating impact on her experiences of another. We cannot be realistic about any war if we just look at discreet categories of violence—as politically innovative and as emotionally demanding as that is to do. We have to pay serious attention to the wartime experiences of individual women.

When Maha left Saydia in 2006, taking her four children with her to what she hoped would be the safety of Syria, she joined thousands of Iraqis who had become wartime refugees over the last twenty years. Some had left Iraq during the earlier Iran-Iraq War, while others had left during the increasingly oppressive later years of the Saddam Hussein rule. Maha was among those added thousands of Iraqis who were driven out of their country by the escalating violence of the third and fourth years of the U.S.-initiated Iraq War. In Jordan, Egypt, and Syria, whole city neighborhoods in Amman, Cairo, and Damascus were becoming known as "Little Iraq." Other Iraqis had fled to Lebanon, Turkey, Iran, or one of the Gulf States. Many Iraqis hoped to emigrate to the United States, but the Bush administration accepted only a relative handful of people fleeing the war zone it had created.

High proportions of the recent arrivals to neighboring Middle Eastern countries were women, usually with their dependent children. Most found themselves in Maha's situation: a husband dead, divorced, detained, or missing, children to care for, no social safety nets, meager finances, and no working papers. UN monitors, struggling to keep up with the scores of Iraqis fleeing their country, reported that by 2007, when Maha was trying to make ends meet in Syria, 2.8 million Iraqis had fled their homes but stayed in Iraq, moving to what they hoped would be safer places to live within the country. Another 2 million had become refugees, leaving Iraq altogether.[28]

Though it would provide no solace to Maha and the other Iraqi women who had been dislocated by the war, their condition confirmed a pattern that had developed worldwide in the early twenty-first century. In 2002, on the eve of the Iraq War, the UN High Commission for Refugees (UNHCR) estimated that there were 50 million refugees and internally displaced people around the world, and that 75–80 percent of them were women with their dependent children.[29]

Many of the Iraqis fleeing the country in 2006 were, like Maha, from Iraq's middle class, which had expanded rapidly over the last three decades. Most of the poorest Iraqis did not have the resources to leave the country. But in exile, middle-class Iraqis such as Maha were being impoverished. The governments of the host countries such as Syria were overwhelmed, unable to fund the humanitarian assistance needed to provide minimally safe and sanitary conditions for the Iraqis seeking refuge in their midst. Syrian officials refused Iraqis legal refugee status, assigning them instead the temporary status only of "guests." Syrians were fearful, too, that the intensified competition between refugees and their own citizens for jobs and resources would destabilize their own delicately balanced political system. The UNHCR, similarly, was strapped for money, able to provide what amounted to only about $30 to each Iraqi refugee.[30]

War-generated refugee crises always are caused by and shaped by gendered dynamics. Once again, to leave those dynamics unexplored—and then to choose one's actions based upon such simplistic scenarios—is naively to imagine causes and consequences of wars as simpler than in fact they are. It is not just that in the Iraq War, as in other recent conflicts, women with their dependent children were the majority of persons who became refugees. The gendered dynamics also determined whether men experienced such dislocations as a loss of masculine pride and how they behaved toward their wives as they tried to cope with that loss. Gendered dynamics simultaneously shaped women's understandings of their maternal roles when their family status had been jeopardized. Likewise, presumptions about masculinity and femininity determined what steps men and women each took to provide for themselves and their families economically.

Sajida was a refugee in 2008, forty-three years old, an Iraqi mother divorced and caring for her two sons. She tried to make a living to support herself and her children in Damascus, Syria, after she fled Iraq in 2006, the same year that Maha left. UN officials in Syria estimated that a quarter of all the Iraqis registering with the UNHCR were in women-headed households.[31]

Sajida described to a woman reporter how a militiaman belonging to the Shiite Mahdi Army had raped her in front of one of her sons in their Baghdad home. She believed he assaulted her and sought to humiliate her as a mother because she was Sunni.[32] Many women who have been raped during the war, however, have remained silent about their experiences, fearing that their neighbors and family members would see them as a source of familial shame. If these women who survived rape still had living husbands, those men sometimes resorted to violence against their wives whom they now saw as tainted.[33]

When Sajida first arrived in Syria, she found a place for herself and her two sons to live in a suburb of Damascus that already was filled with Iraqis. With only a middle-school education, Sajida managed to get a job as a seamstress in a Syrian factory, working eleven hours each day for $4. Her expenses in Damascus amounted to $220 a month. Thus when a male café owner offered her a seemingly better-paying job working in his café, she accepted. But the owner then seized her passport, a precious document to any refugee, and pressured Sajida not only to banter with the café's male clientele but offer them sexual services.[34]

An official with the UNHCR trying to provide support for Sajida, Maha, and the more than one and a half million other Iraqi refugees in Syria cautioned against labeling the growing number of Iraqi refugee women engaging in sex for money simply as prostitutes: "We call it survival sex."[35] She and other international humanitarian aid workers sought to create safe spaces for Iraqi refugee women, not shunning any woman because she had been sexually assaulted or had engaged in commercial sex. Doing their own feminist analysis of the Iraq War, these UNHCR staff people had had to rethink the politics of wartime sexuality, feminized respectability, who should be deemed "worthy" of assistance, and what sort of assistance would be most valuable.

The risks for Sajida and other women of adopting such a sexualized survival strategy, nonetheless, were high. The widowed and divorced women often felt their own self-esteem plummet. Male customers, furthermore, could be abusive, employers could be exploitive. Parents and relatives, if they discovered what a woman in the family had done in order to survive and feed her children, might interpret such actions as having dishonored her entire family, justifying rejection or even violence against the trespassing woman. Consequently, during the Iraq War humanitarian aid workers in Syria, Jordan, and Lebanon began to think about the causal links between wartime displacement, the politics of gender, honor killings, women refugees' impoverishment, patterns of rape, and the expanding commercial sex industry.[36]

At this particular point in the ongoing gendered evolution of the United Nations, women continued to be dramatically underrepresented at its senior levels. Yet women, many of them with feminist tools of analysis, were making headway in the middle levels and field operations of particular UN agencies. Since the 1980s, women's groups outside the UNHCR had pressured the agency to stop lumping male and female refugees together, to start asking whether women and men experienced displacement differently: how did women's and girls' unequal access to literacy, to control of reproduction, to public participation, to money, to physical integrity each and all together shape their abilities to cope with displacement? The answers, feminist policy experts argued, should produce new UN refugee assistance operating practices. These activists' research and lobbying bore fruit.

By the time of the Iraq War, staff people for UNHCR had taken on feminist concerns about violence against refugee women and refugee women's and girls' vulnerability to trafficking. They had begun to redesign refugee camps so that women wouldn't be so subject to assaults when going to the latrines or collecting water or firewood. They reconceptualized refugee participation so that the male head of household would not automatically be the family's recipient of food aid or the family's sole representative in refugee affairs. Thus it was not happenstance that in 2006–8 Damascus UNHCR staff people were concerned about not stigmatizing those Iraqi refugee women being drawn into prostitution and were setting up safe houses where Iraqi refugee women could come and find support in an environment of confidentiality and without judgment.[37]

To make sense of any war, these international feminist staff people had learned, one should ask about prostitution. It is unhelpful—unrealistic—to pretend that prostitution is the "oldest profession," that is, an industry that has no changing historical causes, an industry that has always remained the same. Rather, they had learned that, by taking seriously the experiences of women who had become prostitutes in wars as disparate as the U.S. Civil War, World War II, the French and U.S. wars in Vietnam, and the wars that broke apart Yugoslavia, women become—or are pushed into—wartime prostitution at particular moments during a prolonged war.

Thus, too, Iraqi refugee women resorting to prostitution and men seeking them out as paying clients were not ahistorical constants in Iraqi society. Prostitution grew during the period of international economic sanctions. It grew even more rapidly with the wartime impoverishment of Iraqi women as single mothers and widows and with men's wartime assumption that they should have women's sexual services commercially available to them.

It was these feminist-informed activists, nongovernmental organizations, and UN staff people who conducted the gendered analyses of wartime refugees and displaced persons that persuaded the UN Security Council's state delegates to pass UN Security Council Resolution 1325 on Women, Peace, and Security. The historic resolution was passed by the Security Council in October 2000, in the aftermath of feminist research and activism during and after the armed conflicts in Cambodia, former Yugoslavia, Rwanda, Sri Lanka, South Africa, El Salvador, Guatemala, and East Timor. It was the first Security Council resolution in the history of the United Nations that focused specifically on women, on their rights to take meaningful part in all peace negotiations, and on their particular vulnerability to sexual assault in war zones, as refugees and as displaced persons.[38]

The thinking that went into SCR 1325 built upon the work of feminist lawyers, health care workers, aid agency staffers and local women's advocates who, throughout the 1990s, had lobbied to make governments and international judges and prosecutors treat rape as a distinct war crime. The inclusion of "systematic wartime rape" as well as both forced births and forced abortions in the list of prosecutable war crimes under the international Treaty of Rome authorizing the new International Crimes Court came about through these feminists' years of research and activism. Such political gendered transformations are not the result of mere passage of time. Progress in human affairs never is.

Despite this new feminist-promoted international awareness of the roles that violence against women have played in justifying and perpetuating wars and the alarming reports drawing attention during the same years as the Iraq War of scores of women being raped by male combatants in the Darfur region of Sudan and in the eastern Congo, there was little sustained attention devoted to the wartime incidences of, motivations for, perpetrators of, survivors of, and political consequences of sexual assault of Iraqi women. There were stories circulating, however, such as that told by Sajida, of women being raped by sectarian and criminal gangs engaged in kidnappings and in ethnic cleansing campaigns. (Simultaneously, as we will see in chapter seven, there were multiple reports surfacing of rapes of American military women perpetrated by their own American male military colleagues, though these stories unfortunately were not being analytically connected to the stories of Iraqi women being raped.)

As in many other societies, women who have survived sexual assaults have not reported them because they have distrusted the authorities and/or feared that such public knowledge would only stigmatize them. Wartime struggles were hard enough for refugee, internally displaced, and kidnapped Iraqi women without their enduring the added charge that, by making their survival of sexual assaults public, they had dishonored their families.[39] In addition, according to investigators from Human Rights Watch, Iraqi women found that the Iraqi police were too distracted by what their senior officials deemed higher-priority missions, as well as too-ill-equipped—as were hospital staff—to respond sensitively and effectively to reports of rape by those women who dared to submit reports.[40] In some instances, women told investigators that it was men of the Iraqi Ministry of Interior's security forces who had been their assailants, making it all the more problematic for them to report the rapes to the Iraqi authorities.[41]

Those women who became refugees in Jordan, Syria, and Iraq's other neighboring countries feared that if they reported rapes to those governments' authorities, they would expose themselves as refugees without the proper papers and be sent back to Iraq. Only a few women rape survivors found their ways to supportive clinics, local women's rights groups, or the women's centers of the UNHCR.[42]

Maha made no mention of sexual assault or threat of rape when she told of her reasons for fleeing Saydia, nor did she mention any Syrian employers offering her sexualized jobs. Maha fled what she saw to be the escalating sectarian violence that made living on in Saydia untenable, taking her children with her across the border to Syria. She didn't possess the necessary working papers, she had four children to feed, and she was competing for scarce Syrian jobs with thousands of other Iraqi refugees fleeing Iraq's wartime violence. She pawned her wedding ring and other jewelry, but her savings quickly dwindled. She had hoped that her uncle would be able to join her in Syria, but he was unable to acquire the needed visa. After a year, Maha felt she had no choice but to return to Baghdad.

Back in Baghdad on Haifa Street in late 2007, Maha promised her uncle that she and her children wouldn't stay long at his crowded apartment. At forty years old and with children to support, however, Maha needed a paying job in order to afford her own apartment. Her meager finances were stretched to the limit. After all, Maha was now the head of her household. She had become a war widow.[43]

Women lose their husbands in both peacetime and wartime. As widows, though, they become an especially salient political category in wartime and afterward because they so frequently are used by political and intellectual

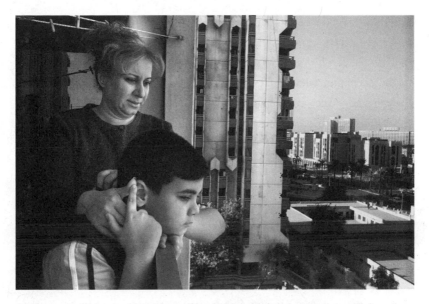

FIGURE 2. Maha on the balcony of her uncle's Baghdad apartment with her son, December 2007. (Photo: Scott Nelson)

elites to symbolize the nation's sacrifice. Citizens are urged to grieve collectively with each of the government's favored wartime widows, women whose husbands died honorably for the approved cause. To support these widows, it is claimed, is to support the nation and, by extension, its government, and its war. Flowers, tears, memorial flags, words of encouragement and gratitude offered to selected wartime widows are seen to be contributions to national unity. Grieving along with these widows confirms the meaningfulness of the cause for which their husbands died.

In reality, most wartime widowed women on all sides of a conflict are left to cope on their own with their grief, their impending impoverishment, and their multiplying responsibilities. Wartime widows simultaneously must navigate their country's sexist inheritance laws, the bureaucratic red tape, and the not-always-altruistic expectations of relatives. Only occasionally, as in postgenocide Rwanda, are women able to organize as widows and become a public force to be reckoned with.[44] When women do organize as wartime widows, they can make men in power nervous. There are usually official efforts to co-opt the widows groups' members and to round off the sharp edges of their analyses. After all, women as wartime widows are hard to use as galvanizing symbols of feminized national sacrifice if they are holding protests outside the government's offices, charging officials with neglect, secrecy, and unfairness.[45]

Organizing during wartime is never easy. If they do not remain solitary and silent, widows risk losing the sympathies of both officials and their fellow citizens. To organize as widows is made all the harder and thus unlikely if, like Maha, they have become their families' sole income earners, have been displaced from their own home neighborhoods and web of social contacts, and know that violence makes it risky for them to leave home or temporary shelter, especially when newly emboldened militiamen are taking upon themselves the authority to police women's public behavior.

In Iraq some widowed women overcame these formidable obstacles to form the wartime Iraqi Widows' Organization. Its leader was Raja al-Khuzai. In 2006, she explained her motivation for activism: "I didn't like to see Iraqi women humiliated like they were during the Saddam [Hussein] time.... I don't like to see them begging in the street, and taking their kids out of school."[46] Other widowed women were supported by Iraqi women's rights groups, whose activists saw providing practical support for widows to be a part of their larger campaign to gain fair treatment for all women during turbulent times.[47]

One woman who had sought out an Iraqi women's group was Khalida Shakir Salih. Her husband had been killed when his food delivery truck was shot as he tried to make a delivery run from Baghdad south to Basra. Even before the current war, Khalida had had to cope with caring for their six children for a whole year when her husband had been jailed by the Saddam Hussein regime. Now, newly widowed at forty-one, Khalida had come to rely on the meager income from her teenage son's falafel stand. She had no widow's pension and no employment of her own: "I wish I could find a job but my sons refused that. Because of our traditions, they said, 'We'll not let you work because it's shameful for us that you work and we just watch.'"[48]

Masculinized shame, feminized silence, gendered understandings of "tradition," maternal care, women's access to paid work, the proprieties and economies of widowhood—each of these are at work shaping the lived realities of women and of men in any war.

By the sixth year of the Iraq War, Maha was struggling to get back on her feet while living with her uncle in another Baghdad neighborhood. She was an internally displaced returnee, a widow, a single mother, unemployed, and crowded with her four children into an uncle's apartment. Maha and other newly widowed women augmented the numbers of Iraqi women who already had lost their husbands in the prolonged Iran-Iraq War of the 1980s and in the 1990–91 Gulf War. They had become so prominent on Iraq's social landscape that Haifa Zangana titled her book about the history of Iraqi women's political resistance *City of Widows*.[49]

The Iran-Iraq War alone had cost the lives of five hundred thousand male Iraqi soldiers. Thousands more men returned from the battlefields in the late 1980s seriously wounded, not able to work, and needing daily care from women in their families.[50] Added to their numbers now were thousands more Iraqi veterans, wounded as Iraqi government soldiers during the 2003 U.S. invasion or as soldiers in the U.S.-created new Iraqi military. Many of these male veterans received minimal medical care and little in the way of promised government pensions. They too relied on handouts from relatives and the care and meager incomes of their wives.[51]

An Iraqi woman named Ruba told a Red Cross interviewer in 2008 how it felt to be simultaneously a widow, an internally displaced person, and a wartime head of household. Ruba was thirty-eight, living with her cousin's family—twelve adults and children in one room. She thought back to the times when "we always sat down together for lunch and laughed." She longed now, she said, just for a bit of normalcy, especially for her children to go to school:

My children and I left my home in Anbar governorate almost two years ago. My husband had been killed right in front of us. I had to protect my children, so we fled the same night with nothing but some money. For me, today, there is no past and no future, only a horrible present. I only wish I had some photos of my husband and my family. I can see it all in my mind but I don't know for how long I will remember.[52]

And just when more and more Iraqi women were being widowed, trying to make ends meet without a second adult bringing home a salary, the Iraqi economy went into a tailspin and sexist discrimination in the job market became more acceptable and widespread. To economically provide for families, women as widows (or as wives of men who had disappeared into the sprawling detention systems of the U.S. and Iraqi security forces) had to compete with unemployed men in the shrunken and increasingly sexist job market. By mid-2007, Sarah Muthulak, a spokeswoman for an Iraqi women's group, Women's Rights Association, reported, "In about fourteen percent of families in Iraq women are the main breadwinners and often they care for a large number of children."[53]

A year later, in early 2008, it was estimated that one million formerly married Iraqi women were widows or divorcees or were living without husbands who had been taken in gang kidnappings and military detentions.[54] The International Committee of the Red Cross noted that "tens of thousands of Iraqis, almost all of them men," were being held in detention by the Iraqi authorities, often without their wives and mothers being able to find out their whereabouts, what charges they were being held on, or even whether they were alive.[55] The wives of these men were forced to live in a netherworld between wifedom and widowhood, yet their daily lives were lived as women heads of households.

During the Iraq War losing one's husband and home and neighborhood often happened simultaneously, as it did for Maha. For instance, Sabriyah Hilal Abadi had been a seamstress before the war. Her husband had worked in a government-owned factory. Together, the couple had brought home enough income to support their four children and pay the rent on their apartment. Then Abadi's husband became a victim of the kidnappings that sowed fear in urban neighborhoods. In July 2005, after armed men pushed her husband into a car, she never saw him again.[56] Now husbandless, she had been forced out of her apartment. Being resourceful, Abadi had taken shelter with her children in an empty, dilapidated Baathist Party building in the Zayouna neighborhood of Baghdad. Soon other newly homeless women and their children joined her. But then the new government's soldiers forced her out, claiming that Abadi and the other women and their children were squatters, that this was a government building, and that squatters like her were the cause of crime in the area. At that point Abadi accepted an AK-47 rifle from friends who were worried about her security. Before the war, she told a reporter, she never would have held a rifle. But times had changed. Gendered expectations can shift as a war proceeds. She commented, "The women now take on the responsibilities of men and women."[57]

As the Iraq War wore on, more Iraqi women acquired guns for their own protection. Many of them were working women, lucky to have jobs and needing to travel back and forth to their employment. Some were divorced or widowed women who felt doubly vulnerable: not only were they living in a war zone, they were living without the protection of a father or husband. And still other women were encouraged by their husbands to carry and learn how to use a gun for their own protection.[58]

Hence by year five of the Iraq War, with more guns in circulation in Iraq society, the gender politics of gun owning had somewhat changed. Many of the guns had been imported by the U.S. government, to be distributed to the newly reorganized Iraqi security forces. But there was no question of female armed militias. Rather, as more and more of the masculinized groups in Iraq turned on women and more and more women felt vulnerable and unprotected, increasing numbers of Iraqi women, though still a minority, came to believe that they had to provide for their own protection. The gendered politics of protector/protected is one of the cultural cornerstones of any political system, but a cornerstone set in sand is not stable.

The Iraqi state had had an elaborate welfare service. Until the international economic sanctions of the 1990s and the subsequent Iraq War, Iraq's had been one of the most extensive welfare states in the Middle East. The causes included both Iraqi women's years of political lobbying and the Saddam Hussein regime's initial aspiring to modernity and its later worries that Iraqis' fall into impoverishment in the aftermath of the Iran-Iraq War and the Gulf War would further undermine the government's tenuous legitimacy.

Thus it was to the Ministry of Labor and Social Affairs that women who had become widowed were supposed to apply for and collect a small state pension allocated for widows. The ministry employees struggled to keep up with the demand. A widow with no children was eligible for a monthly stipend of $34. A woman widowed and caring for five or more children could claim $81 per month. Neither amount would keep a woman out of poverty, but it was something.[59]

Maha or any other widow would have to overcome daunting challenges if she were to collect even these modest pensions. First, she would have to travel to Baghdad—or from one of the capital's neighborhoods to another—in order to appear in person at the ministry. This would cost money, and travel itself—through areas under militia control, and through military checkpoints staffed by nervous gun-wielding American soldiers who spoke no Arabic, who misread Iraqi hand gestures and who looked at any car carrying Iraqis with suspicion—jeopardized a woman's safety. Second, a widow would have to possess the necessary documents to prove to the ministry's officials that she was eligible for a widow's pension, a requirement hard to fulfill if one had had to flee from one neighborhood to another in the face of sectarian or military violence. If a woman were internally displaced, living temporarily with a relative or occupying an abandoned building, she would not even have a legally recognized home address. Moreover, the bodies of many Iraqis who had been killed never made it to the morgue, leaving some widows without an official death certificate to show to the ministry officials. And, even if these multiple challenges could be somehow surmounted, a woman would have to trust that the increasingly politicized and sectarian ministry officials would treat her application fairly. Would they ask her religious affiliation? Would they be hostile if she had been in a mixed marriage? Had her husband been on the "wrong side" during the Baathist era? Would giving the name of her former hometown or neighborhood set off political alarm bells in the ministry?

In December 2007, five years into the Iraq war, Maha and eleven of her relatives were sharing two bedrooms in a neighborhood of modern apartment buildings on Baghdad's Haifa Street. In the lexicon of international law, while outside Iraq, Maha had been a foreign "guest" and a "refugee"; now that she was camping out in her uncle's overcrowded Baghdad apartment, Maha had become, instead, an "internally displaced person."

Displacement wasn't what the Iraqi government's officials had envisioned when, in the fall of 2007, they confidently urged Iraqis to come home from abroad.[60] They naively had imagined that what they judged to be the country's improved security would itself allow Maha to return to her former beloved Saydia neighborhood, where she would be known and accepted.

When the Iraqi government began to urge Iraqis to return home, promising renewed security and providing buses from Syria and Jordan, Maha decided to take the risk and invest her remaining funds in bus fares for her and her four children. What she discovered when she returned to the capital, however, was that her Saydia neighborhood remained so dangerous that she dared not return to it.[61] Another woman from Saydia demonstrated how hard it would be to recover a former home in the neighborhood. Since returning to Baghdad in mid-2008, Um Ali described how she had collected all the documents to prove she owned the Saydia house now occupied by another family, how she had spent days going from ministry to ministry to acquire all the signatures and official stamps needed. But still she was short of reoccupying her Saydia home.[62]

In Cairo, Adnan Abdel-Jabbar was another of the Iraqi refugee women who, like Maha, had become a maternal refugee, the sole caretaker of her children. Also like Maha, she had decided to return to Iraq less because she shared the prime minister's optimistic assessment of Iraq's security improvement than because her money had run out. As she stood among other returning Iraqis in the crowded Cairo airport in September 2008, she explained, "Of course, we are afraid. But we are at the end of our rope."[63]

By February 2009, when the Iraqi and U.S. governments had begun to congratulate themselves on the handover of responsibility for maintaining security to Iraqis and the formal setting of a date (December 31, 2011) for the departure of all U.S. troops, women as widows were still a major sector of society left in a state of profound insecurity. Many war widows were internally displaced persons living in desperation and isolation in a government-supplied trailer park. Officials chose to situate the trailer park in one of Baghdad's poorest neighborhoods. Despite the outspoken critiques by Iraqi women members of parliament, government ministries were distributing public assistance to only one in six of the estimated 780,000 Iraqi war widows.[64]

Commonly during wars, policy makers and media observers frame debates in terms of whether there is progress toward ending the armed conflict and, if the chosen measures are tending in a hopeful direction, what actions should get credit for achieving that progress. In Iraq, few commentators made the sense of security experienced by displaced Iraqi widows their criterion for progress. Fewer still studied the numbers of Iraqi displaced women in prostitution to determine the current direction of the conflict.

Rather, many observers chose as their criterion the incidences of overt public violence. For instance, at the end of November 2008, the Iraqi Interior Ministry released figures showing that, while 148 Iraqi civilians had been killed by bombs in the month just ending, compared with a lower number, 118, who had been killed in October, yet a higher figure, 156, had died in September. It wasn't a clear line of progress, but it could be interpreted as some progress.[65] Taking a multimonth view, and seeing those deadly incidences declining in relative number, U.S. government officials and their military commanders pointed to the increase of U.S. military personnel deployed to Iraq in 2007 and 2008—the "surge"—as the cause: the policy of sending thousands more U.S. troops to Iraq's urban areas should be credited with the relative decline in public violence.

An American geographer, John Agnew, decided to test this causal claim. Using a carefully calibrated mapping of nighttime light (a sign, he thought, of a neighborhood's access to public services and of people's sense of security) in Iraq's principal cities from 2006 through 2007 and overlaying that with a time-sensitive mapping of neighborhood-by-neighborhood ethnic cleansings, he came to a surprising conclusion. His night light data strongly suggested that the reason for the decline in public incidences of urban violence was not the U.S. military surge. Instead, the decline, he believed, was the result of so many urban neighborhoods having been repopulated during 2006–7 in ways that made them each homogenously sectarian and thus unlikely to be the sites of new public violence. That is, by the time the U.S. government sent new infusions of military personnel into Iraq's cities, the segregating damage had been done. Moreover, his mapping revealed that neighborhoods that were primarily Sunni or were once mixed in their populations—such as Maha's Saydia neighborhood—had not enjoyed any increase in access to public electricity.[66]

By 2008, Maha's once-beloved Saydia neighborhood was so transformed that this widowed mother of four saw little chance of her ever returning. And those few lights that were brightening the nighttime sky over Saydia? Perhaps some of them came from the militia-controlled brothel.

CHAPTER FOUR

Safah

The Girl from Haditha

Safah Yunis Salem was thirteen when it happened. She was a teenage girl then, in November 2005, living with her parents, brothers, and sisters, aunts, and uncles in the provincial city of Haditha.[1] Until that day, Haditha had been just a city like many other cities in wartime Iraq, its residents caught up in the town's own distinctive local political and sectarian allegiances and conflicts, each magnified by the operations of the occupying U.S. military. Haditha is located 150 miles north of Baghdad, in the northeastern region of Anbar province. It sits on the banks of the historic Euphrates River. Farms on the outskirts of Haditha had been known for their abundant harvests of food crops. Not far away, a dam on the river was a major source of Iraq's hydroelectric power.

Two and a half years into the war, Anbar province had become defined by American wartime strategists as the heart of the armed insurgency against both foreign occupation and the emergence of Shiite-affiliated parties' control of the central government. American strategists and journalists referred to Anbar and Haditha as within the "Sunni triangle." Thirteen-year-old Safah was coming into her adolescence in an intensely militarized city.

Yet it was only on November 19, 2005, that Haditha became "Haditha." The name became a popular shorthand for massacre. It joined the ranks of other places where people's complex and dynamic lives have been shrunken into popular shorthand for politically salient violent events. One thinks of "My Lai" or "Srebrenica" or "Wounded Knee." Safah, a teenage girl in Haditha, was one of the few survivors of "Haditha."

That morning on November 19, 2005, a convoy of U.S. Marines was returning to its heavily fortified base in Haditha when one of its trucks hit a roadside bomb. One marine was killed instantly. He was a popular young man in his close-knit squad. The other marines in the all-male infantry unit leaped out of their vehicles, thinking that they had come under hostile fire. That deadly supposition would become a point of intense debate over the next three years. In the heat of the moment on that November day, the American marines turned their attention and their firepower toward two neighboring houses not far from the side of the road. Four marines stormed the houses. They were led by Staff Sergeant Frank Wuterich. This was his first experience of live combat. But several of the other enlisted men he led that day were veterans of the 2004 house-to-house battle of Falluja, another city within the Sunni triangle. These veterans of the battle of Falluja knew how to "clear" potentially hostile houses. Over the next several hours, the four American marines killed nineteen Iraqis within the two houses and another five Iraqi men standing nearby, outside a taxi.

All twenty-four Iraqis killed by the marines turned out to be civilians. They included women, young children, and an older man in a wheelchair. None had been wielding weapons. None had posed a threat to the Americans. The senior American commanders to whom Staff Sergeant Wuterich reported the incident, including the killing of civilians, conducted only a cursory investigation. They dismissed the Iraqi civilian deaths as merely an unavoidable part of any war, as "collateral damage."

It was only months later, due to the protests of Haditha's enraged Iraqi witnesses and central government officials, together with dogged questioning by a reporter for *Time Magazine,* that the details of the marines' shootings that day—as well as the dismissive response of their senior officers—surfaced. They prompted the Defense Department to conduct a thorough but belated investigation. By 2006, as the investigators' findings made their way into the media and the halls of Congress, Haditha was on its way to becoming "Haditha."[2]

As "Haditha," the event caused many Americans to ask far-reaching, if uncomfortable, questions. Were American military personnel, especially those deployed in combat units, effectively trained to distinguish between civilians and combatants, and to take the necessary precautionary steps to protect civilians—even in the heat of what they might imagine to be battle? Or, alternatively, were the U.S. military's carefully honed "rules of engagement" honored more in the breach than in practice?

Interviews with American men who had served in Iraq during these years suggested that protecting your comrades came first. Shoot Now, Ask Questions Later was not just a military tactic, it was, many American soldiers and marines had become convinced, the only way to be a "good buddy." Bonds of friendship among soldiers in the midst of a war could prove a danger to civilians.[3]

Moreover, not only many of the American men on the ground, but their commanding officers as well, believed that by 2005 the Iraq War had become a conflict where no one should expect ordinary American soldiers to be able to tell with any certainty the difference between civilians and combatants. American commanders, investigators, and the officers sitting in judgment in criminal hearings back home in the United States, it was commonly believed, should accept an inescapable reality: combatants and civilians are indistinguishable in the "fog of war."

Collateral damage, the fog of war, cover-ups, combat stress, soldiers' loyalties, rules of engagement, military justice, the politics of occupation—they all converged in "Haditha."

By late 2008, U.S. military courts had dismissed most of the charges against the four American male enlisted marines who had fired the shots into the houses in Haditha on November 19, 2005. The case was too "cold," observers said, by the time the Naval Criminal Investigation undertook a serious investigation.[4] Still, damning evidence had been collected. That evidence revealed that several of the Iraqi women, men, and children had been shot at point-blank range by American marines that November day. It also confirmed that the five Iraqi civilian men who had been forced out of their taxi had been shot from a few feet away; they did not try to run. This evidence notwithstanding, there still was not sufficient evidence to convince a U.S. military judge and jury. By late 2008, three years after the killing of twenty-four Iraqi civilians at Haditha, only one man, Staff Sgt. Frank Wuterich, still was standing trial. And many analysts of the military justice system expected that he would be acquitted or that his case also would be dismissed for lack of sufficient credible evidence.

As in the cases of "Tailhook"—the 1991 Las Vegas convention of U.S. aircraft carrier pilots and their superiors and corporate suppliers at which civilian and military women were systematically sexually harassed[5]—and of "Abu Ghraib"—the 2003 incidences of abuse of Iraqi prisoners by U.S. enlisted military male and female guards—so too in "Haditha": the event's legacy would not flow from the convictions of the accused perpetrators or of their military and civilian superiors. Instead, the legacy of "Haditha" would lie in hoped-for institutional lessons learned and perpetual questioning— questioning about the nature of war, about militarized masculinities, and about the causes and consequences of political impunity.

Thus in 2007, two years after the killings in Haditha, when a platoon of thirty U.S. marines deployed to Afghanistan killed at least ten Afghan civilians, among them a young woman and an elderly man, and wounded thirty-three other civilians in Ningarhar Province, a *New York Times* journalist who had closely covered the Haditha investigations thought he saw a parallel. As in Haditha, the American marines in Ningarhar had begun shooting in immediate reaction to the explosion of a bomb (sparked this time by a single suicide bomber, rather than by a roadside bomb). Once again, no one took precautionary steps to determine whether the targets of their fierce shooting were the source of the bomb. This violent Afghan incident of American soldiers opening fire precipitously was, the journalist Paul von Zielbauer wrote, "an episode that bore some striking similarities to the Haditha killings and suggested that the lesson had not taken."[6]

Where is Safah Yunis Salem in all this? Safah had joined the Vietnamese villagers in My Lai, the American women harassed by pilots in the Las Vegas hotel corridors, and the Iraqi male prisoners abused in the U.S.-run prison: each had been pushed aside intellectually and emotionally by most observers.

What had been imagined to matter most, especially to Americans, but also to many other commentators, in "My Lai," "Tailhook," "Abu Ghraib," and now "Haditha" had been the American military perpetrators—their motivations, their failings, their fears, their worldviews, their loyalties, their punishments, their impunity. Observers' preoccupation, even if critical, stemmed from a risky parochialism. The American soldiers and their superiors outrage us, worry us, appeal to our sympathies, fuel our outrage, and inspire us to write our reams of political analysis.

Taking Safah seriously can help us make fuller sense of girls and girl-hood in war. Paying attention to Safah can shed light on how local male and female civilians cope with foreign military occupiers. Refusing to let Safah slide out of the frame can make us more realistic about the prospects for sustainable postwar peace, about the weak mechanisms for accountability, about measures of progress in the midst of a war—and about the length of any postwar era.[7]

Safah, the thirteen-year-old Iraqi girl, told observers that she had sur-vived the marines' attacks on that November day by pretending she was dead. She pretended she was dead after she had witnessed the camouflaged, helmeted, armed American men kill her aunt point-blank there in her own home. She wasn't merely a victim; she was a girl who observed and took action despite severe constraints.[8]

Months after the marines' killing of her relatives, Safah was interviewed by an American military investigator, working with an interpreter. She was the sole survivor in what investigators referred to as "House 2." Next door, in "House 1," two other younger children, a nine-year-old girl and her six-year-old brother, also had survived. The investigators did not inquire about the other members of Safah's family, which relatives were supporting her, how they were faring. Their fates remained uncertain.

The investigator recorded only Safah's account of the shootings she wit-nessed that day:

Safah Yunis Salim Rasif (Safah) statement through an interpreter claims
a Marine threw a grenade into the room and closed the door. The
grenade did not explode. The grenade caused them all to move to the

FIGURE 3. The bodies of Safah's relatives killed by U.S. Marines in Haditha, November 2005, shrouded and awaiting burial. (Photo: Lucian Read/Rapport)

back part of the room near the bed. After hearing what sounded like pipes bursting and running water from down the hall, her Aunt opened the door and saw Yunis lying on the ground. Her Aunt started to scream and was then shot through the doorway by a Marine. The Marine continued into the room and started shooting at everyone on the bed. She described the Marine as being shorter than her at somewhat around 5 foot 8 inches. She also has several inconsistent statements with regard to small details but ultimately her version is that a Marine sprayed the room with M16 fire after shooting her Aunt. Because she dove to the side of the bed she did not see the actual shooting. After the shooting she passed out and remembers pretending she was dead when some Marines came into the room. She heard a Marine say "they are all dead." When the Marines left she went to her Uncle's house.[9]

It has been rare to hear—even if secondhand—an Iraqi girl's account of a U.S. military house raid. More common have been photographs taken by foreign photographers embedded in military units. Photos taken in the heat of a military raid show girls in a family home huddled in a corner, usually, with their mother or aunt, while large, heavily armed American soldiers with guns poised rapidly search the house for weapons and for suspicious men. Sometimes the photo is taken after one of the girls' older brothers or father or uncle has been hooded and handcuffed to be taken away in the back of an American truck to a destination unknown for a time unspecified. Unlike the daytime raid on Safah's home, most American and Iraqi military raids that have been filmed or photographed have occurred in the middle of the night—in Baghdad or Falluja or Mosul or Haditha—when family members have been awakened from sleep. The award-winning American documentary film *The War Tapes*, filmed by male soldiers of the New Hampshire National Guard, shows them carrying out their unit's neighborhood nighttime operations. The American soldiers break down the home's door, shine strobe-strength bright lights, and bark commands at Iraqi civilians, some of which are translated by the soldiers' Arabic translator, as women and girls of the family huddle together.[10]

Time after time in press photos, we see a girl in her nightclothes, looking stunned. We hear nothing at the moment or afterward from the girl, what she is thinking, what she later tells her friends, what she asks her mother, what she writes in her diary, what she keeps bottled up inside herself.

This common wartime image of the frightened silent girl, huddled to one side as the male soldiers seem to take up all the space in every room they occupy and as they challenge those Iraqi men of the family whom they deem threatening, communicates a core message: this is a men's war; women and girls, mothers doing their best to protect their daughters, naturally will be pushed to the side. In their huddled marginality, however, they matter. They are crucial to the nighttime war tableau: these mothers and their daughters in their nightclothes, sitting on the floor against the wall, underscore the dominant centrality of militarized masculinities.

Riverbend, the young woman Iraqi blogger, provides us with one of the few firsthand accounts in English of what it has been like to endure a nighttime military raid. It was February 11, 2006, four months after the killing of Safah's family members in Haditha.[11] Riverbend and her parents had traveled from their own Baghdad neighborhood to Riverbend's aunt's and uncle's house to celebrate the sixteenth birthday of "J.," Riverbend's female cousin. J.'s mother had cooked a delicious lunch of rice and meat wrapped in grape leaves (*dolma*), along with biryani rice and stuffed chicken. Everyone had sung "Happy Birthday" to J. and given her small presents—the most unusual being a Swiss army knife, given to J. by her father, who told his daughter it would provide useful protection. Riverbend, looking on, thought to herself that when she had turned sixteen, no one had thought to give her a shiny new knife.

Riverbend's parents went back to their own home that evening, but Riverbend stayed on to keep her cousins, J. and T., company. The girls changed into their pajamas; there was no electricity, but they stayed up late talking, listening to songs on the battery-powered radio, and finishing off the last of the birthday cake. It was 2:00 A.M. when they first noticed that something unusual was afoot. The girls' mobile phones had stopped picking up signals. When they lifted the receiver on the home telephone, they found it had gone dead. The last time this had happened, one of Riverbend's cousins recalled, there had been a raid. They sat still and listened intently. At first, they could hear only the neighbors' home generators and a barking dog. Then the girls heard the distant rumble of trucks. One of the girls ran to wake up her father. No one knew whether the raid would be by American or Iraqi soldiers. By early 2006, it could have been either.

Thanks to the girls having been awake, Riverbend's aunt and uncle had a few minutes to make their preparations. Her uncle unlocked the house doors and the garden gate. He explained: "The animals will break down the doors if they aren't open in three seconds and they'll be all over the garden and the house . . . last time they pushed the door open on poor Abu H. three houses down and broke his shoulder."[12] Her aunt made the bed, got dressed, and woke up her infant son.

Riverbend's cousins and their parents lived in a neighborhood that had grown rapidly during the 1980s. Its residents were a mix of Sunnis, Shiites, and Christians, people who had known each other for two decades. Her aunt was angry: "This is the third time the bastards raid the area in 2 months. . . . We'll never get any peace and quiet. . . . We don't know what they are looking for."[13]

Riverbend and her teenage cousins changed into their jeans and sweaters. They all sat together with Riverbend's aunt in the living room, waiting. They could hear the raiding soldiers moving from house to house, getting closer. The last time they had raided this neighborhood, the soldiers had taken away four men, one of them a grandfather, two of them university students in their twenties. Everyone knew that none of the four arrested men had been heard of since. It was thus important for everyone to suppress their anger and do nothing that could possibly provoke the raiding men. Riverbend's aunt orchestrated the family's response, while sitting on the couch and holding her infant son in her arms: "'There will be no problem,' My aunt said sternly, looking at each of us, thin-lipped. 'You will not say anything improper and they will come in, look around and go.'" She then looked pointedly at her husband—he had started smoking again after having quit—and asked if he had all his papers ready to show the soldiers. He nodded.[14] There was nothing left to do now but wait.

"Suddenly the house was filled with strange men, yelling out orders and stomping into rooms. It was chaotic. We could see flashing lights in the garden and lights coming from the hallways."[15] This time the raiders were Iraqi male soldiers, part of the new government's army trained by the Americans. Riverbend's uncle went outside to try to talk to them. Two of the soldiers came into the living room. They wielded Kalashnikov rifles. Riverbend's aunt answered their brusque questions. One of Riverbend's female cousins put up her hands to shield her eyes from the bright lights the soldiers were shining at them, but dropped her hands when one of the soldiers shouted at her. "I squinted in the strong light," Riverbend recalled, "and as my eyesight adjusted, I noticed they were wearing masks, only their eyes and mouths showing. I glanced at my cousins and noted that T. was barely breathing. J. was sitting perfectly still, eyes focused on nothing in particular. I vaguely noted that her sweater was on backwards."[16]

Then someone called from outside, doors started slamming, the masked men rushed out. Suddenly it was over. Riverbend and her aunt and cousins were left in the dark.

Her aunt, so seemingly collected during the raid, now was sobbing quietly.

One of her daughters tried to comfort her. "Houses are no longer sacred," her aunt explained. "We can't sleep.... We can't live.... If you can't be safe in your own house, where can you be safe? The animals ... the bastards."[17]

Hours later, as neighbors began to exchange experiences and information, Riverbend and her cousins discovered that one elderly local man had suffered a heart attack during the raid. The soldiers wouldn't allow his son to take him to the hospital; he died. Piecing together other local accounts amongst themselves, neighbors tallied up the number of men taken away by the soldiers: a dozen. On one nearby street not a single household was left with an adult male. This would have dire economic consequences for their families. Among those men taken away were lawyers, engineers, students, ordinary laborers; almost all were Sunnis. Riverbend also learned that, while the soldiers who came into the homes had been Iraqi, the soldiers who had been hovering a few blocks away, securing the outer boundaries of the neighborhood, were American: "It was a coordinated raid."[18] Under the terms of the new U.S.-Iraq security agreement, hammered out by the Bush and al-Maliki administrations, which went into effect on January 1, 2008—the so-called Status of Forces Agreement, or SOFA—both American and Iraqi military and police forces would have to obtain search warrants from an Iraqi judge before raiding an Iraqi residence. Officers in both forces worried out loud about the constraints this new rule would impose on their separate and joint efforts to track down and detain alleged insurgents and terrorists.[19] For Safah and other civilian Iraqis, the question remained open: would these new rules, dependent on a judge's discretion and on the transformed attitudes among military and police personnel, reduce their nighttime terrors?

The independent Web site iraqbodycount.org was generally considered a credible (to some, overly cautious) source of information on the number of Iraqi civilians killed in the Iraq War. In August 2008, iraqbodycount.org estimated that, in 2007 alone, at least 658 Iraqi children had been killed in incidents related to the war.[20] As notable as that 658 number was, it left uncounted all the girls and boys who had been left physically wounded by military operations and insurgent bombings. The casualty figure also did not cover those boys and girls, such as Safah and Riverbend's teenage cousins, who might have suffered severe mental health problems as the result of witnessing acts of wartime intimidation or violence.

Posttraumatic stress disorder—PTSD—became a topic of growing American alarm by 2005, as thousands of U.S. male and female soldiers began returning home from deployments to Iraq and Afghanistan. PTSD was treated by most Americans as if it were an American disease, maybe even an American male soldier's disease. Many feminist activists and health professionals working internationally with women survivors of rape have hoisted warning flags, noting how PTSD can be equally disabling for the women wartime rape survivors they work with. Nonetheless, it still was American male military sufferers of PTSD who monopolized popular attention. The reality is quite different.

In August 2008, a new clinic opened in a Baghdad hospital. It would be the first to specialize in serving the health needs of Iraqi children suffering from posttraumatic stress disorder. The Iraqi girls and boys who were treated by the clinic's doctors couldn't sleep at night, were afraid of the dark, and endured perpetual anxiety. Some of the children had been kidnapped. Some of the girls had been kidnapped and raped. "Especially in children, especially in the female, any psychological problem is a stigma," according to Dr. Haider Maliki, Iraq's sole child psychiatrist working at a government hospital.[21] Parents and relatives of those girls and boys showing these trauma symptoms, as is so common everywhere, were puzzled, worried, and afraid. Yet enough of them were seeking help that this one underfunded public hospital's staff decided to devote one of their wards solely to treating these wartime traumatized children. Still, it would have been difficult and risky for relatives of a girl living in Haditha to travel all the way down to the capital to seek these specialists' assistance.

Simultaneously, another Baghdad hospital's staff was trying, in mid-2008, to muster the resources to attend to the growing numbers of Iraqi civilian adults—perhaps the aunts and fathers of the traumatized children—who showed signs of PTSD. This was in 2008, at a time when major news media were describing the decline in violence in the country. There were only two psychiatric hospitals in the country. In one hospital, Ibn Rushid, seven of the eleven staff psychiatrists had left Iraq or fled north to Kurdistan, having been threatened with kidnapping or assassination.[22] Those staff members who had remained were dealing with their own losses. As one Iraqi social worker, Khalida Ibrahim, explained, "Sometimes we are talking to them [patients] and trying to comfort them, but inside our hearts we feel pain because we also face the same problems. . . . We also have lost people, but we must pretend to be another person, to hide our real feelings and our real suffering."[23]

Sometimes it was a daughter who brought her mother to the hospital for treatment. One morning in May 2008, a fifteen-year-old girl brought her mother to Ibn Rushid hospital. The girl was worried because her mother was drinking too much alcohol. Her mother, Hana al-Dolaimi, acknowledged that she was having a difficult time coping. Her husband had been missing ever since he had left home one day during the war to visit his sister. Several days later armed gunmen had come to her house demanding money. She couldn't tell if they were Sunni or Shiite. She had heard rumors that her husband was dead but was unable to go to the morgue to identify the body. Was she a widow? She didn't know. Now, Hana al-Dolaimi explained, "Everything makes me sad. My houses are gone. My husband is gone. Everything sweet in this life is gone."[24] Yet she had her teenage daughter. The short-staffed hospital required that anyone who was brought in for treatment had to be accompanied by a family member who had to stay close to the patient at all times and help keep the patient clean. For Ms. Dolaimi, her hospital companion and aide would be her fifteen-year-old daughter.

In the last decade we have learned to pay a lot more attention to girls in war. Groundbreaking research by scholars such as Dyan Mazurana, Susan McKay, Helen Brocklehurst, Joni Seager, and by feminists within organizations such as UNICEF and Plan International has taught us to beware of lumping girls and boys together as "children" when we are trying to understand how wars are launched, how wars are waged, and how wars sputter to their often inconclusive ends.[25] During peacetime—in their caloric intake, housework, schooling, literacy, geographic mobility, media imagery, paid work, respectability, honor, sex trafficking, marriage, sexuality, and gun access—girls are not boys. Similarly, women are not girls; boys are not men; and men are not women. In the early twenty-first century:

- Girls and their mothers are more likely to be the collectors of water and firewood than are boys and their fathers.
- More girls marry before they are eighteen than do boys.
- More girls than boys under eighteen become parents.
- Girls' sexual purity is more likely than their brothers' sexual purity to be made the measure of a family's public honor.
- In a few countries today—for example, the United States and Iran—girls who graduate from secondary school are more likely than boys to enter university.
- Girls are more likely than boys to be internationally trafficked by prostitution syndicates.

In time of war these peacetime inequalities become a platform from which to launch even further differentials. That is, when a war breaks out, it does not start from an ungendered childhood blank slate:

- During wartime scarcity, within most households, women and girls, mothers and their daughters eat less, even relative to their fathers' or brothers' declining food consumption.
- As violence escalates, parents are especially prone to keep their daughters inside.
- Girls and women are more likely than boys and men to be the wartime targets of sexual assaults by the men in the multiple rival armed forces.
- Girls in fighting forces are more likely than boys or men to be used as sex slaves ("wives") by older men in those forces.
- Boys are more likely to enter postwar international health, training, and reintegration programs for young ex-soldiers than are girls.
- Girls who have been in fighting forces are more likely to come out of those forces with young children of their own to care for.
- Girls who are refugees are more likely to be lured by civilian

assistance staff members and men in security forces into exchanging food and other necessities for sex.

- Girls who have spent part of their girlhood—willingly or unwillingly—in fighting forces are more likely than are boys to have their respectability—and thus future marriageability—questioned by civilians in the postwar era. [26]

In other words, "children" and "child"—as in "displaced children" or "child soldier"—turn out to be explanatory concepts that hide as much as they reveal. In this sense, "children" is similar to "households," "families," "refugees," "bankers," and "militias": the workings of each cannot be realistically understood if their internal gender dynamics—relations between males and females, and contested understandings of masculinity and femininity—are made immune from investigation.

In November 2005 Safah was, in one sense, an Iraqi adolescent. In international law, however, including under the terms of the international Convention on the Rights of the Child, Safah would be considered a child until 2010, when she would turn eighteen. But Safah had been more than that. She had been raised to meet her parents' and others' expectations of youthful femininity. In the uncertain aftermath of the traumatic loss she experienced at Haditha, she still was likely to be imagined a young girl in the eyes of her uncle and her other remaining relatives, as well as the American military investigators, her neighbors, and the Iraqi authorities.

Girlhood in Iraq has its history, as it does in every country. It is historically specific. But to recognize its historical dynamism is not to say that the conditions of girlhood are always on an upward swing. Violence against girls can escalate over time, not just drop. In the 1990s, prepubescent girls became more sought after by traffickers and brothel owners than they had been in earlier decades because more men thought that they could avoid AIDS by having sex with them. Likewise, pressures on girls to become unhealthily pencil-thin can increase over time. The likelihood that a girl will have the chance to learn how to read and write may improve from one generation to the next, but there's no guarantee.

Hence girls are *in* history—products of their times, shapers of their times—as much as militiamen are, as widows are, and as hairdressers are. And "history" is not shaped by forces of nature; it is shaped by the actions of humans. More often than not adult men are the ones who have determined the conditions under which girls experience their particular girlhoods. Male-dominated legislatures, judiciaries, civil services, and media in any country, for instance, have determined the "age of consent," the distributions of budgets for boys' and girls' schooling, the criteria for the "honorable girl," and the rules governing marriage and child labor.

In their roles as mothers, grandmothers, and aunts, as well as social reformers, teachers, and campaigners, women too have helped shape standards of feminine propriety, modern girlhood, and dutiful daughters. Of course they have. But rarely have women in these capacities had the first or final word about what constitutes the resources devoted to and standards for evaluating the sort of girlhood imagined to best serve the community and the nation.

Safah was thirteen in 2005. Just as Nimo and Maha experienced each of Iraq's three recent wars at particular points in Iraq's gendered history, so too Safah experienced war at a particular moment in the ongoing history of Iraqi girlhood.

Safah was born in 1992. The modernist Baathist laws were at the time still on the books, providing some basic protections for girls as they approached womanhood. Yet the 1990s was the decade marked in Iraqis' lives by the immediate aftermath of the Gulf War and the devastating effects of the international economic sanctions. It was a postwar era of increasing economic hardship and growing regime oppressiveness. Safah would have been eligible to start elementary school in 1997, when Iraqi girls' school attendance was declining. Eight years later, in November 2005, she was of an age when she might attend a Haditha secondary school.

The Iraq War has been one of several wars in recent history in which girls' school attendance has been held up prominently by some policy makers as evidence of the success or failure of a military intervention. Interestingly, girls' school attendance was not so politically salient among Americans during the U.S. war in Vietnam, nor was it during the intense U.S. military intervention in Central America in the 1980s. Similarly, Russian officials did not make girls' school attendance a featured measure of military success or failure during the Russian war in Chechnya. Instead, girls' school attendance made its debut as a high-profile measure of military success—even as a war-waging justification—with the U.S.-led NATO invasion of Afghanistan in October 2001.

The Taliban's 1996–2001 regime had, among its many draconian rules, banned girls from attending school. International outrage at this policy gave Afghan girls' schooling a new international political high profile. To some, it became one in a package of justifications for launching military intervention. In 2007 and 2008, as Taliban militiamen regained control of several Afghan provinces, attacks on schools increased. From January to November 2008, according to UNICEF, 256 schools were attacked, leaving 58 dead and 46 wounded.[27] In early 2009, the challenge faced by Afghan schoolgirls escalated as men attacked schoolgirls, throwing acid at their faces, leaving some of the girls blind and all of them seriously burned. These attacks on schoolgirls could still make the front pages of some American newspapers.[28]

After their military invasion in March 2003, American policy makers made Iraqi girls' school attendance a measure of military success in Iraq, erroneously implying that the histories and current politics of girlhood in Afghanistan and Iraq have been identical. They have not been. According to UNESCO's assessment of Iraq's primary-to-university schooling, "the education system in Iraq, prior to 1991, was one of the best in the region," with many boys and girls, as well as women and men having had access to basic literacy training, as well as advanced education.[29]

The international economic sanctions, followed by the U.S.-led invasion, would change this.

Girls' access to formal education has been on the activist agendas of many women's rights campaigners around the world for a century and a half. Even before organizing to win the vote, women activists in many countries had pressed for girls to have the right accorded to their brothers to learn to read and write, to do mathematics, to gain knowledge of the world, its history, its scientific laws, its geography, and its political economies. Western colonizers in the late nineteenth century tried to co-opt this feminist agenda, arguing that their (and their Protestant and Catholic missionary allies') building of schools for girls as well as for boys, was proof of their imperial mission's civilizing benefits.

What appeared to be new during the Iraq and Afghanistan wars was promoting girls' schooling to justify military intervention and, as both wars dragged on, turning girls' rising school attendance—or its decline—into a measure of whether the militarized security strategies were succeeding or failing.[30]

In June 2003, Paul Bremer, President Bush's recently appointed head of the coalition's Provisional Authority, wielded unparalleled power over the early direction of Iraq's reconstruction. One day Bremer headed out of the fortified Green Zone to make what he hoped would be a widely covered "photo opportunity" appearance at a site of American-backed Iraqi reconstruction efforts. He chose a girls' elementary school. His convoy was surrounded front and back by vehicles of heavily armed private contractors, suggesting that the trip to a Baghdad girls' school in June 2003 was not without its risks.[31]

Coming to primary school age in Iraq in the mid-1990s and reaching secondary school age in Haditha in the years of the U.S.-led military occupation and the Sunni armed insurgency in Anbar province made it very likely that Safah would confront far more formidable obstacles to gaining an education than had her mother a generation earlier. If Safah's mother was born in the early or mid-1970s, she would have come to school age when Iraqi girls were nearing the peak of their government-supported access to formal schooling. It would have been a time when the Baath party leaders were making schooling and paid employment pillars of their own brand of nationalist modernization. In 1980, between 66 and 80 percent of Iraqi girls were formally enrolled in primary and secondary schools.[32] Young girls in 1980s Turkey, Syria, and Egypt had about the same opportunities for primary education, for gaining basic literacy and numeracy skills. By contrast, their young female counterparts in Iran and especially in Afghanistan and Pakistan then faced much narrower access to primary schooling.[33]

Of all Iraqi teenage girls in the early 1980s, 38 percent were attending secondary school. At the same time, 32 percent of Iran's girls and 35 percent of Syrian girls were attending secondary schools. Across the border in Jordan, 66 percent of that country's girls were pursuing postprimary education.[34] If Safah's mother was growing up in the 1970s and 1980s in a town such as Haditha, rather than in an Iraqi rural village, her chances for gaining primary and even secondary schooling were even better than the Iraqi national girlhood average.

Sanguine is the view that pictures daughters as always better off in their access to literacy and schooling than their mothers. It is not uncommon today for mothers—women who came into their girlhoods and adolescences in the preceding decades—to have had more, not fewer, opportunities to attend and stay in school than have their daughters.

In 2005, the year of "Haditha," UNESCO reported that the gap between Iraqi boys' and girls' secondary school enrollment rates had reached an alarming 18 percent. Other countries in the region had continued to develop their education systems throughout the 1990s and early 2000s in ways that had narrowed the gaps between girls' and boys' accesses to schooling. Iraq, by contrast, had slid backward and had done so in a way that disadvantaged girls more than boys. This 18 percent gap in 2005 secondary enrollment rates between boys and girls amounted to the widest gap of any Arab state: while 54 percent of secondary school-age Iraqi boys were enrolled in secondary school, only 36 percent of secondary school-age girls were enrolled.[35]

A war can cause that backward slide, if waging that war destroys school buildings, sends teachers into exile, decimates electric power and bus services, makes streets unsafe, reduces families' money available for schoolbooks, or persuades parents that a daughter's security is better provided for by early marriage than by schooling. Any one of those conditions can reduce a girl's chances for an education. Several of them wrapped together can make school attendance for girls almost impossible. A war can further cause this backward slide from a mother's generation to a daughter's if waging that war persuades a dutiful daughter to leave school to take up household responsibilities after a parent has been killed in wartime violence, or if it empowers those gun-wielding men who see those girls remaining within the confines of home as the girls most likely to help restore the nation's social order.

In other words, as much as the notion may go against the grain of our optimistic intuitions, it is all too possible for a literate mother to have an illiterate daughter. It is possible today for a mother who graduated from secondary school to raise a daughter who never gets much beyond primary school.

"Beatrice Sirkis, 14, wanted to be a teacher, but with her father hurt and out of work she had to leave school." So read the caption to a *New York Times* story reporting on the shrinking spaces of Iraqi girlhood after the first fifteen months of the Iraq War.[36] At fourteen, Beatrice had become an income earner for her wartime family. She had an older brother, but her parents decided that it made more sense for him to stay in school after her father, a retired soldier, had been injured. Thus it was that Beatrice, the teenage girl hoping to become a teacher, was becoming a wartime worker. In June 2004 she was employed as a sweeper in a Baghdad ladies' beauty salon.[37]

The Iraq War was being waged when the conflicting pressures on Iraqi girls, especially urban teenage girls such as Beatrice and Safah, were perhaps more intense than they ever had been. During the 1990s, conservative notions of girlhood had gained a new purchase, as Saddam Hussein, weakened by two failed wars, sought out allies among conservative clerics and male tribal leaders. But the early 2000s wartime genderings had created even more contradictory conditions for Iraqi girls to navigate. On the one hand, girls in their early teenage years in 2005 had grown up in an era when girls attending school had become the s++ocietal norm. They had seen many of their mothers, aunts, older sisters, and female cousins delaying marriage, pursuing not only secondary, but university educations and professional careers of their own. By 2004, moreover, many urban teenage girls had access to the Internet, cell phones, and satellite dishes, each of which transmitted a globally manufactured image of adolescent consumerist, sexualized girlhood. But a year into the Iraq War and its accompanying American military occupation, these same teenage girls were experiencing the pressures of a more confidently articulated religious patriarchal conservatism—often expressed by their own male schoolmates—as well as rumors of rape and kidnapping and subsequently growing parental supervision.[38]

Yosor Ali al-Qatan, a fifteen-year-old girl in Baghdad, had been confined to her home in 2004. She spent hours in her all-pink bedroom. Yosor "stares longingly at a hip-hugging pair of pink pinstriped pants. The new Iraq, her mother warns her, is far too dangerous to be seen in such pants."[39] While Yosor might have measured the impacts of the war on her girlhood in terms of fashion policing, it was at least as telling that she had stopped going to school. She was not alone. At the start of the 2004 school year only 700 girls had enrolled in her secondary school. The year before 850 girls had registered.[40]

Three and a half years into the Iraq War, in late 2007, Iraqi education analysts were more worried than ever as they charted wartime's widening gender gap. A spokesperson for Iraq's Ministry of Education reported that, while in Baghdad in 2006, there had been signs of girls' school attendance improving, during 2007, the capital's gender schooling gap had widened. Simultaneously, in the country's southern provinces the ratio of girls to boys attending school had dropped markedly. In recent years it had been two girls to every three boys. Now in the south the school attendance ratio had plunged to only one girl for every four boys.[41]

More regional differences within the country were apparent. In northern Iraq, in the provinces where the Kurdish political parties were in control and where incidences of wartime combat were considerably fewer, the gap between girls' and boys' school attendance was not as wide. Nevertheless, even in the north it was in the towns where sisters came closer to matching their brothers in school attendance. "In many villages," the ministry official noted, "either girls have never attended school or they have been forced by their parents to leave school."[42] The education officials worried that in the postwar era this gender gap would lead to more young men than young women being equipped with the skills and credentials to take on responsibilities for rebuilding the country and for making authoritative public decisions.[43] The consequences of girls' losing two or three years of schooling would ripple forward into the next decade and, in turn, produce more inequality within future marriages.

A year after the U.S. military's infusion of thousands of extra troops into Iraq and its arming of Iraqi male local Sunni militias called Awakening Councils, a strategy that seemed to reduce the incidences of violence, a California journalist decided to return to Haditha. It was 2008. He was curious to see whether local residents still were preoccupied with the killings of twenty-four civilians three years earlier. He found that the people of Haditha were interested in more mundane affairs: "Schools are open, shops and markets are bustling, the streets are crowded.... In front of one shop I saw mannequins dressed in tight, Western-style women's jeans.... At a florist shop—a florist shop in Haditha!—I watched a young Marine on patrol admiring the flowers."[44]

Since the initial stories of her survival of the marine massacre and later account to the American military investigator, Safah seemed to drop out of sight. As her city of Haditha came to be a frozen moment of violence in a longer war, Safah's ongoing experiences of teenage girlhood appeared beside the point. During the intensely fought 2009 provincial council elections in her province of Anbar, what made news were the rivalries between adult men, the Sunni male tribal chiefs who had turned their Awakening Councils into the Awakening Party, on the one side, and their male Sunni opponents holding office on the other.[45]

We do not know what ideas and feelings Safah would carry with her into late girlhood and then into young womanhood. What would become her own memories of the violence that tore apart her family that November morning? She would craft her own lessons. How Safah experienced girlhood in 1990s postwar Iraq and early 2000s wartime Iraq would influence how she sees the causal flows of history and how she understands herself in that history. We have learned from listening to other girls in other war zones that however Safah crafts her memories and her lessons, they are likely to influence her adult efforts to shape her country's future. Safah should not be imagined to be frozen in time. The city's image may be fixed, but Safah remains a dynamic, complicated Safah.

CHAPTER FIVE

Shatha

A Legislator in Wartime

Shatha al-Musawi had known for a long time that she wanted to become involved in politics. Perhaps the desire had its seed in losing her father to political violence as a young girl. In 1980, when Shatha was thirteen, her father was killed by gunmen working for Saddam Hussein's regime. Two years later, the government's police struck again. Shatha, now fifteen, was thrown into prison, together with her mother and several other relatives, all branded "undesirables." When eventually Shatha was told she would be released, she recalled she didn't want to leave: "I didn't think life was a secure place."[1]

So it was with great relief that Shatha saw the regime of Saddam Hussein overthrown in March 2003. Though her own family identified as Shiite, she was then living and working in a tailor's shop in the mixed Baghdad neighborhood of Adel. Shatha had known Sunnis whose families experienced violence and loss at the hands of the Saddam Hussein regime. She expected her post-Saddam relief to be shared by Iraqis of all ethnic and religious backgrounds. Thus she felt disappointed, and then disillusioned when, during the months following the U.S.-led invasion, she saw the growing distrust and even open violence between local Sunnis and Shiites. Sunnis, even those who had suffered at the hands of the regime, became fearful that those political privileges they, as a group, had enjoyed during the previous decades—access to houses, jobs, social status—would evaporate in the post-Saddam era. Many Iraqi Shiites, by contrast, even if they didn't blame every Sunni for the oppression and marginalization they had experienced under Saddam's rule, felt that now, in the wake of the U.S. military's invasion, their time finally had come. When witnessing one act of attempted abduction in her neighborhood, Shatha yelled at the young assailants, all of whom she had known since they were boys, "Are you crazy? . . . Have you lost your mind?"[2]

It was at this point, in the early months of the Iraq War, that Shatha began to take political action. She recalled later how she thought that politics might provide a "way to restore some sanity."[3] First she formed a local women's group. This activism brought her local attention and helped her win popular votes when she ran for a seat on the newly elected neighborhood district council.

In the 1990s, Shatha had become a divorced mother with children. She had to interrupt her education; as a single mother, her first priority was to find paid work. A private sector job, working for a neighborhood tailor, was risky for her status as a respectable woman, but it was the only one available then. Once her children were grown, Shatha went back to school, learned English, and graduated from university. At the time, she couldn't have known that learning English would prove especially useful in dealing with an American occupation. Despite her years of loss, Shatha's self-confidence grew along with her political consciousness. Thus in the midst of war she became an activist and then an elected official.

Shatha's progression from divorced working mother to political activist provides a valuable reminder: wartime does not necessarily put gendered political consciousnesses on hold. For many women, wartime poses such daunting challenges that it is all they can do to support their children, search for their missing husbands, find shelter after becoming displaced, and obtain minimal employment. To move beyond these pressing responsibilities to take political action seems impossible. Yet, for some women, these same experiences of life in wartime—enduring immeasurable losses, being displaced, having extra responsibilities, witnessing injustices, feeling powerless to prevent acts of violence, coping with a shredded social safety net—prompt them to become politically engaged.

Some of these newly politicized women tackle the challenge of providing for women's and girls' immediate wartime needs—health care, trauma counseling, shelter, food, employment. Other women politicized by war create groups to press for political change. Some make the journey from the first kind of activism to the second. That is, they may start out concentrating their efforts on meeting women's immediate wartime needs but gradually become convinced that women's wartime needs can be met only if foreign intervention and local masculinized communal violence are directly resisted or if society's existing sexist laws and conventions are overturned.

Three Iraqi women's advocates met with Maha Muna, an official from the United Nations Development Fund for Women (UNIFEM), in November 2003. They described their own efforts and their concerns eight months after the U.S. invasion.[4] Lina Abood, a medical doctor who had taken part in Awakening Iraqi Women and the Iraqi Women's League, the latter one of the country's longest-standing women's groups, was working in Baghdad. Abood and her colleagues were trying to provide services for orphans, as well as literacy and computer training for women. Sawsan Al-Barak, trained as an engineer, focused her wartime activities on the rights of women in Iraq's central and southern provinces. Her activities included an Internet café for women, programs to teach women their rights and ways to further peace processes. The third activist, Ala Talabani, after being fired from her engineering job for being Kurdish and for refusing to join the Baathist Party during the Saddam Hussein era, had to flee to Britain. Once back in Iraq, she concentrated on promoting the rights of Kurdish women.

Together, the three Iraqi women weighed the U.S. occupation officials' outreach to Iraqi women activists such as themselves, while they also closely monitored the actions of those Iraqis whom the Americans were selecting to fill posts in the interim governing bodies. They described the contradiction between the two: on the one hand, the Americans seemed to be saying that they wanted Iraqi women to take part in building the new, post-Saddam political system; on the other hand, the occupation-appointed Iraqi

Governing Council (GC) was cut off from those women. Along with the other women activists in their respective groups, they had tried to lobby those Iraqis placed in the new positions of influence on the twenty-five member council but found the three women unconnected to popular movements and the more influential men unreceptive; some of the men would not even shake the women's hands. Moreover, women activists had no way of knowing what political strategies the council's members were pursuing, since they were meeting in a U.S.-controlled military compound with no phone connection or way to contact them: "My uncle is the leader of the GC, another speaker's [one of the three interviewees] brother is on it, and we don't know anything—imagine the situation of other women."[5]

Nevertheless, these activists, together with the less-well-connected locally engaged women such as Shatha al-Musawi, were attempting to build the foundations of civil society in the midst of war. They implicitly rejected the notion of constructing civil society only after the war is over. Iraqi women who became politically active in the throes of the Iraq War were following in the footsteps of recent women wartime activists in Serbia, Bosnia, East Timor, Columbia, Kashmir, Afghanistan, Haiti, Congo, Georgia, Northern Ireland, Cyprus, Argentina, Chile, Mexico, Palestine, Israel, and Sri Lanka.[6]

When Shatha decided in late 2003 to try to start a local women's group, she also was following in the footsteps of earlier Iraqi women activists. In fact, Iraqi women had been taking part in political life since the 1920s, both as allies of Iraqi men in male-led organizations and as founders of and activists in independent women's groups. Ignoring these eight decades of Iraqi women's organizing allowed many outside observers and policy makers in 2003 to imagine that it would take foreign intervention and military occupation to show Iraqi women how to build a civil society. Hence commentators misread at what point in Iraq's gendered history the Iraq War was being fought: in reality, it was being waged in the middle of Iraqi women's political organizing, not at the start of it.

Haifa Zangana, whose own activism began as a young woman in the early 1960s (when she was imprisoned by the Baathist government), decided to resurrect Iraqi women's activist history as one step in critiquing the 2000s foreign occupation. She found that one group of Iraqi women, daughters of prominent Ottoman imperial officials and military officers, had created the Society for Women's Awakening as early as 1923. This was in the midst of Britain's rule of Iraq via its mandate from the post–World War I League of Nations. Five years later, officials' wives founded the Kurdish Women's Foundation.

As happened in Egypt, Turkey, France, the United States, Britain, and Russia, women in these early groups combined charitable activities and training in income-generating skills for girls and women along with raising public awareness of women's social conditions.[7]

Activist women also sought out the new media. *Layla,* the country's first women's magazine, was launched in 1923. It carried articles on art, literature, home economy, and the status of women. By 1929, one Iraqi newspaper was devoting a full page each Saturday to articles about women and girls. The articles were far more political than mere "human interest" stories; their authors described the obstacles facing Iraqi women when they demanded access to their rights, including access to formal education. Often publishing under male pseudonyms, the writers called on other women to become active in demanding their rights, to join the emerging Iraqi nationalist movement, and to look abroad for inspiration. In the newspaper *al-Bilad,* one woman in the 1920s wrote fervently to fellow Iraqi women:

> Dear sister, what are you thinking of now and tomorrow? Tell me.
> Haven't you been hibernating long enough in this deep sleep . . . ?
> Rise up and start working for your dear homeland. Take a look at
> the daughters of Turkey, your neighboring country, who are always
> enthusiastic for nationalism armed with science and faith.[8]

Those Iraqi women who became activists—as in other countries, disproportionately from the cities and from the expanding, modernizing middle class—were not homogenous in their political strategies and alliances. Despite a shared opposition to British interference, by the 1950s and 1960s some activists took nationalism as their goal, others pan-Arab nationalism, and still others made a class-based social revolution their goal. In 1958 a military reformer overthrew the Iraqi monarch, King Faisal II, and declared Iraq a republic. Iraqi women activists, though united in anti-monarchical sentiments, were not uniformly confident that supporting republican national independence or class-based revolution would secure women's rights—to political voice, to equality in marriage, to education, to paid employment.

In this questioning, Iraqi women of the 1920s–70s had abundant company around the world. Women active in nationalist and revolutionary movements in Mexico, France, Russia, India, Egypt, Vietnam, China, Korea, South Africa, Nicaragua, Cuba, Indonesia, Iran, Ceylon (now Sri Lanka), the Philippines, Kenya, Ireland, and Quebec all had struggled with this analytical and strategic puzzle. How exactly would freedom from foreign domination or from class-based oppression guarantee that all women and girls would be treated as first-class citizens in the public arena and within their homes? And the corollary quandary: How risky was it for women activists to accept the assurances of male nationalist or revolutionary leaders that women's rights wouldn't slip (or be shoved) off the table when issues of women's welfare and influence might offend, anger, or politically alienate strategically important groups of men? The stakes in reaching the correct answers were high.[9]

In Iraq, as in so many other countries, how any activist woman crafted her own answers to these difficult questions determined which organizations she allied with during the politically charged 1950s–70s. It would determine whether she joined a male-led mixed-gender nationalist, socialist, or communist movement or political party, on the one hand, or, on the other, chose to help organize an all-women's group that was consciously independent from—even if it on occasion allied with—any of the male-led movements. And, although she might have decided to invest her energies in a mixed-gender nationalist or class-defined movement, it might lead her and other women to form a women's caucus group inside the wider organization to keep its leaders and members attentive to women's issues.

Nadje Al-Ali interviewed Iraqi women of an older generation who, as young women, had taken part in Iraq's heady, often dangerous gendered politics of the 1950s–70s. She wanted to make visible the little-known stories of Iraqi women who had sorted out these complex questions, women who had chosen their political affiliations based on the conclusions they had reached. One woman, Soraya, described to Al-Ali how, as a university student in the 1950s, she had co-founded an activist group called Rabitat Difa Huquq al-Mara' (the League for the Defense of Women's Rights):

> We opened a small factory as our meeting place. It was close to al-Rashid Street. We would go into the countryside and distribute medicine to the women. We would ask them about their lives and their needs. We provided literacy classes. As time went by, Rabitat got bigger and bigger, mainly through word of mouth. I think we were successful because we touched on the most important things in these women's lives: their welfare, their children's health, and their problems with their husbands. . . . The Ba'athists and the Arab nationalists had a joint women's organization called *Nisa' al-Jumhuriya* (Women of the Republic). They had a voice, but not as strong as Rabitat. They did not do our work.[10]

During the 1950s–70s, the government's personal status laws became one of the primary objects of Iraqi women's political activism. This early campaigning and its results would come to play a crucial role in Shatha al-Musawi's and other Iraqi women activists' debates and alliances thirty years later as they sought to establish women's public influence in the middle of the Iraq War.

In many parts of Europe and the Middle East, personal status laws have defined women's condition, especially relations with their husbands, children, male relatives, male religious authorities, and the state. They set forth the terms of marriage, divorce, inheritance, and child custody. Many women's rights thinkers and campaigners concluded that, so long as the state sanctified women's subordination inside the family, advances in women's status and opportunities in politics and the economy would be tenuous at best, subverted at worst. As a result, women activists in Algeria, Egypt, Tunisia, and Iraq made the reform of their respective states' personal status laws a primary goal of their organizing.[11] That is, marriage, widowhood, and motherhood were understood by women's activists to be political, in peacetime as well as in wartime.

The Iraqi women who in the 1950s sought equality for women in marriage and in parenting were denounced in the mosques and in the male-dominated media and mosques. Still, they used a combination of popular organizing, campaigning, and alliances with key male political figures to win the all-male legislature's passage of a reformed Personal Status Code of 1959. Nonetheless, despite its drawing on both Sunnis' and Shiites' more progressive interpretations of religious texts to establish women's right to consent in marriage, the restriction of polygamy, and the provision to women of more access to inheritance, the new personal status laws left some women campaigners disappointed. They assessed the reform as only partial, as still too rooted in religious understandings of women's relationships to men. Yet they strategically concluded it was as much as they could achieve at the time.[12]

Iraqi women won the right to vote in 1967 and to contest legislative seats in 1980. In the name of modernizing nationalism, the Baathist male party leaders pursued government policies that expanded the opportunities of girls and women: universal free education and expanded jobs in the paid labor sectors.[13] During the 1970s, however, the women who had chosen to channel their activism into the ruling Baathist Party's own women's federation became more and more dissatisfied with the persisting patriarchal constraints women experienced.

The scenario is familiar: male party leaders believe that mobilizing women supporters through their own intraparty organization—such as the party's women's federation or women's committee—simultaneously will demonstrate the party's concern about women's issues, bring more women into the party's ranks and co-opt women party members to support the party's male leadership's own priorities. Such a masculinist assumption, however, may prove naive. Women organizing within a party may continue to do their own monitoring of women's actual conditions, may develop their own analysis of what policies are needed to adequately address those realities and may use this analysis to critique the party's male leadership.

Thus in 1978, Baathist women in the party's General Federation of Iraqi

Women (GFIW) pressed for a more radical secularization of the country's Personal Status Code. Saddam Hussein, a Baathist army officer, would seize control of the regime a year later, in 1979. The most radical women among the GFIW members called for a complete ban on polygamy, a ban on divorces enacted outside the state's courts, a more explicit minimal age set for marriage (not just "sanity and puberty," as under the 1959 law), more genuine equality for women and men in inheritance, and a more thoroughly secular basis to undergird the code.[14] The intertwined party and government male leaderships, by contrast, feared totally alienating the male Sunni and Shiite religious clerics, who, under the 1959 Personal Status Code, had retained considerable authority in family matters. Baathist leaders also were anxious not to provoke an angry backlash among Iraqi men, who were the beneficiaries of the remaining patriarchal family structures blessed by the legal system.

So it was a considerable achievement for the women of the GFIW to have persuaded the Baathist leadership to institute any reforms in the code. The revised 1978 Personal Status Code widened the conditions under which a woman could seek divorce, outlawed forced marriage altogether, curtailed the power of uncles and male cousins over girls and women, and prescribed punishment for any marriage contracted outside the state's court.[15]

It was these 1978 revised personal status laws that would be in effect when the Iraq War began in 2003. They significantly shaped the relations between women and men and the state during this wartime. The product of decades of political activism by women lobbying inside and outside the dominant party, they were in jeopardy under the new Iraqi political party wartime alignments fostered by the U.S. occupation.

The most conventional way to think historically about the timing of the Iraq War is to frame it as having happened at a particular point in the history of Iraq's colonization and subsequent national independence, wars, and coups—the 2003 invasion, thereby, stands as the latest event in a series of major political events: 1920, 1932, 1958, 1968, 1979, 1980–88 and 1990. However, there is an alternative way to position this war. That is, to understand this armed conflict as occurring at a distinctive point in the ongoing history of

Iraqi women's organizing to establish their rights within marriage and the family. In this telling, 2003 follows in succession from 1959, 1978, and 1991. Such a feminist rethinking of wartime history might help us grasp why the political contest over Iraq's personal status laws became so fierce in the middle of the Iraq War. Adopting this gendered historical lens, in turn, might enable us to see how this rivalry helped shape the course of the war itself. Shatha would find herself in the middle of this gendered wartime fray, influencing the next major benchmark in Iraq's ongoing gendered history.

In the 1980s and 1990s, the Baathist Party, by then dominated by Saddam Hussein, tightened its grip on power. The Iraqi political arena shrank. Women activists of all persuasions had far less room to organize and lobby. Many were imprisoned, others went into exile abroad. The Baathist Party's own women's federation, portrayed as representing all Iraqi's women's interests, was reined in by the party's male leadership. What little political autonomy its members had garnered for themselves in the 1970s contracted. By the time of the Gulf War in 1990–91, and the subsequent international sanctions, which together dramatically worsened Iraqi women's condition, there was no effective political voice left for women.

Did Shatha al-Musawi realize that she was following in these earlier Iraqi women's activists' footsteps? If not, she shared a lack of historical awareness with women of most other countries. In fact, it is frequently the mobilization of women in their own generation that inspires efforts to make newly visible to women themselves—and thus strategically usable—earlier generations' political analyses, dilemmas, tactics, and strategies. Engaging in academic and popular women's historical investigations into their mothers', grand-mothers', and even great-grandmothers' efforts may motivate those who read or hear the findings to become politically engaged themselves. More typi-cally, however, it works the other way around: women's political mobiliza-tion provokes a new dissatisfaction with the orthodox telling of the country's political history.

Women's current politicization inspires fresh skepticism toward the "offi-cial story," the standard narrative that makes the country's men seem to be the past's sole actors or that makes women's winning voting rights, access to schooling, rights to consent in marriage, and opportunities for decently paid work appear to be the gifts of enlightened men, or to be the "inevitable" (i.e., nonpolitical) fruits of disembodied "progress." How many girls and women—and boys and men—are required to study in school their country's history of ending male-only voting or the history of reversing women's exclusion from the professions as routine parts of their learning about their country's political and economic history?

Thus in Japan, Russia, Britain, Korea, Canada, the United States, Germany, Turkey, South Africa, and India, women's recent political activism has been not just the outcome of learning about their mothers' and grandmothers' political organizing. Rather, it often has been a reverse causality: recent women's activism has sparked a determination to unearth the ignored and buried history of women's past theorizing and activism. In Iraq, as well, it was unlikely that Shatha and her contemporaries, who were becoming politically active after the U.S.-led invasion, had had any chance to learn about the women of Rabitat Difa' Huquq al-Mara', Rabitat al-Mara' al-Iraqiya, and the GFIW. School curricula in 1980s–2000s Iraq, paralleling school curricula in most countries, did not explore debates among women and between women and their male allies over nationalism, over modernity, over the role of religious clerics, over the laws governing marriage, divorce, child custody, and inheritance. Girls and boys—and their teachers—were left to assume either that such debates never happened or, if they did, that they were inconsequential.

Many Iraqi women, even though opposed to a new round of foreign domination, a repeat of Iraqis' experiences with Ottoman and British rule, initially perceived the toppling of the authoritarian Saddam Hussein regime in March 2003 as providing a new opportunity for women's organizing, a chance to reassert their rights within a newly opened political space. Iraqi women who had fled abroad during the years of war and repression returned to Iraq to join those women who had never left the country but had been driven into silence as they began to speak out.

Yanar Mohammed was one of the former. As a young woman in 1993, she and her family had sought refuge in Canada. She had trained there as an architect, had watched Canadian feminists demonstrate for economic equality and against domestic violence, and returned to Baghdad hoping to be of use. By 2004, Yanar Mohammed, then forty-three, had decided that providing services for Iraqi women trying to escape violence at home would be the focus of her activism. She helped found a group called Women's Freedom in Iraq, started publishing a newspaper, *Equality,* and with other Iraqi women opened women's shelters in Baghdad and the tense northern city of Kirkuk. She saw her advocacy work not only as providing immediate services, but also as challenging the losses in security and rights that Iraqi women had experienced over the previous twenty years, as wars and impoverishment frayed the social fabric and an ever-more nervous Saddam Hussein sought allies among patriarchal male tribal leaders and male clerics. Yanar Mohammed doubted that the American occupation officials were genuine in their concern about Iraqi women as wartime widows, as wartime single mothers, as wartime unemployed, as wartime victims of domestic abuse wielded in the name of "honor." She went further and criticized the occupation for having worsened the already desperate condition of many Iraqi women. Yanar Mohammed's work attracted positive media attention in North America, much of it from feminists, attention that helped support her efforts.[16]

By 2007, in the wake of the 2005 national elections, the intensification of sectarian violence, a change in prime ministers, and the intense constitutional drafting negotiations, Yanar Mohammed was describing the political system that Iraqi women had to cope with as having regressed: "We used to have a government that was almost secular. It had one dictator.... Now we have almost 60 dictators—Islamists who think of women as forces of evil. This is what is called the democratization of Iraq."[17]

Yet her activism limited Yanar Mohammed's political effectiveness. Her outspoken, explicitly feminist advocacy of a secular legal and political system alienated many of those Iraqi women, including a number of politically active women, who either insisted, strategically, that the most persuasive discourse would have to be more nuanced or who genuinely believed that religion could play a positive role in reestablishing a peaceful social order.

Shatha al-Musawi was among the latter. She and Yanar Mohammed would find themselves on opposite sides of Iraq's constitutional debate. Moreover, Yanar Mohammed's ability to gain overseas feminist support provoked some misgivings among those Iraqi women activists whose networks were more firmly rooted inside the country.[18]

This mixed-blessing of overseas networking was not unique either to Yanar Mohammed or to other Iraqi women activists cultivating foreign contacts. In Afghanistan, Nicaragua, Chile, Argentina, Honduras, Russia, Poland, Egypt, Palestine, Korea, Serbia, and East Timor local women's advocates in recent years have had to stay acutely attuned to the costs and benefits—financial and political—of seeking or accepting support from foreign donors and feminist groups. It has not been uncommon for women's advocates' local patriarchal opponents to tar women activists who have received foreign support with the nationalist brush, labeling them "puppets," even "traitors." Most local women's groups are too politically fragile to risk such charges. At times, however, funds from abroad have kept the doors of a marginalized women's center open. On occasion, too, the publicity provided by overseas women's rights groups, groups with computers, paid staff, and e-mail lists, has prevented the execution or extended imprisonment of an outspoken local women's advocate.

The source of overseas assistance has mattered. The Dutch, Norwegians, Swedes, and Spanish frequently have been the most adept at providing aid to local women activists in ways that do not jeopardize the local recipients' tenuous legitimacy. Some of the most effective external support is offered intraregionally: Thai women activists helping Indonesian activists; Algerian women activists giving advice to Palestinian women activists; Honduran women activists providing training to El Salvadoran women activists; Women Living Under Muslim Laws sending out their international alerts of impending threats to women's rights in Middle Eastern or South and Southeast Asian countries.[19]

Iraqi women's advocates had been drawing inspiration and strategic lessons from abroad for decades. As early as the 1920s, they were in touch with, and gaining useful ideas from their counterparts in Egypt and Turkey. Yet the U.S.-led military invasion, followed by its political occupation—symbolized by its fortified military bases scattered throughout the country, its truck convoys, checkpoints, and nighttime raids, as well as its off-limits 5.6-square-mile Green Zone, taking up a large swath of downtown Baghdad, with its highly paid contractors, pizza parlors, computer banks, heavy armaments, flowing liquor, hair salons, and swimming pools—would make Iraqi women's decisions about who to turn to for money, advice, and moral support excruciating throughout the Iraq War.[20]

This already difficult set of wartime choices was made even more risky for Iraqi women activists by the emergence on the American political landscape of a new brand of conservative "feminism." Starting in the 1990s and burgeoning in the years of the George W. Bush presidency, these new Washington-based conservative women's groups utilized their deep connections to Republican officials at the highest levels of the administration to become well-funded actors in the occupation's attempts to make Iraqi women's advancement a hallmark of the U.S. invasion. The Independent Women's Forum (IWF) was especially prominent. One of the IWF's founders and leading members during the years of the Iraq War was Lynne Cheney, the wife of Vice President Dick Cheney and a longtime conservative anti-feminist activist in her own right. It was the Independent Women's Forum that the Bush administration chose to make its leading women's group in what the Bush administration called its "Iraqi Women's Democratization Initiative." Making Iraqi women's alliance choices all the harder, the IWF activists sometimes described their work as "feminist."[21]

As Nadje Al-Ali and Nicola Pratt point out in their invaluable study of how diverse Iraqi women's groups navigated the dangerous shoals of the U.S. occupation, the American neoconservative Independent Women's Forum had developed an ideology that was at odds with what most Iraqi feminists—and American, Egyptian, Turkish, and British feminists—understood to be necessary for women's genuine liberation. The IWF representatives came to Iraq with the U.S. occupation authority's funding to teach Iraqi women to embrace a contradictory package of "women's empowerment, free markets, strong families, and strong national defense."[22] This unusual positioning of women's empowerment within a dual embrace of women's primary role as within the family and support of the U.S. occupation's military and privatization missions made the IWF an ideal vehicle for the Bush administration and yet a confusing and questionable ally for local Iraqi women's advocates.

Iraq's January 2005 interim legislative elections and the subsequent contest over a new constitution would throw Iraqi women activists' strategic dilemmas, risks, and choices into sharp relief. Ordinary women talked among themselves about whether it was worth taking the risk to go out to the polling stations to vote.

One American radio journalist decided to visit another beauty parlor in Nimo's home Baghdad district of Karada in order to cover the election campaign of 2005. There in Dena and Mena's Hair Salon, she found several women getting their hair done. One patron, Nasrin Misir, identified herself as Shiite. Although it was the Sunni leadership that was calling for a boycott of the upcoming election, Nasrin Misir also was not interested. She wasn't planning to vote. "When asked about female candidates, she shrugs.... 'The situation in our country is not suitable for a female leader.... You can't change the situation.'" One of the hairdressers joined in: "We are walking the street and we are worried. We don't know if when we walk out the door we'll make it back."[23] While women activists were lobbying to ensure that a significant number of women were nominated by the male-led parties and were elected to the new legislature, many women made their decisions on whether or not to vote based on their security calculations. Physical security and voting each are gendered, and they are entwined in women's political thinking.

It was with satisfaction, therefore, that Shatha al-Musawi, divorced single mother, local organizer, and city councilor, found she had been was selected to run on one of the Shiite parties' tickets in the elections. If successful in the January 2005 elections, she would help shape the representative assembly in drafting the country's new constitution. The American authorities, themselves divided over whether these elections were premature, presented the contest as evidence of the occupation authorities' commitment to democratization. For this reason, they deemed it crucial that Iraqi women be prominent among both the candidates and the ultimately elected legislators. While the Bush administration repeatedly had declared racial and gender quotas anathema, it accepted gender quotas for the January 2005 Iraqi election.

The January 2005 legislative election was a wartime election occurring at a particular point in both Iraqi and international gendered histories. During the 1990s and early 2000s, feminist electoral activists in a number of countries—for instance, France, Britain, Sweden, India and Argentina—had successfully pressed for the imposition of gender quotas on political parties. Their argument was this: no matter whatever else they disagreed over, political parties shared masculinized internal organizational cultures; their leaders might practice occasional tokenism with women candidates, but never, left to their own devices, would they nominate a significant proportion of women to contest the plum seats (constituencies deemed winnable by that party). Women activists had made gender quotas a topic of shared analysis—the justifications for them, the actual workings of them, the results they produced—through their networks in the European Union, the UN, and the Inter-Parliamentary Union.[24]

In the version of the gender quota system adopted in Iraq, each political party had to field a national list of candidates of which every third nominee was a woman. Still, the inability of the occupation authorities to ensure the safety of candidates led to the decision to keep candidates' names and photos secret during the campaign. Public appearances, especially by women candidates, were confined to a few small gatherings in secure places. Thus one of the intentions of imposing gender quotas—to foster the popular acceptance of women as publicly engaged in political life of a country—was compromised. Still, in the smaller gatherings, women candidates could spell out their positions and their hopes at greater length and often with nuances that moved away subtly from their male party leaders' own platforms. For instance, in the southern Shiite-dominated city of Najaf, home of some of the country's most esteemed Muslim clerics, several women candidates on rival Shiite party lists began their presentations by noting the family members they had lost to Saddam Hussein regime's campaign of oppression against Shiites in the south but then went on to emphasize less their religious credentials than their intentions to promote women's economic well-being—promising classes in "computers, languages and job skills."[25]

Shatha was successful in her January 2005 parliamentary candidacy. She became one of 87 women legislators in a male-dominated wartime Iraqi legislative body that would draft the new constitution: male politicians held the other 188 seats. Shatha and her female legislative colleagues made up over 31 percent of the total, exceeding the legal requisite 25-percent minimal quota.

The new legislature's evolving institutional culture began to take on the hallmarks of a masculinized culture. Moreover, it met inside the fortified U.S.-controlled Green Zone, which did not give ordinary Iraqis much of a sense of connection with their representatives.

Comparing the new Iraqi parliament with other national legislatures around the world, Iraqi women's legislators' one-third proportion was notable. In that same year, 2005, in the United States—the country whose government had set itself up as a model for the new Iraq—women held a mere 15 percent of congressional seats (this would grow to a modest 17 percent after the 2008 congressional elections). Women in Britain, the American government's chief military ally, fared a bit better; in 2005, they made up 20 percent of the House of Commons. By contrast, voters in Rwanda, the Scandinavian countries, the Netherlands, Spain, South Africa, Angola, and Costa Rica all elected higher percentages of women to their national legislatures than did those in either the United States or Britain. In Afghanistan's 2005 elected lower house of the National Assembly women accounted for 25.5 percent of the total delegates.[26]

In every country, after the numbers are revealed, the question that must be posed is, how independent are any legislators? How able are they to represent both their own regional constituents' best interests and their cross-regional demographic groups' best interests? In Iraq, some women's advocates, even those in favor of quotas, expressed skepticism about the capacity of the women elected to stand up for women's concerns, since so many of those women legislators had been handpicked by male party leaders and were beholden to them, often even members of their own families.[27] Investigation alone, legislature by legislature—using an explicitly gendered curiosity about how and when ideas about masculinity and femininity are wielded—can determine issues of political autonomy in the intralegislative workings of political party discipline, patronage, and patriarchal control.

Shatha was elected on the ticket of a coalition of Shiite groups called the United Iraqi Alliance (UIA). It was by far the largest of several parliamentary party groupings in the newly elected body. Twenty different—and often rival—political groups had come together to form the UIA. Its two most influential parties were the Islamic Dawa Party and the Supreme Council for the Islamic Revolution in Iraq (SCIRI). Although they generally adopted policy positions friendly to Islam's role in the country's political life, the UIA's two most powerful parties often were at odds on other crucial political questions, including whether the country's southern provinces should have significant political autonomy from the central government. Nominally allies, each of them continually sought to attract the other's supporters into its ranks. The outspokenly anti-occupation cleric Moqtada al-Sadr's party remained a barely digestible member of the UIA.

The two Kurdish parties, which for decades had been rivals for political influence in northern Iraq, joined together in early 2005 in a parliamentary coalition, the Kurdistan Alliance. Generally in favor of a secular legal system, the Kurdish male and female members of the new national legislature were committed to the Kurdish region of the north's exercising autonomy and effective control over Kirkuk's oil reserves. In addition, a coalition of secular-identified parties, the Iraqi National List, held seats in the National Assembly, claiming to be nonsectarian in both its identity and agenda. Most Sunni voters had heeded the call of their leaders to boycott the January 2005 election, producing a notable underrepresentation of Sunnis in the legislature that would draft the new constitution, and leaving the coalition of Sunni parties with little negotiating leverage.[28]

Twelve months later, on December 15, 2005, Shatha had to run again, this time for a seat in the permanent national parliament, the National Assembly. She again ran on the ticket of the Shiite-identified United Iraqi Alliance. The gender quota formula remained in place. But this time women of all parties managed to garner in toto only 70 of the legislature's 275 seats, men

FIGURE 4. Shatha meeting with her parliamentary male colleagues in Baghdad, August 2007. (Photo: Marko Georgiev/for the *New York Times*/Redux)

gaining the other 205 seats. Hence women held 25.5 percent of the total, a slippage from their earlier 31 percent. The mere passage of time is no guarantor of progress toward gender equity.

The next crucial elections were held in late January 2009. Seats on Iraq's eighteen provincial councils were being contested. As the campaigning became more intense in mid-January, incidents of violence increased. The most hostile campaigning occurred in the south, where the two main Shiite parties, Dawa and the Islamic Supreme Council of Iraq, alleged coalition partners, vied for provincial council seats.[29] Women activists noticed that, as a result of the political bargaining between the male party leaders in parliament, the male-led electoral commission, and the male-led presidency council—each of which had a say in the crafting of rules for provincial council nominations and campaigning—the rules governing the quota for women had been diluted.[30] In the end, in January 2009, out of 14,400 provincial council candidates nationwide, 4,000 (28 percent) were women. Some of these women candidates reported facing intimidation and feared to put up posters; others defied expectations and campaigned openly.[31]

All the new parliament's party coalitions proved fluid. During the three years following the 2005 national elections, there would be perpetual jockeying for position, efforts by each party to expand its support base at the expense of its supposed allies; parties would change their names; and personal rivalries would spark disputes among parties' male leaders. Shatha's United Iraqi Alliance continued to be both dominant in its number of seats and fraught with internal tensions during 2005–8. The leader of its Dawa Party, Nuri Kamal al-Maliki, became the prime minister in 2006. The following year, SCIRI changed its name to the Islamic Supreme Council of Iraq. Sunni voters had ended their electoral boycott and cast ballots in the December 2005 election. In 2007 Sunni Arab parties came together in a new parliamentary coalition, the Iraqi Consensus Front, also known as Tawafiq.

For an outsider, perhaps for many Iraqis too, it was a challenge to keep abreast of all the rival parties and coalitions. For Shatha al-Musawi and the other women legislators, it meant being forever aware of shifting lines of influence. Most urgently, the multiplicity of male-led parties in such an unstable partisan landscape made the creation of a cross-party women's legislative alliance a daunting task.

In any legislature, it has taken stamina, commitment, and courage to create bonds of trust and legislative agreement among women of different parties. For one thing, women legislators have affiliated with a particular party for a reason; they do not automatically see eye-to-eye with representatives of other parties simply because they too are women. Shatha chose to cast her electoral and legislative lots with the United Iraqi Alliance, not, for instance, with the more secular, less explicitly sectarian Iraqi National List, just as American Congresswoman Nancy Pelosi chose to tie her legislative career to the Democrats, not the Republicans. It was because of Pelosi's Democratic Party loyalty that she rose to become the first woman Speaker of the House of Representatives. In virtually every legislature, party leaders judge their members' loyalty based on their adherence to that party's policy choices. It also becomes the criterion for distributing party rewards, especially entrance into inner decision-making circles and renomination when the next election comes around.

In wartime, especially when militias and security forces clash inside the country, the stakes of party loyalty rise even further. Cross-party women's policy consensus building and strategic legislative maneuvering become all the harder. Thus it came as somewhat of a surprise that in 2007, the male Speaker of the Iraqi parliament, Mahmoud al-Mashhadani, announced the formation of a women's bloc within the National Assembly. It wasn't clear whether this was the product of some women legislators' own cross-party organizing; or whether the bloc would be able to bring partisan-divided women together. Yet one woman parliamentarian, Safiya al-Suhail, a legislator and advocate of women's rights, who four years earlier had joined with other women activists in pressing Paul Bremer to include a quota for women in the interim government formula in 2003, said that the goal was to "resist a male-dominated parliament."[32]

At the time of the January and December 2005 elections—and during the constitution-writing negotiations in between—neither gender nor class categories, however, were being used to piece together political alignments and to structure political contests. By that point in Iraq's wartime evolution, sectarian and ethnic affiliations overshadowed all other affiliations. Not only Iraqi men at the heads of the emergent political parties, but also the American officials in the Green Zone and back in Washington, were weighing their alternatives by looking at society through a sectarian/ethnic lens.[33]

If clashing sectarian and ethnic interests are seen by senior officials and party leaders to be the most potentially explosive and thus the most urgent to address, then, regardless of the occasional rhetorical nods in women's direction, concerns about gender inequities, especially concerns about women's distinctive needs and rights, will be pushed on to the proverbial back burner. "Not now, later," echoes in women's ears: *when* the war is won, *when* the revolution has been consolidated, *when* the territorial calculus has been hammered out, *when* ethnic groups have found a way to trust each other, *when* the constitution is ratified, *when* the oil revenues have been distributed, *when* the occupiers have left, *then* we will turn our attention to women's demands, *then* we will consider gender inequalities, *then* we can enjoy the political luxury of worrying about violence against women, *then* . . .

In practice, what this meant for Shatha during the crucial years of 2003–9 was that, although her alarm at the dissolution of her mixed neighborhood into sectarian distrust and violence led her into politics, she now was being tagged principally by her membership in the United Iraqi Alliance, a Shiite-identified political party coalition.

This wartime political development was especially disappointing to many of the Iraqi women who had been active in earlier decades. Looking back, they had drawn a political lesson: Iraqi women made the most sustainable and meaningful political gains when they had come together across sectarian and ethnic lines. The new wartime salience assigned to sectarian and ethnic affiliations—and the power of the parties and armed militias which claimed to represent them—subverted efforts to revive the successful women's political strategy of earlier generations.[34]

The question of women's legal place in the new political life of Iraq came to a head in the midst of sectarian violence, foreign occupation, and the daily operations of both Iraqi and foreign militaries. By this phase of the drawn-out Iraq War in fact, the number of masculinized actors in the Iraqi political arena had proliferated:

the U.S. military

U.S. civilian authorities

foreign private security companies

American-owned supply contractors

Iraqi political parties

Iraq government's ministerial chiefs

Iraqi religious clerics

Iraq's new military

Iraqi partisan and sectarian militias

Iraqi anti-U.S. insurgents

the United Nations' own small security force

Iraqi criminal gangs

Iraqi tribal sheikhs

Iraq's new police

Masculinization is a step-by-step process by which any group or any institution both becomes more dominated by men—as its ordinary members and as its leaders—*and* becomes more thoroughly imbued with a masculinized culture—its established rituals, its accepted criteria for wielding influence, the skills deemed valuable for rising within its ranks, the shared jokes among its members. Any group, consequently, is becoming masculinized insofar as it is composed overwhelmingly of men (even if there are a few women, perhaps up to 20 percent, inside the group), led by men (even if it occasionally selects a woman for a senior position), adopts strategies and goals derived from hegemonic notions about manliness, and develops internal hierarchal and horizontal bonds among its members based largely on their assumptions about shared manhood. A host of groups all can be masculinized without being natural allies. Masculinized groups and institutions can be, and usually are, rivals: the military versus the police; the legislature versus the executive; one intelligence service versus another; each of the political parties versus one another. In fact, the very construction of intergroup rivalry usually further deepens the masculinized culture of each rival.

In this regard, the Iraqi National Police deserves more comment. Starting in 2007, more Iraqi women were recruited into the expanding Iraqi police force. Was the blatant masculinization of the Iraqi National Police being rolled back a step?

Women always have a stake in police forces. Police officers either take domestic violence and sexual assault seriously or dismiss each as a private or trivial affair. Police officers either measure the security of a neighborhood by ascertaining how safe women and girls feel when walking along its streets after dark or pick other controls to gauge local security. Police officers deem women working in prostitution as unworthy of protection under the law or as due police protection. Police officers can abuse women they take into custody or see professional policing as including respectful behavior of women in detention. From the 1970s onward, feminists in many countries—notably, Brazil, Britain, India, the United States, Ireland—began to make the transformation of their local police forces a political movement goal. These activists wanted not only to bring more women into the ranks of the police, but to compel male police officials and rank-and-file police to take seriously women's charges of domestic violence and sexual assault.

Then, during the 1990s and early 2000s, feminists in countries as diverse as East Timor, Afghanistan, and Liberia, often in alliance with feminists working inside and around the UN, began to argue that in peace keeping and national reconstruction efforts, it was important not to focus just on the reform of the country's military; reforming the police force was equally important. In international discourse, this came under the rubric of "security sector reform." If police forces kept to their existing patriarchal forms—dominated by men and dismissive of women's and girls' security—genuine peace would not take root.

The Iraq War was being waged at a time when feminists internationally were paying close attention to policing in wartime and to the transformation of policing culture as essential to creating meaningful security.[35] In a later gendered stage of the Iraq War—from 2007 onward—some American military men and their Iraqi male counterparts in the nascent police force made a deliberate effort to roll back the existing police masculinization, which marked policing not only during the Saddam Hussein regime, but also during the first four years of the Iraq War and U.S. occupation. For 2008–9, by contrast, the new Iraqi national police academy graduated several hundred women from its one-month police training course. Were domestic violence and sexual assaults against women to be taken more seriously during wartime? Were local women's measures of security to become the police commanders' measures of security?

Such an outcome did not seem likely. Instead, American commanders and their Iraqi police colleagues saw admitting more women into the Iraqi police force as a strategy to cope with the rising number of women suicide bombers being deployed during 2007–9 by Iraqi male insurgent leaders. By mid-2009, the number of women in the police force reached 120—less than

1 percent of the police force's total of 45,000 (also less than 1 percent of the total security force)—and male commanders were chiefly assigning women police to staff check points, specifically to search civilian women for explosive devices.[36] Thus, as women came increasingly to be imagined as terrorists, women police came increasingly to be imagined as useful instruments of counterterrorism.

At the same time that the Iraqi police force took over the lead in civilian house raids from the U.S. military, commanders decided that more women police would be necessary to deal with women whose homes were being raided. But there appeared to be no American or Iraqi official plan to use the new Iraqi women police officers to protect women from violence. Demasculinization of the police, this crucial public institution, therefore, would go no farther.[37]

After 2006, added to the already-formidable list of masculinized groups and institutions among which Shatha and other Iraqi women activists would have to navigate were the Awakening Councils (also called Sons of Iraq), new groups of Sunni men loyal to particular tribal sheikhs, in provinces such as Anbar, young Safah's home province. The Awakening Councils were armed and funded by U.S. commanders (via both direct payments and lucrative reconstruction grants funneled to those male Sunni sheikhs American commanders favored). The American objective was to mobilize Sunni sheikhs to resist the Sunni male-led insurgency. The strategy was at least partially successful. From 2007 to early 2009, many male insurgents moved out of Anbar to carry on their operations further north. It was unclear, however, whether the sheikhs' armed male followers would be, as the Americans had promised, fully incorporated into—given paid jobs in—the central government's Shiite-controlled security forces. At least part of the American counterinsurgency plan was continued militarization of many of the Sunni sheikhs' male loyalists.

Early in 2009, some of the Awakening Councils' tribal sheikhs turned their own councils into political parties to compete for seats on the increasingly powerful provincial councils. Controlling a provincial council would bring with it influence over patronage, and patronage was a salient political currency in a society with such high unemployment. While to some observers this transformation from tribally based militia into tribally based political party was a positive development, it did little to roll back the masculinization of Iraqi political parties.[38]

In the wake of the provincial elections and in the lead-up to the December 2009 national elections (when American commanders in Afghanistan were beginning to adopt the Awakening Councils as a model for engaging local men in U.S.-led counter terrorism), the masculinized politics of the Awakening Councils took another turn. The Sunni men equipped with American-supplied guns became increasingly suspicious that Prime Minister al-Maliki's government would not fulfill its earlier promise to hire Awakening Council members into the government's paid security forces. Jobs, especially jobs for unemployed men, were as politically loaded in wartime Iraq as they were in other countries suffering economic recession. Added to this common masculinized political saliency of male unemployment was the news of yet another new layer of masculinized politicized organizations. In an effort to ensure his own control of the government's armed forces, Prime Minister al-Maliki had created two new military forces: the Baghdad Brigade and the Counterterrorism Task Force. The armed men in each would, allegedly, be part of the state military, but they would be handpicked by, and report directly to, the prime minister.

The array of masculinized organizations and institutions in any country is rarely static. Its varieties and numbers can proliferate. Occasionally, with deliberate effort on the part of politically engaged women, some of the groups—for instance, the courts—can be somewhat demasculinized. If any masculinized group loses political power, its rivals might even call it feminized. Masculinization often fuels a particular form of intense competitiveness—ridicule of feminization is one of its weapons. The rivalry between masculinized groups thereby excludes women from meaningful public influence and regards them chiefly as objects of symbolism or control.[39]

In a gendered understanding of the history of warfare—years before Shatha's legislative and constitutional struggles—October 30, 2000 stands as a milestone. On that day, in the UN's famous glass building on the banks of the East River in New York City, the delegates of all the governments then holding seats on the Security Council, the UN's most powerful body, voted for a resolution on women, peace, and security. For the first time in the UN's fifty-five year long existence, the Security Council voted to commit not just the UN's myriad agencies, but all of its member states, to a process of demasculinization in the name of peace building and postconflict national reconstruction: to include women's issues and women's advocacy groups inside decision-making circles at every stage of efforts to end wars and to rebuild countries and their states after wars.

The measure was officially designated "UN Security Council Resolution 1325 on Women, Peace and Security." Its name didn't sound very dramatic. It quickly came to be called simply "1325" by local and transnational women activists organizing in current and recent war zones from Bosnia, Haiti and Liberia to East Timor, Palestine, Sierra Leone, Afghanistan, and Congo. Women activists in transnational organizations—Women's International League for Peace and Freedom and Women's Environment and Development Organization, along with staff people pressing for feminist policies inside Amnesty International, International Alert, Oxfam, Human Rights Watch, UNIFEM, UNHCR—developed the evidence that underlay the argument for taking this innovative Security Council action. They went further, they helped draft the resolution itself and lobbied the Security Council delegates, country by country. Most of these activists were from war-torn countries or had worked in war-torn countries, often in alliances with local women's groups.

As soon as the Security Council's positive vote was taken, these transnational activists turned on their fax machines. They began faxing copies of 1325 to women activists all over the world. Now women's advocates would have a document to put under the noses of those male officials and political power wielders who clung to the notion that ending wars was as much men's affair as was launching them.[40]

These women activists heralded the passage of SCR 1325 in October 2000 as a potential turning point in the gendered history of warfare: no longer could women be treated as silent, supposedly naive bystanders in the "serious business" of peace negotiations and in the planning for postwar reconstruction. No longer could women's particular experiences of warfare, especially their experiences of sexual assault, either be swept under the militaristic rug or, if acknowledged at all, be used as an excuse to treat women as mere victims, symbols of suffering who, it was imagined, had no ideas of their own about the causes of war, the formulas for ending wars, and the priorities for reweaving social fabrics and constructing new public institutions in the aftermath of war.[41]

The U.S. government (led by the Clinton administration), a permanent member of the UN Security Council, voted in favor of 1325. Then U.S. officials promptly ignored its commitments. Those American authorities in Washington and Baghdad, architects and justifiers of the U.S.-led military invasion and each of its many steps during the 2000–2008 Bush administration, never mentioned SCR 1325. Nor did the Iraqi male political figures who, after 2005, became increasingly influential in shaping the country's political life. Yet, because of the Iraq War's place in gendered international history, both local and transnational women activists had available to them a newly credible standard, the provisions of 1325, as they assessed developments in wartime Iraq.

In post-2001 wartime Afghanistan, by contrast, the requirements of SCR 1325 became salient. Though NATO—and within NATO, especially the United States—had control of the military operations in Afghanistan, influential feminists within United Nations agencies and independent humanitarian groups were able to make their presences felt far more effectively than either could in the U.S.-led occupation of Iraq.

During the 2005 drafting of the country's new constitution, faced with the array of masculinized actors and the dismissal of 1325, Iraqi women legislators and activists had to take concerted action to have any voice in the deliberations. Nor were all the Iraqi women activists in agreement. As in any other country, they differed in their perceptions of the nation, of ethnic community, of class relations, of religious faith, of political parties, of tribal and family commitments, of generational experience, of the sources of their own security and insecurity. Therefore, even though the resultant constitutional bargaining was likely to determine every Iraqi woman's relations with her father, her uncle, her husband, and her children with religious clerics, the courts, and state officials, there was nothing automatic about Iraqi women's solidarity during the 2005 constitution drafting process.

In these constitutional negotiations, Iraqi activist women's achievements of 1959 and 1978 were once again placed on the table. They were made negotiable. At this gendered stage of the Iraq War, Iraqi women's legal status became one of the spoils of war.

No women had been appointed to the nine-member committee, charged in 2004, with drafting the interim constitution. The fifty-five-member committee appointed after the January 2005 elections to draft a permanent constitution included forty-four men and only nine women.[42]

Women dedicated to a secular legal code were already on their guard. Iraqis appointed by the United States to the Governing Council back in late 2003 had tried to issue a decree to replace the 1959 Personal Status Code with sharia, Islam's legal code. "Women inside and outside Iraq issued press releases outlining the implications of the decree, which were distributed widely by e-mail. In Baghdad and the Kurdish region, thousands of women protested, calling for the decree to be repealed."[43]

Responding to the mobilization of Iraqi women's civil society groups, Paul Bremer, the American head of the coalition's Provisional Authority, refused to sign the Governing Council's 2003 sharia decree. Yet this evidence of their wartime political muscle did not persuade activists that they could exert enough influence on the crucial 2005 constitution writing process to keep sharia from being incorporated into the country's new basic law.

Shatha al-Musawi took a different tack. During the war, Shatha had become convinced that Iraqi society would be a more stable, safer place for women if the government's laws were brought into line with Islamic traditions. During the spring of 2005, at the height of the constitutional debates, Shatha spoke out in the parliament in favor of sharia law—to be administered by male Muslim clerics—being incorporated into the new constitution. She cited the plight of so many Iraqi women left single or widowed by the succession of wars that had killed so many thousands of men. She said that she believed these women were "living lives of lonely misery," because of being left outside the security of the family. Institutionalizing Islam's sharia law, she argued, would bolster the family. As for the dangers of men's rights to polygamy under sharia, Shatha noted that one of the most influential women's rights advocates, Nasreen Barwari, was the third wife of one of the male legislators. On the question of sharia endorsing unequal inheritance, Shatha defended that principle on the grounds that Iraqi men were expected to support their poorer relatives and thus needed more resources. Noting an American journalist's skepticism, she retorted, "We have different traditions. . . . What is acceptable to you is not acceptable to us."[44]

Many Iraqi women's rights advocates agreed with Shatha al-Musawi that U.S. and western European models of politics and of the state were not appropriate for Iraq and, further, that heavy-handed foreign influence only served to taint locally developed ideas and practices of gender equality. Of course, not all Iraqi women engaged in the constitution-drafting political process were as sanguine as Shatha about the alleged ameliorative effects of incorporating sharia into the new government's basic law. Some of the debate among women could be heard on a newly launched Baghdad Arabic-language radio program, *Cup of Tea,* on Radio Al Mahaba, 96 FM. The station called itself "the Voice of Iraqi Woman." During the constitution-drafting months, *Cup of Tea* became a lively call-in forum for women's discussions of marriage, careers, divorce, physical abuse, dress codes, and the constitution. Its producer, Ruwaida Kamal, while promoting open public on-air discussion, herself saw the station as affirming women's rights: "We are in a dangerous period. There are many movements, many groups that aren't taking women's rights seriously. Women are being marginalized."[45]

When the draft of the new constitution was leaked in July 2005, it was particularly Article 41 that raised alarm among those Iraqi women who believed that the Personal Status Code of 1959 and 1978, with all its imperfections, should be the starting point for women's place in the recreated polity. Article 41, as hammered out by the legislators, would allow for Islamic law and clerical judges—Sunni or Shiite, depending on the apparent affiliation of the couple involved—to settle disputes over marriage and divorce. Scores of women came to downtown Baghdad on the hot July midday to protest the constitutional provision. They had written fliers, which they handed out to passersby, and they raised banners for drivers and pedestrians to see. One read "We want to be equal to everybody—we want human rights for everybody."[46] Dohar Rouhi, president of the Association of Women Entrepreneurs, found an especially worrisome assumption embedded in the draft constitution: that every woman would be identified by her supposed Shiite or Sunni background. "We want a law that can be applied to everyone. We want justice for women."[47] One of the organizers of the July protest was Hanaa Edwar, founder of the Iraqi Women's Network. She called for a meeting between women critical of the constitution and members of the drafting committee.[48] On the other side of the street women affiliated with Moqtada al-Sadr's conservative movement demonstrated in favor of the draft constitution.

Throughout that summer and autumn and into the winter, negotiations and debates and public lobbying persisted. Questions not just of oil and regional autonomy, but of marriage and divorce continued to be hotly contested.[49] The constitution that was ratified in the fall of 2005 included a version of the family law that was ambiguous. It left many women's rights advocates nervous. Several months later, Hanaa Edwar decried the constitution as inadequately protecting women's rights and called for Iraqi women to become more politically engaged.[50] In London, the overseas feminist group Act Together, comprised of U.K.-based Iraqi and non-Iraqi women, held a series of discussions, to explore what its members saw as the rolling back of the 1959 personal status laws and to mobilize support for continuing to challenge the constitution's Article 41.[51]

However, such mobilizing among Iraqi women inside Iraq, critics of the constitution admitted, would not be easy. Insecurity made it difficult to spread the word about the constitution and its implications for women. Insecurity likewise made organizing to pressure elected politicians and party leaders a daunting prospect.[52] So many women in Iraq, moreover, had little time or energy to worry about constitutional or religious issues while the daily work of maintaining households in wartime remained so preoccupying. One local activist summarized many Iraqi women's responses to the constitutional political struggles: "Screw the constitution, where is my water?" Or, as another woman declared in frustration, "I'll wear clothes from top to bottom and paint myself black if you give me electricity."[53]

In short, it is precisely the gendered politics of wartime insecurity that often enable patriarchal relationships to be inscribed into a wartime-negotiated new constitution.

During all these months, Shatha sought to carve out a reputation for herself as an independent political actor. On the one hand, she was a member of a conservative political party parliamentary coalition and was said to have close ties to aides to the Shiite cleric Ayotollah Ali al-Sistani who, from his enclave in the southern city of Najaf, wielded perhaps more moral and political influence than any other single Iraqi during the wartime years.[54] On the other hand, Shatha spoke willingly, in English, to foreign journalists, providing her own analyses of what was motivating sectarian conflict. She was vocal, for instance, when, in 2006, two women legislators were the targets of gunmen and kidnappers. She spoke out forcefully within the legislature, not hesitating to criticize the more prominent male legislators. She blamed both the Americans and senior Iraqi officials, including men belonging to her own multiparty coalition, for the lack of progress in stopping violence: "My people are dying for you. . . . You have to take responsibility. . . . Al Qaeda was not here till the Americans came."[55]

The life of a legislator, protected inside the Green Zone, never absorbed all of Shatha's daily energies. She continued to organize local women, especially widows, who were being traumatized by ongoing violence. She herself had been forced out of her own home in the Adel neighborhood by Sunni armed militias. She had had to move to another, less mixed neighborhood. Shatha al-Musawi was not only a national legislator; she had become one of the five million Iraqis who, by 2008, were internally displaced persons. Instead of concentrating on getting just her own home back, however, she led a group of widows, all of whom had been displaced by the "ethnic cleansing" of 2006–7, in an attempt to repossess their homes.[56]

To achieve her goals, Shatha contacted Iraqi male politician Ahmad Chalabi, once the Pentagon's favored Iraqi exile, now responsible for helping

Iraqi refugees return home. She also contacted an American major general. Not only Shatha's own forceful personality, but also her position as a member of the National Assembly, helped to open doors. She achieved modest success. Some of the women she had been working with returned to their home neighborhoods, though they had to be accompanied there by Chalabi and Iraqi soldiers.

In early 2008, Shatha met face-to-face with the militiaman who was occupying her own house. "He said he was just taking care of the house for me," she reported afterward, "but I told him I do not need anyone to take care of my house." At that point the journalist, who had interviewed her previously, noted that Shatha "uncharacteristically" broke down in tears. Pulling herself together, Shatha went on. She was determined to have people return to their homes in a way that did not set off another round of violence: "It was the hardest thing I have had to do in my life. But I have to do this and keep inside my anger because I want a future for Iraq."[57]

The American Women

CHAPTER SIX

Emma and the Recruiters

Emma Bedoy-Pina already had one son in the U.S. military. Now military recruiters were trying to persuade her to encourage her second son to enlist. She wasn't easily persuaded.[1]

It was October 2005. The U.S.-launched war in Iraq was in its third year. It had been three years since the sharp upsurge of American patriotism after the attacks on New York and Washington in September 2001, followed just months later by the U.S.-led military toppling of Afghanistan's Taliban regime and the first flush of militarized euphoria when American troops rolled into Baghdad in April 2003. By late 2005, Americans' wartime story had turned grim. An Iraqi anti-American insurgency had become deadly. Rising sectarian violence had left many Americans bewildered about divisions among Iraq's religious sects. "Body armor" and "IEDs"—roadside bombs—had joined "Humvees" in ordinary American conversation. The army was falling short of its enlistment goals in 2005. The job of an American military recruiter had soured.

Still, Emma Bedoy-Pina lived in San Antonio, Texas. Situated on the border with Mexico, San Antonio was supposed to be a good town for recruiters. The military's presence there dated back to 1845, when Americans fought Mexicans for control of the large Texas territory. Up in Massachusetts, people still admired naturalist Henry David Thoreau for having gone to jail for a night to protest that American expansionist war, but here in San Antonio stories of past soldiers' heroism were woven tightly into the collective local memory. After all, San Antonio was the home of the Alamo fort. Every American school child knew the defiant shout, "Remember the Alamo!" Over the last hundred and fifty years, it had gained a firm foothold in American patriotic lore.

Paying close attention to Emma Bedoy-Pina may help us think like a recruiter—a locally deployed military recruiter and his or her Washington superiors. Taking Emma seriously reveals how much gendered strategizing it took to raise and sustain an American military force—even one stretched thin—capable of waging a prolonged war.

Military forces are composed of thousands of men and women, and persuading each of these individuals to enlist and then reenlist is not easy. In other words, taking as a given a government's unquestioned ability to have at its disposal soldiers to deploy will produce an unrealistic analysis. Furthermore, any analysis that treats the recruitment of a military force as problematic but still leaves the gendering of recruitment politics unexamined is equally unrealistic. Making feminist sense of any government's war, thus, involves investigating just how a government goes about manipulating ideas not simply about manliness, but also about ethnicized and classed femininity in pursuit of raising and reproducing its fighting force. To ignore Emma is to risk grossly underestimating the complex gender calculus developed by the U.S. government's "manpower" strategists during the early 2000s. To ignore Emma is also to risk underestimating their and their superiors' war-waging anxieties. Most of all, to ignore Emma is to underestimate the agency of mothers of teenage sons and daughters in any militarized society.

During the early 2000s, Emma became the object of considerable Defense Department conceptualizing and strategizing. Quite often, she was diced up into particular demographic categories. As we will see, sometimes she was imagined (by military recruiters) chiefly as a mother of a high school son. At other times, she was targeted by her ethnicity. And, at still other times, she was seen as the mother of a military son.

Of course Emma was not a mere pawn to be moved at will on a wartime chess board. She was a complex person with her own hopes, her own experiences, and, as will become apparent, her own sources of loyalty and motivators to public action. Emma would become a public figure in San Antonio's political life during the Iraq War.

City boosters had proudly labeled San Antonio "Military City, USA."[2] Emma's hometown was certainly not the only city in early twenty-first-century America whose economy, politics and popular culture were threaded with military history, military participation, and military interests. New London, Connecticut, along with Fayetteville, North Carolina, Tampa, Florida, Newport News, Virginia, and San Diego, California were among the country's most deeply militarized towns.[3] Observers noticed that in the era of the Iraq and Afghanistan wars the towns most deeply connected to the military—through the presence of military bases or the local economic importance of private military manufacturers—increasingly were located in the South and Southwest.[4]

Given San Antonio's long history of military presence and militarized local civilian pride, perhaps it wasn't surprising that the military's recruiters found young people in Emma Bedoy-Pina's hometown still willing to volunteer for various branches of the military, even when teenagers in other parts of the country in 2005 were becoming disenchanted with soldiering, seeing enlistment as an automatic ticket to Iraq.

In fact, during fiscal year 2004 (October 2003–September 2004)—in the midst of the Iraq War—Texas as a whole ranked sixteenth out of all fifty states, plus Puerto Rico and the District of Columbia, in its proportion of new army (active duty and reserve) enlistees per 100,000 of each state's seventeen- to twenty-four-year-olds. The top three states in that year—that is, the three states yielding the year's *highest* per capita army enlistees—were the District of Columbia, Hawaii, and Kansas.[5]

By 2005, Emma's older son already was serving in the U.S. Air Force. Emma was proud of him.[6] However, it wasn't the air force—or the navy— whose men and women were appearing on the evening news covered with Iraqi dust, crouching behind their trucks, peering nervously upward looking for insurgent snipers. It wasn't air force or navy men and women who most typically were smiling bravely into the cameras as they were being interviewed in a military hospital's amputee ward. The dust-covered, rifle-carrying, and the severely wounded soldiers were members of the army and the marines. The army's recruiters faced the greatest challenge. First, the army, the U.S. military's largest branch, constantly needed high numbers of fresh recruits. Second, in American twenty-first-century popular culture, the army did not enjoy the marines' elite and manly cachet. Going into the third year of the Iraq War, the army's recruiters were having to work the hardest to fill its ranks with volunteers.

Moreover, in 2005, Emma's older son was stationed on an air force base up in Alaska.[7] Alaska seemed to an anxious Texan mother a safe distance from both Iraq and Afghanistan. But the army's recruiters were scouring San Antonio's urban landscape for recruits. They had easy access to the city's high schools. In some parts of the country, school administrators, often under pressure from parents, were putting tight limits on recruiters' access to schoolchildren. For instance, parents in some school districts became alarmed when they discovered that, under the less-publicized provisions of the Bush-era "No Child Left Behind" law, local school administrators were required not only to allow military recruiters access to students within their schools, but also to pass along to the Defense Department the names and addresses of all their high school seniors, leaving some parents puzzled when their sons and daughters began to receive personally addressed communications from the military urging them to enlist. As word spread about the law, some mothers and fathers began to look more closely and discovered that they could explicitly request that their sons' and daughters' names and home addresses *not* be shared with the Defense Department. It was up to parents, however, to take action. One might characterize this wartime education law as a step toward incorporating American public schools into war waging.

Those American mothers and fathers who believed that service in the military offered positive experiences for young people, or who were daunted by the law's fine print, or who lacked facility in English, or who were uncomfortable contacting authorities—perhaps because of their own uncertain immigration status—were inclined to let the No Child Left Behind law work its way unimpeded. In some American wartime towns, on the other hand, mothers and fathers convinced their local school officials to inform all parents about how they could opt out of this information sharing, with notices of this parental option spelled out in large print in both English and Spanish.

In other towns during the Iraq War, parents went further. They began working together with local peace activists, some of the latter members of veterans' groups such as Veterans for Peace, others in pacifist organizations such as the Quakers' American Friends Service Committee, to permit peace advocates to have as much time in the schools and meeting with students as the military's recruiters did. They argued that young women and men deserved to be informed about the full range of their postschool options and about the implications of their choices. Some peace activists referred to their efforts as "counter-recruiting."[8]

Rachel Rogers, a single mother in the upstate New York town of High Falls, for instance, said that she had not thought much about the Iraq War until 2005. Then she learned that some recruiters were teaching students how to throw hand grenades. She decided to become involved in the affairs of her son's school. She pressed school administrators to impose stricter limits on military recruiters' access to the school's students. Meanwhile, across the country, in Southern California, truck driver Orlando Terrazas started to hang posters critical of enlistment at his son's school. He was inspired to take action when he heard that recruiters were promising students that if they enlisted they could become musicians.[9]

Occasionally, these local efforts provoked new public questioning of the Defense Department's Junior Reserve Officer Training Corps (JROTC), an in-school military cadet program for high school boys and girls. That questioning was often joined by a new parental curiosity about school guidance councilors' common practice of using the military's own career aptitude test for testing their school's students and then sharing the test's results with the Defense Department. Some parent and student activists began talking about "de-militarizing" their local high schools.[10]

By mid-2005, twenty-seven months into the Iraq War, a shift in American mothers' and fathers' attitudes toward military service was under way. The Defense Department, using the tools of social science, had been conducting opinion surveys. Its November 2004 study already had revealed that "only 25 percent of parents would recommend military service to their children."[11] This was a notable drop. In August 2003, when the Iraq War and the war in Afghanistan both looked as though they would succeed in a finite time span and at the cost of relatively few American casualties, 42 percent of American parents whom the Pentagon surveyors questioned said they would recommend military service to their children. It was a different story in mid-2005. Defense's recruiting strategists decided to step up their efforts to persuade mothers and fathers.[12] A new American phase of the gendered war was beginning.

Though markedly different in important ways, in the United States as in Iraq, schools were becoming the sites for war waging in the early twenty-first century. In Iraq, violence and threats of violence determined if mothers and fathers would risk sending their sons and, especially, their daughters off to school each day. As a result, elite observers made the numbers of Iraqi girls attending school one measure to determine whether, month-by-month, wartime security for ordinary Iraqis was improving or whether the U.S.-led war in Iraq was worth the carnage. In the United States during the same years, some schools had been sites of civilian youth violence, while other public high schools had become the wartime contested ground for parents, students, school administrators, military recruiters, and peace activists. The militarization of schools—and of children's lives—can come in varied forms.

In San Antonio, the army's recruiters, dressed in camouflage fatigues, were free to enter the schools' cafeterias and talk with students during lunchtime. The city's high school guidance counselors also seemed willing to help recruiters make contact with their students. [13]

Emma's younger son, Jacob, was just finishing his senior year of high school in San Antonio in 2005. Army recruiters were interested in Jacob. But Emma wasn't so sure. Comparing Jacob's prospects with those of her older son serving in the air force and deployed up in Alaska, Emma wondered out loud, "What if he's not as lucky as his brother?"[14]

Back in Washington, the Department of Defense's recruiting planners were devoting considerable attention to women such as Emma. To them, Emma was the mother of a teenage son. They also thought of her as Latina. Each of these conceptualizations figured into the Pentagon's wartime thinking.

Since Congress had ended the U.S. government's all-male military conscription ("the draft") in 1973, a perennial topic of military strategizing had become acquiring and retaining the numbers and types of military volunteers that Defense, White House, and congressional decision makers thought the country needed. Young women—of all races and ethnicities—seemed suddenly attractive to these recruiting strategists. They, it appeared, would help make up for the loss of the middle-class white young men, out of high school and newly released from the draft, who would be more likely now to seek their futures in colleges and civilian workplaces. Young African American young men, with fewer civilian workforce opportunities and usually less money for college, these strategists calculated, could also be encouraged to volunteer, especially if the military's racism could be effectively tackled. (Both women's and African Americans'—and particularly African American women's—experiences in the U.S. military will be explored in more depth in the next chapter.)

Nonetheless, all this recruitment strategizing would not bear fruit if parents couldn't be persuaded that enlisting in the U.S. military was good for their own sons, for their own daughters. Yet parents, the Defense recruiting command concluded, had to be approached with gender sensitivity. Distinct recruiting campaigns would have to be designed for mothers and fathers. A mother's standing in the community—the criteria used by neighbors, the press, fathers, teachers, and other mothers to evaluate her parenting—reflects her responsibilities and resources in caring for a son or for a daughter in ways that are unlike those experienced by a man who becomes a father. The U.S. military's recruiting strategists have distinguished between persuading mothers and persuading fathers when they have designed their enlistment campaigns. This tactic was apparent throughout the Iraq War.[15]

On the U.S. Army's Web site, www.goarmy.com, wartime viewers could click on a page for "parents." There they could see its "Real Life Stories" of soldiers and their parents. Of the eleven stories of soldiers offered by the army during the Iraq War, five were of soldiers and their parents or families. Even more, six, were of soldiers and their mothers. None of the eleven stories were of soldiers and just their fathers.

For instance, there was the story of an African American mother, Tanya Forbes, and her son, Jonathan. According to the army's online narrative, "Tanya knew her son had the tools to be successful but realized he didn't always apply himself. Much to her surprise, Jonathan decided to talk to an Army Recruiter, which led to him enlisting in the army." A year later, Tanya summed up her assessment: "Since he's been in the Army, he's matured quite a bit. It's teaching him that he needs to move forward in his life."[16]

Another of the stories offered on the army's www.goarmy.com Web page for parents was of Molly Anderson, a white woman and mother of Autumn. By the time of the army's Web story, her daughter had not only enlisted but been promoted to the rank of sergeant. The army identified Molly as "a single mother raising a family on her own." She described herself on the Web site as having a "protective mother bear instinct." According to Molly, when Autumn "told me that she was joining the Army Reserve and she was for sure doing it, I was in shock." This was a wartime recruiting message crafted by an army whose strategists had become increasingly sophisticated. The army was acknowledging here that a mother's initial reaction to her offspring's interest in enlistment during wartime might be surprise, even resistance. Yet the army's Web narrative was quick to provide a mother's firsthand reassurance that her son's or daughter's choices ultimately must be their own. Looking back, Molly Anderson recalled for the Web site, "Eventually I did see it Autumn's way. I had no choice but to allow her to create her own world."[17]

On the same www.goarmy.com Web site, viewers also could click on "Ask a Soldier Discussion Board," to receive personalized replies to their own questions. The discussion board was gendered in its design. The army dedicated one page to questions from "mothers, girlfriends, and wives." All the worried questioners identified themselves as either girlfriends or wives, none as mothers. On the page dedicated to fathers, there were fewer questioners. Its principal theme seemed to be fathers' worries about what their soldier-daughters would face.

In the minds not only of the officials back in Washington, but in the eyes of the army recruiters assigned to wartime San Antonio, Emma was a mother, a mother of one military son and of another civilian young son who was a potential army recruit. By 2005, they had refined their approach to Emma further. They now conceived of Emma as one of the "influencers."

The recruiting strategists in the U.S. Defense Department created a list of those Americans whom they considered twenty-first-century influencers: mothers, fathers, teachers, athletic coaches, guidance councilors, and clergy. These were the people imagined by recruiters and their Pentagon superiors to be able to persuade a young man or young woman— if under eighteen, under the UN's Convention on the Rights of the Child they were girls and boys—to look favorably on enlistment in the U.S. military. Alternatively, these were the people who might most effectively discourage a young person from signing up. Each of these influencers—and the relationships between them—was gendered. A male football coach giving advice to a young high school boy, for example, might seem credible to the young man but lack credibility in the eyes of his mother.

While American military recruiters in the era of the Iraq War might have worked hard to find potential enlistees among high school students by developing strategic alliances with athletic coaches, pastors, teachers, councilors, mothers, and fathers, they had no guarantee of control over the web of dynamic gendered relationships in which each of these alleged influencers was embedded. Thus each recruiter was trained to develop multiple relationships with all the available influencers. The American military recruiters' wartime goal: to "own" the high school in their district.[18]

By mid-2005, when recruiters were walking through the corridors of San Antonio's high schools, the recruiters' job was becoming one of the most stressful jobs in the U.S. military. Nobody was shooting at them, but they were likely to fail. Each one had a monthly enlistment quota to fill. The U.S. war in Iraq wasn't going well, however. American casualty rates were rising, the American media's early approval of the Iraq invasion was waning and the U.S. civilian economy at that point was healthy enough to offer reasonable job opportunities to many young people. The Defense Department estimated that any one recruiter had to talk to 150 young people before finding just one who both met the military's requirements and expressed some serious interest in enlisting.[19]

So much in a wartime recruiter's life depended on where she or he was deployed. First Sergeant Olympio Magofina, for instance, had been assigned to the Northern Marianas, one of the U.S. Pacific island territories. He found it easy in 2005 to fill his monthly quotas. Many young men and women there—like those on American Samoa, the Marshall Islands, and Guam—believed that joining the U.S. military was their only viable economic alternative, given the lack of civilian job opportunities in their poor island communities. In the Marianas, a job at a local McDonald's paid an hourly wage of $3.25. According to Sergeant Magofina, he was lucky compared to his mainland counterparts: "In the states, they are really hurting. . . . But over here, I can afford to go play golf every other day."[20]

The U.S. mainland, of course, was far from homogeneous. While recruiters in San Antonio and in the Marianas had local cultures and economies working in their favor, those deployed to New York City were finding their Defense Department-dictated monthly quotas almost impossible to meet in 2005. Some military recruiters even were tempted to fake potential recruits' qualifications so that the young people could meet the army's entrance requirements. According to one journalist, "As long as the war continues to scare people from serving, recruiters said yesterday in interviews, the 80-hour weeks would continue, along with the unyielding pressure to find recruits, which they say has already bred depression, broken marriages and rule-breaking among the ranks."[21]

Military street-level recruiters, however, weren't on their own. They had the entire Defense Department's Recruiting Command behind them. And it, in turn, had major segments of the American advertising industry as its clients and allies. During the years 2003–9, advertising agencies vied for Defense contracts. American advertising techniques and the ideas about persuasion drawn from social psychology had become more refined since their origins on the eve of World War I. From their early days, both the advertising industry and social psychology had been gendered. Advertisers' images and messages aimed at female consumers and at male consumers had been differentially designed because, they believed, the messenger who was deemed most credible by men and boys might seem less credible to women and girls.[22]

The U.S. Defense Department, known among military professionals around the world for its unusually close relationship to the civilian social sciences, was sensitive to these gendered psychological and commercial refinements. The Iraq War era's recruitment campaigns thus were being designed at this moment in the ongoing gendered development of social psychology.

In 2005, when Emma was weighing what maternal advice to offer her younger son, the army decided to invest more of its substantial advertising budget in televised ads during stock car racing events. These sites had a particularly masculinized appeal in wartime America's popular culture. NASCAR—the National Association for Stock Car Racing—became a prime market for the army's efforts to recruit young men and help fathers encourage their sons to enlist. At NASCAR races, moreover, the army's advertisers could communicate more directly with white, working-class, and rural men, those considered by Washington recruiting strategists to be particularly positive in their attitudes toward soldiering. "Indeed, the connection between NASCAR and the military seems seamless," according to one journalist who observed NASCAR's Nextel Cup races in Brooklyn, Michigan: "From military fly-overs before the Nextel Cup races, to a fireworks-punctuated rendition of the national anthem, to the army-sponsored car that posted the fastest qualifying time before last Sunday's race, the combination of screaming stock cars and the flag-waving fans," this was a promising event for attracting male military volunteers. It wasn't irrelevant, furthermore, that rural Michigan at the time was suffering economic hardship. The U.S. Army in 2005 spent $16 million on NASCAR advertising, displays, and sponsorships, 6 percent of its annual advertising budget.[23]

"Y Ustedes . . . Sus Orgullosos Padres . . . And You . . . His Proud Parents."
The parent pictured here on the army's bilingual brochure was a mother,
wearing a crucifix, standing with her son. The army identified her: "Sra.
Ma. Luisa Hewitt, Madre de Private First Class Howard F. Hewitt, Military
Policeman."

> Para sus hijos, su opinion es lo mas importante y cuando se trata de
> tomar decisions siempre piden su consejo porque saben que ustedes
> siempre desean lo major para ellos.
>
> Your children value your opinion. When they need to make a decision,
> they come to you for advice because they know that you only have their
> best interests in mind. . . .
>
> Asi como ustedes, el U.S. Army quiere darle lo major a sus hijos y les
> ofrece el entrenamiento y la experiencia necesaria para ayudarles a
> lograr el exito que merecen.
>
> Just like you, the U.S. Army wants to give your children the best,
> offering the training and experience that will help them to achieve the
> success they deserve.[24]

In the eyes of the army's recruiters, Emma Bedoy-Pina was not only a
mother, she was a Latina. Since the 1980s, when the Reagan-era U.S. military launched its extensive operations in Central America, the Defense
Department had become increasingly interested in enlisting Latino young
men and women. The Iraq War, two decades later, was being waged at a
time when the proportion of all Americans who identified as "Hispanic"
or "Latino" had grown to 15 percent. The percentage of all American
people under twenty-five years old who were Latino was even higher.
Demographers were forecasting that, by 2050, Latinos would comprise 30
percent of all Americans.[25] The Department of Defense was paying close
attention to these demographic shifts. Its recruiters became more explicit
than ever about attracting Latino enlistees.

By the time of the Iraq War, more of the Defense Department's recruiting
brochures and Web sites' messages were appearing in Spanish. More of its
recruiting advertisements showed up in Spanish-language publications and

on Spanish-language television stations. The Pentagon was paying greater attention to high schools in cities with large Latino communities, such as Los Angeles, San Diego, and San Antonio. According to the 2003 census, San Antonio's population of 1.6 million was 53 percent Hispanic.[26]

The Defense Department's interest in recruiting young Latino men and women was further fueled during the Iraq War years by a shift in African Americans' attitudes. Since the end of the draft in 1973, the military had come to count on African American young people and their parents—and their aunts, uncles, and grandparents—viewing enlistment in the military positively and matching their positive attitudes with enlistment. Especially after President Harry Truman's 1948 order to desegregate the armed forces—two decades before lunch counters, rest rooms, movie houses, and buses in the American South were desegregated—the military, even with racialized discriminatory ideas and practices, appeared to many African Americans to offer a better chance for equal access to training, pay, benefits, and upward mobility than did most other sectors of American life. Those calculations could change, however. The Iraq War seemed to be causing just such a change.

In 1996—between the Gulf War and the start of the war in Iraq—41,185 African Americans volunteered for the army. Nine years later, in the middle of the Iraq War, that number had plummeted: in 2005, the army reported only 17,399 African American new enlistees, the same number as new Latino enlistees.[27] Still, the numbers of African Americans in all branches, and especially in the army's rank and file remained high. Although African Americans were only 13 percent of all Americans between eighteen and forty-four years old, they were 19 percent of all four services' active-duty enlisted personnel.[28]

More worrisome to Pentagon recruiters than the numbers of African American military personnel, however, were the new community attitudes. There seemed to be a sea-change under way in African American influencers' attitudes. Not long ago, African American adults had seen enlistment in the military as providing black young people with a road to economic security, upward social mobility, and community respect. By contrast, in 2005, many African American adults had come to the conclusion that the Iraq War was a mistake and that the community's young people should not take risks to help their government wage a mistaken war.[29] The Defense Department became all the more determined to cultivate mothers, fathers, and young people in Latino communities.

Latinos' contributions to the U.S. military and their wider political experiences of U.S. wartimes had been long overlooked.[30] By the early twenty-first century some Latinos had started to challenge this historic neglect. Thus when, in 2007, the celebrated documentary filmmaker Ken Burns and his co-director Lynn Novick produced their Public Broadcasting Service multipart series on the American experience of World War II, *The War*, many Latinos objected to Burns's and Novick's cinematic slighting of the Latino experience.[31] Latino activists succeeded in persuading the filmmakers to produce an extra segment devoted to Latinos' wartime service. After all, returning Latino veterans in the post–World War II era had formed the American G.I. Forum and become prominent organizers of Latino electoral and civil rights political movements in the Southwest, just as Japanese male veterans had been leaders of the Japanese American political ascendancy in post–World War II Hawaiian politics. The controversy over the Burns and Novick film, coming as it did in the middle of the Iraq War when more Latinos were weighing military enlistment, gave new energy to Latino veterans' efforts to become more visible in contemporary American public life and in the country's collective memory.[32]

As in Iraq, so too in the United States—and in Britain (where the British army, by 2008, was 8.8 percent black and Asian), Afghanistan, Iraq, Sri Lanka, Rwanda, South Africa, Lebanon, India, the former Yugoslavia, Russia, Guatemala, Israel, Turkey, Canada, and Malaysia: the state military's particular relationships to each of the country's ethnic or racial groups took on heightened saliency during wartime. Did Sunnis think they—their men— had a special historic place inside Iraq's military? Did Shiites think that the time had come for their men to control the ranks of the Iraqi armed forces? Had Iraqi Kurds—and Turkish Kurds—developed a deep-seated distrust of their respective central governments' militaries? Did many white American soldiers try for decades to informally subvert Truman's racial desegregation order? Had African Americans come to believe that generations of service in the U.S. military earned them first-class citizenship? Did Puerto Ricans see military service as a path to upward mobility in American society yet simultaneously resent the U.S. Navy's years of jeopardizing the territory's fragile environment by using the island as a heavy weapons firing range?

Whenever any country engages in warfare, that war is happening as a distinctive episode in that country's military-ethnic/racial gendered history.

The Iraq War occurred at just such a distinctive moment in Iraqi Sunnis,' Shiites,' and Kurds' gendered relationships not only to each other, but to the state's military—its old military and its new, U.S.-reconstituted military. Likewise, it occurred at a distinctive phase in the ongoing patterns of African American, ethnically diverse white American, Japanese American, Jewish American, Chinese American, native American, Arab American, and diverse Latino communities' gendered relationships to the U.S. military.

In neither Iraq nor the United States during the years 2003–9, moreover, did the military act as a passive mirror. In each country the military took steps to shape the society's current ethnic and racial cultural and political dynamics. Many senior military officers and their civilian superiors in each country had a stake in its citizens adopting the passive mirror analogy. Such a portrayal of a country's armed forces might have lowered popular expectations of its military's responsibilities for any racial or ethnic tensions or inequalities. In reality, during the Iraq War, Iraqi and American military officers and their immediate political civilian superiors took deliberate steps to encourage members—especially young men—from certain ethnic and racial communities to join their all-volunteer militaries.[33]

By spring 2002, eight months into the U.S.-led military operation in Afghanistan, and as the Defense Department was hammering out plans for a U.S.-led military invasion of Iraq, Latino men and women accounted for 13 percent of the army's new recruits. Overall, Latinos by then made up 9.7 percent of all the army's soldiers. Both figures represented increases. As the *Wall Street Journal* reported in its "Advertising" news column, these increases were the result in part of the Pentagon's having "boosted the marketing dollars dedicated to Latinos."[34] By 2006, the Defense Department reported a further increase: 11 percent of all of its active-duty enlistees were Hispanic/ Latino. This percentage, however, still was less than Latinos' proportion of the total U.S. population.[35]

Making the jobs of Defense Department recruiting strategists and advertising executives more challenging was the fact that Latinos in the United States in the early twentieth century were not homogenous. In particular, Latinos had quite disparate experiences with U.S. and foreign militaries. Many Latinos who had recently immigrated from Guatemala, El Salvador, or Honduras, for example, had vivid memories of their home countries' militaries as instruments of brutal repression. Mexican Americans, by contrast, might not harbor such memories—unless they recently had immigrated from Mexico's most militarized states, Oaxaca or Chiapas. Still, many Mexican immigrants or their relatives might have experienced rough handling by the U.S. Border Guard, which had become increasingly militarized during the years of the Iraq War.[36] Longer-established Mexican Americans might have thought back with pride to their grandfathers who, as World War II veterans, used their new-found status as a launch pad for greater Latino local political participation and influence. Then there were the members of Florida's large and highly politicized Cuban American community. Many of their influencers perhaps saw the U.S. military as a defender of their freedom and as the instrument of future Cuban liberation from Cuba's communist regime. Puerto Ricans living in New York, Hartford, and New London might have had uncles, aunts, and grandfathers who had served in the U.S. military and belonged to veterans' social clubs.

By the time of the Iraq War, Latinos in the United States were more diverse than ever.

Among the large national advertising companies that had won lucrative Defense contracts to launch appeals to Latinos were Young and Rubicam and Leo Burnett. One of the advertising firms that had won an army subcontract to work with Leo Burnett was Cartel Creativo. It was based in San Antonio and thus matched the Pentagon's prioritizing of Los Angeles and San Antonio as cities for their wartime recruitment efforts.[37] Cartel

Creativo's chief executive, Victoria Varela, had her advertising sights set on San Antonio women, women similar to Emma Bedoy-Pina. According to Varela, "We've got to put as much emphasis on the mothers as we do on the potential recruits."[38] For instance, the recruiting advertisements created by Cartel Creativo reassured worried Latino mothers that their military sons and daughters would be able to stay close to home and remain a part of the local Latino community.[39]

The Iraq War was being waged when Latinos, in all their diversity, were becoming a more significant segment of the country's total population, a larger proportion of the military's personnel and a subject of more intense military recruitment strategizing. It also was a time when Latinos were becoming more politically influential, at both the national and local levels.[40] Latinos were voters and elected officials whose ideas about the Iraq War carried new political weight. Emma Bedoy-Pina was part of this politicization. As we will see, candidates for local office had begun to seek her out.

The evolution of Latinos in the American polity was gendered. Latina feminism and, within that, Chicana feminism, emerged in the 1970s and 1980s. By the early 2000s, Latina and Chicana feminist consciousness was helping to shape wider social movements and academic women's studies programs in American colleges and discussions in public forums.[41] Activist Latinas were calling for an accounting of patriarchy's toll inside their own communities. They also were demanding that women as well as men have a voice in the emergent Latino power movement and that white-led women's organizations pay more attention to immigration and labor issues, each so salient for Latinas. The days when male military veterans could be the chief public spokespeople for the entire Latino community were waning.

Latinos were assiduously courted by both Republican and Democratic candidates during the 2002, 2004, 2006, and 2008 wartime elections for Congress and the White House. As a result of the 2004 congressional elections, for instance, seven Latino women and seventeen Latino men were elected to the House of Representatives. Political party affiliation mattered. A majority of Latinos and Latinas identified as Democrats.[42]

In the historic 2008 presidential election, in which the Iraq War was a featured issue, Latinas and Latinos made their presence felt in both the primaries and the final election. A Latino, Governor Bill Richardson of New Mexico, was an early Democratic presidential candidate and, after dropping out of the race, was intensely wooed by both of the remaining Democratic front runners for his endorsement. In the Texas Democratic 2008 primary election, Latino voters were credited with providing candidate Hillary Clinton her margin of victory in the state, although the Texas primary win was not sufficient to give her the Democratic presidential nomination. On the Republican side, John McCain's candidacy was significantly strengthened by his support among Latinos in his home state of Arizona and in other southwestern states.[43]

In the 2008 final presidential election, states in the Southwest were among those where Barak Obama and John McCain were thought to be running neck and neck in the final weeks of the campaign. Ultimately, in New Mexico, according to exit polls on election day, 72 percent of Latina voters cast their votes for Obama. This was a higher proportion for Obama than was cast by white male voters (43 percent), by white women voters (41 percent), or by Latino men (65 percent).[44]

In hotly contested Nevada on election day there was less of a Latino/Latina gender gap: 76 percent of Latinas voted for Obama, compared with 40 percent of white men, 49 percent of white women, and 76 percent of Latino men.[45] CNN's exit polling data revealed that, across the country, 68 percent of all Latina voters chose Obama, the candidate most critical of the U.S. government's war in Iraq. This was a slightly higher proportion than the 64 percent of Latino men who voted for Obama. Latinas also made their voices heard because they turned out in large numbers to vote. Nationwide, Latinas made up 5 percent of all 2008 voters and voted overwhelmingly for Obama, making Latina political power visible at this later stage of the Iraq War.[46]

Military recruitment efforts likewise never take place on an empty playing field. During the Iraq War, multiple contests were going on that would affect Emma and her son's decisions and that, in turn, their decisions would help shape. Waging the Iraq War, as its casualties rose and its time line stretched into an uncertain future, called for the Department of Defense somehow to acquire large numbers of military enlistees. Potential recruits were sought amid dynamic gendered Latino politics, the ever-changing politics of motherhood, and the political contests over the role of public schools in American society.

Emma's younger son Jacob ultimately disappointed San Antonio's army recruiters. Emma and her son would not help the recruiters meet their enlistment quotas. Despite the recruiters' access to his San Antonio schools during the early 2000s, despite wartime campaigns aimed squarely at Latino young men and their mothers, Jacob decided not to join his older brother in the military. After finishing high school, instead he pursued his studies in college. Emma voiced no unhappiness with her younger son's decision. She reported, too, that her older son's specialty in the air force had kept him safely stationed in the United States.[47]

In any case, American military recruiters soon thereafter became less desperate to acquire Jacob. Their jobs would become easier in the Iraq War's late phase. By fall 2008, the plunging American economy was driving up rates of civilian unemployment and underemployment, as well as the soaring cost of college, which led increasing numbers of American young people—and not-so-young people—to look more favorably on the military as an employer. By early 2009, unemployment overall in the United States had risen above 8 percent, with predictions being made that it would go higher. Latinos' unemployment rates were higher even than the national average. Latino men, concentrated in the construction industry—where the bursting of the "housing bubble" was acutely felt—were especially vulnerable. In late February 2009 the Defense Department announced that the army, which had suffered most during the height of the Iraq War from missed enlistment quotas, driving it to lower its enlistment standards, was exceeding its monthly enlistment quotas for the first time since the Iraq War's start.[48] Studies done by the Defense Department were being confirmed: "for every 10 percent increase in unemployment there is usually a 5 percent boost in military recruitment."[49] If Emma's younger son wouldn't answer the recruiter's call, other young people would.[50]

Also helping American military recruiters in this later stage of the Iraq

War was the fact that American editors had pushed news of combat from both the Iraq and Afghanistan war zones to the inside pages of the American press. Iraq often didn't even make it on to the nightly television newscasts. Newly elected President Barak Obama, though a critic of the Bush administration's invasion of Iraq, was continuing in early 2009 to pledge that he would send thousands of additional American soldiers to Afghanistan, where the U.S.-led NATO forces were losing ground to resurgent Taliban militias. There was to be no let-up in the recruiters efforts. This prospect, however, was not making the sorts of media headlines that might catch the eyes of potential young American recruits. Many of them were thinking of military enlistment as an appealing safe employment haven in the midst of a sagging domestic economy, when money for college was scarce and civilian jobs were drying up.

Yet the news of Jacob's choosing college over enlistment was not the sum of Emma Bedoy-Pina's relationship with the American military during the years of the war.

When her older son had joined the air force, Emma had become active in the San Antonio branch of the Blue Star Mothers. Begun during World War II, the Blue Star Mothers over the succeeding decades had grown into a nationwide organization with locally rooted branches, a congressional charter, and working relationships with the Defense Department and the Veterans Administration.

The women such as Emma who joined Blue Star Mothers had sons or daughters in one of the armed services. Its members saw their role as supporting each other as mothers and supporting not only their own offspring but American military personnel, including veterans, more generally. Among their missions was to "promote patriotism."[51]

However, even embracing patriotism and support for the country's soldiers did not guarantee that any woman in the Blue Star Mothers would recommend that all her children enlist. Nor did membership ensure that a woman would see any given war as worth sacrificing her child. Emma, for instance, remained reassured that her older son continued in 2009 to be safely deployed within the borders of the United States.

The San Antonio branch of the Blue Star Mothers was organized in 2004, initially by city women without any federal affiliation. Gradually, however, its local group became incorporated into the national Blue Star Mothers. During the Iraq War, the San Antonio branch's forty women met at a local Lutheran church, created care packages to send to soldiers, and offered comfort for local families whose sons and daughters had been killed or injured in the war. Although it was a women's group, occasionally a father came to the Blue Star Mothers' local meetings. Many of the group's mothers stayed active in the group even after their own sons or daughters had left the military.[52]

In the middle of the Iraq War, Emma was elected president of the San Antonio branch of the Blue Star Mothers. She compared her own relationship to the soldiers she and her colleagues were caring for with that of other San Antonio military mothers. Her son was stationed in the United States, while many other local mothers' sons and daughters were on their second or third deployments to Iraq. They, more than she, were the mothers who needed extra support. The group adopted as their motto, Till They All Come Home. Emma signed her own e-mails, "Proud mother of an Airman."[53]

Becoming so active in the city's Blue Star Mothers made Emma more visible to San Antonio's journalists. Thus a reporter for *San Antonio Express News* sought her out for a reaction to the 2006 execution of Saddam Hussein. Emma gave her opinion without hesitation: "I think I would rather he die a long and lonely death in squalor and in a run-down prison with no running water, no heat, no windows, where he would have to sleep on the dirt floor . . . and live as long and miserable as possible."[54] In her role as chapter president, Emma also wrote letters to the editor of the San Antonio papers. For instance, in January 2008 she wrote a public letter to thank one of the city's veterans affairs officials for the "the excellent job she has done in educating the public on issues, both personal and general, regarding our military families and their sacrifices."[55]

Political figures in San Antonio added Emma to their Rolodexes. Thus when a Latino candidate sought to raise funds and popular support for his campaign for city office, he welcomed the support of a group of locally prominent Latina women. Emma was among them.[56]

CHAPTER SEVEN

Danielle

From Basketball Court to Baghdad Rooftop

Danielle Green had hoped that the U.S. Army would provide her with the family she yearned for. It had been difficult growing up on Chicago's South and West sides during the late 1970s and through the 1980s. Three decades later, these neighborhoods would become famous for having given Barack Obama the opportunity to hone his skills as a community organizer. In the 1970s and 1980s, poverty here was rife, neglect was palpable. Many African American families came unraveled. Danielle's father was absent, her mother became addicted to drugs. Her aunt took over parenting the young Danielle until she too succumbed to addiction. Danielle then lived with her grandmother, who supported them both with public welfare assistance. Danielle's favorite toy, she later would recall, was "G.I. Joe." He was "cool," she thought. He offered a reassuring image of discipline and focus.[1]

G.I. Joe had his own history. A twelve-inch plastic figure of an American soldier, G.I. Joe was first launched in 1964. The toy in its original incarnation represented a fairly realistic version of an ordinary post–World War II enlisted man. In the wake of the U.S. failed war in Vietnam, G.I. Joe lost his appeal to American children. Its Rhode Island-based toy maker, Hasbro, took G.I. Joe off the market in 1976. But not for long. In 1982, with the coming of the Reagan administration, infusions of new resources into the U.S. military and its operations in Grenada, Panama, Honduras, and Nicaragua, playing with soldiers regained its attraction for American children. G.I. Joe was back on the toy store shelves. He returned, however, as a more fantastic figure, with a story line that pitted him against a formidable and evil foe. He also returned with a new physique. Over the years, Hasbro's designers continued to paint G.I. Joe a pinkish white skin color, but now they made the small plastic figure more muscular. Hasbro marketed him not as a doll but as an "action figure." Boys and their parents were the intended market for G.I. Joe. And American boys didn't play with "dolls." Danielle Green, a young African American girl struggling to give coherence to her roller-coaster girlhood, was not the child whom Hasbro's marketing professionals had in mind.[2]

Toy soldiers and war games long have been part of sustaining the cultures of war. Boys growing up in Europe's aristocratic families had been given toy tin soldiers to play with to prepare them for their adult masculinized responsibilities. Boys and girls in war zones often have made games out of mimicking what they have seen adults around them doing—hiding, pointing guns, shooting, dying. Military recruiters in the United States during the Iraq War sought to interest children in soldiering by introducing video war games into their recruiting campaigns. In 2009, Britain's Ministry of Defense introduced its own series of toys: camouflage-attired, technologically equipped "Action Men."[3] Danielle's 1980s G.I. Joe had had an impressive ancestral line and still was being updated.

Despite the turmoil in her home life, Danielle stayed in school. When she reached high school, she discovered the Junior Reserve Officer Training Corps, or JROTC. Founded in the mid-1990s, the military cadet training program managed by the Defense Department ran courses and activities paralleling those of ordinary courses and activities within high schools. JROTC was intended to be a younger version of ROTC, the program for older students already in existence on many American college campuses. ROTC gave its enrollees college credit for certain ROTC courses, as well as money for their tuition but obligated its cadets, in return, to continue their military service for several years after graduation. By the early twenty-first century, more and more senior officers in the U.S. military had begun their military careers as ROTC cadets in civilian colleges and universities across the country.

Faculty and students at numerous colleges and universities challenged the existence of a Defense Department-run program on their campuses during then 1980s and 1990s, arguing that ROTC compromised the intellectual integrity of higher education and that, moreover, with its bans on gay men and lesbians, ROTC violated what for many colleges by the late 1990s had become a declared principle: nondiscrimination against students, staff, and faculty on the basis of sexual orientation. In response, supporters of ROTC on campus, including many college presidents, contended that banning ROTC on their campuses was unfair to those male and female students who could not have afforded college tuition were it not for their ROTC subsidies.

JROTC carried with it no monetary compensation for its young student enrollees yet also no obligation for them to enlist in the military after high school. But the Defense Department's recruiting strategists did see JROTC's increasing presence in public high schools across the country as playing a crucial role in persuading teenagers to think positively about future military enlistment.

The program was voluntary and open to both boys and girls. The teenage students such as Danielle who joined the JROTC dressed in military-styled uniforms, were taught American history by military veterans, took part in military-like drills and activities, and often were chosen by civilian school administrators to be the students to raise the school flag or perform other patriotic school rituals.

Because American public schools were not required to adopt JROTC, incorporating it into Danielle's or any other public high school often set off a lively debate among parents over whether it would enhance or undermine their children's education. The debates could become heated. Many parents rejected the introduction of military culture and practices into their local schools. Some calculated that JROTC actually cost their resources-strapped schools money. The Defense Department, as well as those school administrators, school board members, and parents in favor of introducing JROTC, argued in response that membership in JROTC fostered patriotism. Furthermore, they contended, JROTC was especially valuable for students in inner city schools—that is, poor young people from racial minorities—

whose neighborhoods and families were seemingly chaotic. JROTC could offer these disadvantaged students, its supporters believed, discipline and a source of needed self-esteem.[4]

Danielle recalled that she had thrived in her school's JROTC. However, she did not do what its Pentagon managers had hoped she would do. She did not enlist in the military directly after graduating from high school. Instead, Danielle went to college. For the other stabilizing pillar of her Chicago high school career had been basketball. Danielle became a good athlete, a high school All-American player. She was good enough to catch the eye of another set of recruiters, college women's sports coaches. Notre Dame University offered Danielle a college basketball scholarship.

By the 1990s, when Danielle was paying for her college education by playing basketball, American women's school sports were better funded than they ever had been in the history of American higher education. The reason: Title IX.

It might strike readers as odd to analyze the Iraq War even partly in terms of the history of American women's sports. Men's and boys' sports' relationships to American war culture and war waging seem a more obvious choice for investigation. By the early 2000s, American masculinized sporting culture had adopted many war analogies and rituals to inspire male athletes' competitiveness: uniformed soldiers and jet fighters were incorporated into the opening ceremonies of many American professional and college men's sporting events; military personnel in uniform were given special attention at games; elaborately designed plays appeared akin to battlefield stratagems. It was not surprising that the Defense Department's recruiters targeted the coaches of schoolboys' athletic teams as among the people who potentially could encourage their young male charges to enlist.

Yet what the expansion of American young women's athletic opportunities offered to many young women in the 1990s and early 2000s was a means to attend college where, a decade earlier, they might have considered military enlistment. And the same hard-won expansion of women's sports during Danielle's generation of American girls had helped to break down the same popular assumptions about women's limited capacity for strenuous physical exertion that previously had justified the U.S. military's imposition of both gendered quotas and job exclusions.

Title IX was a provision of Congress's 1972 Civil Rights Act. It was the product of lobbying by women's rights advocates who became convinced that girls and young women were being deprived of equal opportunity in education in no small measure because so many schools—with the enthusiastic backing of their male alumni—invested such disproportionate resources in male college sports. While scarcely debated at the time of its congressional passage, Title IX became the single most potent engine driving the expansion and flourishing of American girls' and women's sports in the 1990s and early 2000s.[5] Colleges began offering sizable scholarships to women scholar/athletes. Men began vying with women for the jobs of coaching women's teams. Girls' and women's sports attracted more alumni and even commercial media attention. "Soccer mom"—the mother of a soccer-playing *girl*—entered the American political lexicon. She was the busy middle-class mother who devoted hours every week driving her daughter to soccer games, rooting for her daughter's teams, and overseeing her athlete daughter's knee surgeries. The "soccer mom" also was presumed by electoral strategists to be a voter, a voter who might swing between Republicans and Democrats.[6]

Danielle was a success at Notre Dame. Her deft lefthanded maneuvers down the basketball court earned her a campus nickname, "D. Smooth."

After graduating from Notre Dame, Danielle was hired as assistant coach for the girls' basketball program at Chicago's Washington High School. Her head coach was Willie Byrd. Danielle continued to aspire to become the member of a close-knit family. Danielle and Willie began dating. Despite Willie's being twenty years her senior, they enjoyed each other's company, he treated Danielle nicely, and they shared a love of basketball. Danielle told him that she would make a good wife. But at that point in his life Willie was reluctant to become a husband.

Danielle surprised many of her college friends when, five years out of college, at age twenty-six and at the start of a promising coaching career, she decided to enlist in the army. It was 2003. She explained that she hoped that

FIGURE 5. Danielle, "D. Smooth," playing basketball for the University of Notre Dame. (Photo: Joe Raymond/for the *New York Times*/Redux)

the army would give her the family she had never had but had always wanted. Looking back, she said, "I knew I was taking a risk in joining the Army."[7]

Danielle trained to become a member of the military police. She was soon deployed to Iraq. She had expected her service in Iraq to be as part of a humanitarian mission. During the next months, her familial hopes for the army went unfulfilled. When she returned home to Chicago on a three-week leave, she began seeing Willie Byrd again. This time, they got married. Then Danielle returned to duty in Iraq.

A year after President Bush had declared "Mission accomplished," the war had escalated. Danielle's military police assignment was not categorized by the army as a "combat" job. Nonetheless, she served as a gunner with the army's 571st Military Police Company. Often her job was to sit in the turret of the unit's armored vehicle; she felt exposed. Sometimes, however, hours went by when nothing happened. One fateful May day it was a blistering hot 110°F in the sun. Danielle was on guard with her M-16 rifle, standing next to a wooden water tank on the rooftop of a Baghdad police station. She recalled, "I didn't like being alone, but I thought I'd let some of the others cool down below, and then they'd relieve me. It was like I was a sitting duck. But that's the way it is a lot of the time over there. You want to trust the Iraqis—some are such nice people—but you know you'd better not, even the children. You just never know. And they just don't want us there."[8]

Then Danielle heard the explosions of two rocket-propelled grenades. She was hit. She remembered the sound of her own screaming, sand was in her mouth, eyes, and ears, and splintered wood was embedded in her left cheek. She thought, "Please God. . . . I have so much more to do in life. I don't want to die here."[9] Within minutes, other soldiers in her unit were up on the roof covering her body, then carrying her down to a waiting Humvee, which drove her, now wearing fatigues soaked in blood, to the hospital inside the Green Zone. One soldier had found her wedding ring on the roof. Her sergeant put it on a finger on her right hand. Danielle's left forearm and hand, which had helped earn her the name D. Smooth, were gone.

Danielle's injury and evacuation were caught on camera; the images quickly began to circulate around the world.

A month later Danielle was back in the United States, in Washington. She became a patient at Walter Reed Hospital, the premier American military hospital. Four and a half years later it would be Walter Reed that Barak Obama would symbolically visit just days before his presidential inauguration. Danielle Green was in the amputee ward. She had become one of the first American women soldiers in the Iraq War to endure a combat-caused amputation. The hospital's medical staffs were particularly attentive. Journalists were eager to interview her.

Every government's military that became part of the U.S.-led "coalition of the willing" in Iraq had its own gendered politics. While virtually every military in the early twenty-first century remained overwhelmingly male and was infused with its own form of masculinized institutional culture, each nation's troops deployed by their civilian superiors to support the Americans in their war in Iraq had a distinctive gendered history and dynamic.

The British military, the Americans' chief operational partner, had given up male conscription decades ago and was 10 percent women as it conducted its operations in southern Iraq. The Australian military, at 13 percent women, had had its share of sexual harassment scandals but had been less ambivalent than the British about recruiting women and deploying them on overseas missions. The proportions of women in two other coalition militaries—the Portuguese and Dutch—had been miniscule but rising rapidly in the decade just prior to the Iraq War. Both of their proportions of women in uniform had reached 13 percent by 2005. The Japanese military, by contrast, was only 4 percent women, but that proportion was expected to climb. The U.S.-led coalition's Spanish, Honduran, Polish, South Korean, and Ukrainian partners had relatively small proportions of women in their forces. The Italian military had been among the NATO and Iraq War coalition forces whose commanders were most reluctant to end male conscription and to recruit women volunteers.

Thus none of the U.S.-led coalition forces' myriad policies perfectly matched that of the American military in which Danielle Green enlisted in 2003. Nor was the U.S. military the most enlightened or progressive. Some governments and their military commanders allowed women to serve in

jobs labeled "combat," others didn't. The U.S. Congress, White House, and
military maintained, despite mounting critiques, some from retired admirals
and generals, the bans on openly gay men and lesbians serving in the forces.
In some countries, women's pursuit of equality within the military made
headlines but in many scarcely had reached the status of a political issue. In
Germany, South Korea, Turkey, and Russia, for instance, male conscription
still was the backbone of the military; in others it had been replaced by an
all-volunteer force. Some countries' militaries, such as those of Bangladesh,
Ireland, Italy, and the Netherlands, had taken up UN-directed peacekeeping
as among their forces' chief missions. Others, most notably the American,
eschewed the blue helmet, preferring their own or NATO-led overseas missions with what appeared to their superiors to permit a less compromised
style of masculinized soldiering. As Iraqis were reconstructing their wartime
military, they had a host of different gendered models to compare but were
pressured to adopt the American model.

During these same years, but outside the Iraq war zone, other militaries
also were engaged in debates over how many women could be recruited and
distributed in the ranks without damaging the masculinized image of the
state's armed forces. The Russian military, for instance, throughout the cold
war had relied on male conscription and enlisted only a very small number
of women. In the 1990s, however, while still conscripting men but facing
escalating male conscript disaffection, owing in part to its unpopular war in
Chechnya, the Russian military began recruiting substantially more women.
By 2003, women volunteers had reached 10 percent of the Russian forces.

The German military, which also stayed out of the U.S.-led invasion but
contributed its troops to NATO's Afghanistan operations, had inched gradually up to 8 percent women. Male conscription still supplied the German
government with most of the soldiers it required, but conscientious objection was easily available to Germany's male conscripts and was widely chosen and popularly acceptable. The Canadian military, whose government
likewise refused to take part in the Iraq invasion yet had sent its troops to
Afghanistan, had a longer history of recruiting significant numbers of women
into its all-volunteer forces than the German military had and was ahead of

its American neighbor both in permitting women to enter combat jobs and in lifting its ban on gays and lesbians in uniform. By the time of the Iraq and Afghan wars, the Canadian military matched the Australians, Portuguese, and Dutch with 13 percent women. The military with the highest percentage of women in its forces by 2008 was New Zealand's—at 24 percent. As the Canadian, German, and French had, its government declined to join the U.S.-led coalition. The world's second-highest proportion of women in uniform was that of the South African military, another Iraq War nonparticipant, at 21 percent women.[10]

Women's proportion of U.S. active-duty military personnel had increased dramatically since the early 1970s. In the aftermath of World War II, when thousands of American women had been enlisted into the uniformed forces, Congress and the Defense Department had taken deliberate steps to ensure that the country's military was once again a thoroughly masculinized institution. Consequently, the U.S. military that fought in Vietnam during the 1960s and early 1970s was a military shaped by a gender ceiling: no more than 2 percent of the active-duty personnel could be women.

The American military was able to engage in gender manipulation during previous wartime eras because it could rely for enlistments on compulsory male conscription. In practice, the draft worked in ways that bred racism, alienation, and civilian anti-war protest. In its actual operation, it also proved easier for a young man to avoid military service if he was—or his parents were—affluent enough to enroll him in and keep him in college. Nonetheless, the all-male draft did allow U.S. military planners and their conservative congressional overseers to hold on to their 2-percent women limit. The American women who served in the U.S. military in the Vietnam War were confined chiefly to the nursing corps or administrative posts. These women were made virtually invisible to the general public.[11]

Indulging in this masculinist luxury came to an abrupt end when the U.S. Congress ended the male draft in 1973. Members of Congress, overwhelmingly male in 1973, had become concerned about both the unfairness in the actual operations of the military conscription law and, particularly, the growing political alienation of white middle-class voters, mothers and fathers who resented their sons' being drafted to wage the unpopular war in Southeast Asia. The change affected the army more deeply than the other three military services, since the army had the most persistent need to enlist large numbers of new recruits. Thereafter, the post-1973 army would have to rely on volunteers. Setting quotas for recruiters, promoting high schools' adoption of JROTC, inflating expenditures on media advertising, profiting from passage of the No Child Left Behind law, cultivating relationships with sporting associations such as NASCAR—between 1973 and 2009, each became a strategic part of the Defense Department's postdraft formula.

The Defense Department's manpower planners anticipated that the first pool of soldiers to dry up would be white, middle-class young men, those Americans who had available to them other, more attractive, career alternatives than soldiering. This expectation had inspired military planners to take a new interest in young women as potential recruits. The 2 percent ceiling was removed by the late 1970s. Other, less tangible, sexist ceilings remained securely in place, however. They would be charted, challenged, and occasionally shattered over the next three decades. This American anti-sexism activist reporting and resisting would become integral to how the Iraq War was experienced and waged.

Several American women's organizations began to take on the job of monitoring the military's new interest in women volunteers. Starting in the early 1990s, in the wake of the Gulf War, they collected data from the Pentagon. They saw the numbers of uniformed women in all four services grow. They watched more than the sheer numbers, however; they were alert to gendered patterns and questioned the workings of sexism inside the military that caused those patterns. These same women activists took special note of how Defense Department officials—usually with congressional support—defined and redefined an elastic concept that set off clanging patriarchal alarm bells: "combat."

During the two decades prior to the Iraq War, American women activists repeatedly challenged Pentagon officials' attempts to formally categorize scores of military jobs—including, in the 1980s, army carpenter and electrician—as "combat" jobs. The bureaucratic goal seemed to be to ensure that they would remain male-only jobs, off-limits for any uniformed woman. But in the early 1990s, in the months immediately after the Gulf War, as a result of activists' and congressional women's mobilization, more military jobs were opened up for women, including that of fighter pilot. The special forces (Navy Seals, Delta Force, and other units), however—which came to play such significant roles in the American operations in both Afghanistan and Iraq—remained exclusively male.[12]

The official American definitions of "combat" remained problematic. Danielle's military policing job, for instance, still would be deemed "non-combat" by her Pentagon superiors, as if the label provided her and her fellow (male and female) soldiers with protection from wartime harm. Fifteen American military women had been killed in the Gulf War. None were in "combat" jobs. By August 2008, 112 American military women had died in Iraq and Afghanistan, 65 of those from what the Pentagon reported as "hostile fire." Another 600 American women in uniform had received Purple Hearts, the military's decoration for having been physically wounded by enemy fire.[13]

These realities notwithstanding, the masculinization of the concept of combat, while challenged, had not lost all of its gendered political potency in American culture. Congressional conservatives, in control of Congress prior to 2006, still tried to formally restrict women soldiers to "non-combat" roles. They failed.[14] Nevertheless, during the years of the Iraq War, many Americans inside and outside government continued to imagine that combat could be set neatly apart from other war-waging activities in a way that would preserve distinct zones of protected femininity and muscular masculinity. This may help explain why, when journalists and photographers came to Walter Reed to interview Danielle, the very idea of a *woman soldier amputee* would prove so newsworthy and yet so disturbing to many Americans.[15]

The realm of most American feminist activism during the 1980s until the early 2000s did not include the small group of military-focused anti-sexism activists who monitored the U.S. military's and Congress's gendered politics. Most of the activists in the country's women's movement had come out of the 1960s–80s civil rights and anti-war movements and were wary of any engagement with the U.S. military. Only occasionally, as during the post–

Gulf War 1990s Tailhook scandal, which briefly drew back the curtain on the misogynist culture of the American armed forces, did the majority of civilian feminists believe it was worthwhile to devote their scarce resources and overstretched energies to critique the sexist dynamics coped with daily by women inside the military.[16]

During the 1980s and 1990s, when the numbers of women in the armed forces were growing dramatically, those American women challenging military sexism organized conferences of women military personnel. They talked to women in other military forces around the world and especially to the Canadians, British, and Australians. They compared women's experiences in militaries with those of civilian women then beginning to enter formerly male-only fire departments and police departments. They revealed that, year after year, ever since the anti-gay/lesbian "don't ask, don't tell" policy's inception in 1993, women in the U.S. military were far more likely than were their male comrades to be officially investigated and discharged on charges of violating the ban on gays openly serving in the military.[17]

Women advocating for equality of women in the U.S. military made alliances with women in Congress, such as Patricia Schroeder, Democrat of Colorado, Barbara Boxer, Democrat of California, and, later, Heather Wilson, Republican of New Mexico (Heather Wilson was the first woman military veteran to win election to Congress). They were opposed by social conservatives, most of whom were Washington insiders, who argued that expanding women's roles in the military was jeopardizing American national security. It took substantial political energy and bureaucratic attentiveness to turn the U.S. military's normalized sexist thinking, discourses, rituals, and policies into an issue.

Turning any phenomenon into a political *issue*—that is, persuading enough people to stop accepting a phenomenon as normal or as trivial, and then convincing enough people that it is a problem that justifies public intervention—is never easy. Out of all this post–Vietnam War, pre–Iraq War data collection, feminist analyzing, legislative lobbying, and networking, the small band of women activists and their congressional and armed forces allies succeeded in turning into political issues the khaki-tinted glass ceiling, the invisibility of women soldiers in war memorials, the male-exclusiveness of combat jobs, the military's witch hunts directed against women accused of being lesbians, as well as the rampant sexual harassment inside the military.[18]

By the time that Danielle Green was deployed to Iraq as a member of an army police unit in 2004, the U.S. military not only tolerated women in its ranks, it had come to depend on women in its ranks. During the years of the Iraq War, women comprised 15 percent of all American active-duty personnel. Women were, by contrast, approximately 9–10 percent of all the U.S. troops deployed to Iraq and Afghanistan. The gap—between the 15 percent overall and the 9 percent of those deployed to Iraq and Afghanistan—in large part reflected the American government's heavy reliance on the still-masculinized army infantry, special forces, and marines to wage both of these wars.[19]

That is, the four U.S. armed services differed in the degree of their dependence on women personnel. By 2007, compared to the other services, the U.S. Air Force was able to take in the highest percentage of women because it had the lowest proportion of all its jobs categorized as "combat." By midpoint in the war, the active-duty air force was nearing 20 percent—one-fifth— women. The navy had reached 14.7 percent women in 2007. By contrast, the Marine Corps, with its masculinist culture and its high proportion of all jobs designated as "combat," was a mere 6.3 percent women. The army, Danielle's service and by far the U.S. military's largest branch, was 15.3 percent women on the eve of the U.S. invasion of Iraq. By the fourth year of the Iraq War, however, the army as a whole had become somewhat more masculinized, down to only 13.7 percent women. Still, that 13.7 percent amounted to 71,100 women serving in the country's active-duty army.[20]

No major gendered military scandals equivalent to the Gulf War's Tailhook caught the attention of most Americans during the Iraq War. But those activists who continued to watch the U.S. military began to notice a pattern: a significant increase of sexual assaults perpetrated by American male soldiers against American women soldiers. General Janice Karpinski, best known for her role as commander of American military police in U.S.-controlled Iraqi prisons, including Abu Ghraib (the investigation led to her demotion), described in her autobiography how women soldiers on service in

Iraq were afraid to go to the latrines at night for fear of being attacked—by their male comrades. Karpinski also described how senior male commanders dismissed women soldiers' reports, adopting the attitude, "We've got a war to fight, don't bother us with minor complaints."[21]

Women activists outside the military, especially those working within the Miles Foundation, a small independent feminist organization, repeatedly tried to turn rapes of American women soldiers by American male soldiers—and military commanders' dismissive actions—into a political issue. Many of the assaults had occurred while the women were on duty in Iraq or Kuwait. Turning rapes of American women soldiers into an issue during the Iraq War proved hard going.

"Not a day went by that I wasn't sexually harassed." This was the recollection of a woman veteran who phoned National Public Radio during its special program for Veterans Day, November 11, 2008. After describing how the harassment eventually escalated into actual assault, she continued: "I wasn't going to tell anyone. . . . But I was so angry that I had to report it. . . . I felt so trapped."[22]

The women activists who sought to turn rape inside the U.S. military during the Iraq War into a public issue did manage to provide support to several military women survivors of rape and attempted rape that proved effective enough to persuade those women to speak out publicly. They told about both the sexual assaults by fellow soldiers and the dismissive responses of their superiors, responses that had made many of the women feel as though they themselves were "criminals." Many survivors felt too ashamed, too discouraged, or too traumatized to speak out about their experiences, not only of sexual assault, but of the treatment they received from their commanding officers. The feminist activists did manage to persuade several representatives and senators, nevertheless, to hold congressional hearings to investigate the Defense Department's lack of serious response to sexual assaults perpetrated by its male personnel. They also inspired several journalists to publish and air stories about the women soldiers' experiences of sexual assault.

Two decades before the Iraq War, rape, at least civilian-on-civilian rape, had been successfully turned into a political issue in the United States: "date rape," "marital rape" had sounded like oxymorons just a generation earlier but—along with "wartime rape," "rape crisis centers," "rape kits"—had entered into American legal and popular discourses as a result of feminist campaigning. Yet rapes of American women soldiers by American male soldiers—*that* proved to be for many Americans indigestible.

As a result of all their efforts, these activists did manage to get the U.S. Veterans Administration (VA) in 2007 for the first time to conceptualize veteran rape survivors' mental health symptoms as a form of posttraumatic stress disorder. Activists among women veterans and their civilian allies persuaded the VA to develop treatments specifically designed for women veterans who had endured sexual assault. This was a significant moment in the gendered history of warfare. With the support of a handful of members of Congress, they also succeeded in putting the Pentagon on the defensive to the point that its senior officials at least publicly pledged to treat women soldiers' rape charges with more respect and to take those charges more seriously up and down the chain of command. Under congressional pressure, the Defense Department even created a new office, the Sexual Assault Prevention and Response Office, and hired as consultants a civilian organization called Men Can Stop Rape.[23]

Representative Jane Harman, Democrat of California, described her own coming to consciousness. She said that, after talking to therapists and medical personnel treating assaulted women soldiers, as well as listening to the survivors themselves, she had become convinced that rape in the U.S. military during the Iraq War was best understood as an "epidemic."

> The scope of the problem was brought home into acute focus for me during a visit to the West Los Angeles VA Healthcare Center. . . . My jaw dropped when the doctors told me that 41 percent of female veterans seen at the clinic say they were victims of sexual assault while in the military, and 29 percent report being raped during their military service. They spoke of their continued terror, feelings of helplessness and the downward spirals many of their lives have since taken. . . . Numbers reported by the Department of Defense show a sickening pattern. In 2006, 2,947 sexual assaults were reported. . . . At the heart of this crisis is an apparent inability or unwillingness to prosecute rapists in the ranks.[24]

It was only by the fifth year of the Iraq War that enough American women soldiers had spoken out, enough evidence of Defense Department neglect had been collected by those women's supporters, enough women's advocates had persuaded a critical mass of members of Congress and media editors to take the matter seriously—it was only then that American male soldiers' sexual assaults of American women soldiers gained traction as a wartime political issue. But somehow, rape of women soldiers by male soldiers never really gained a purchase on the collective consciousness of the American general public as a major issue of the Iraq War.

Danielle was a young woman in early twenty-first-century American wartime. And she was a young African American woman in wartime. At the outset of the Iraq War, there was a little-noticed reality in the U.S. Army, present, but not yet an issue: African American women had enlisted in the active-duty ranks of the army in such numbers during the 1980s, 1990s, and early 2000s that they were dramatically "over-represented." While African American women were 13 percent of all American women, on the eve of the Iraq War they comprised a surprising 34.3 percent of all active-duty women in the enlisted ranks. They were 16.2 percent of all women active-duty officers. As the Pentagon and the White House were making their plans for invading Iraq, Latina women were 10.1 percent of all active-duty rank-and-file women and 4.3 percent of all women officers.

But it was in the army's ranks—where Danielle Green would serve—that African American women were most dramatically present. By 2002, African American women had become *44.9 percent* of all women in the army's rank and file. That was almost four times African American women's proportion of all American women. Two years earlier, in 2000, their proportion had reached 46 percent, higher than in any of the other three branches of the armed forces. Furthermore, there was a gendered, not simply a raced, dynamic at work in the army's relationship to the African American community. African American *men's* proportion of all active-duty military men was considerably lower, closer to 25 percent.[25]

While stunning, this development was scarcely noticed by politicians, the Pentagon, members of the American public, or by white or African American feminists. When there was any discussion of women in the U.S. military—whether they should be in combat roles, whether the American public would accept "women coming home in body bags," whether women were more likely than men to be accused of being gay, whether women soldiers faced a greater daily threat from their own male comrades than from Iraqi insurgents—the public discussion was framed as if it were about "women" in general.

Thus there was no curiosity expressed, no investigations launched by either the government or by advocacy groups when, during the years of the Iraq War, the proportion of African American women in uniform dropped. By 2007, the fourth year of the Iraq War, according to the Defense Department's figures, African American women had fallen to 30.1 percent of all women in the active-duty forces' enlisted ranks, though their proportion of all women officers had risen slightly, to 17 percent. During the same years, Latinas had risen to 12.5 percent of all four branches' enlisted women and 5.5 percent of all women officers, reaching 17 percent in the rank and files of both the navy and the marines.

Again, however, it was the trends in the army that were particularly puzzling—if anyone had thought to puzzle. While still a higher proportion than they were of the American society as a whole, African American women had dropped to 38.2 percent of all army enlisted women.[26]

Thus Danielle, perhaps without realizing it, enlisted in the American Army at the peak of African American women's engagement with soldiering. She had joined its ranks and was deployed to Iraq at a time when the army was particularly dependent on black women to fill its ranks, to carry out its mission. She also took up soldiering at a particular moment in American gendered war waging—when the military was under intense scrutiny for its sexist, often misogynist, attitudes toward women.

Most of the handful of American women soldiers who made headlines during the Iraq War were white women—Jessica Lynch, the quartermaster corps enlistee whose convoy was ambushed and who was later rescued by other American soldiers; Lynndie England, the low-ranking soldier accused and found guilty of taking part in abusing Iraqi male prisoners in Abu

Ghraib; and Janice Karpinski, the woman general who was charged with failing to keep order in Abu Ghraib.[27] The only African American woman to attract significant, though less, American media notice was Shoshana Johnson. She was captured and wounded in the same ambush on March 23, 2003 as Jessica Lynch. She thereby became the first African American woman soldier to become a prisoner of war.

Shoshana Johnson's and Danielle Green's stories are at once similar and distinct. Like Danielle, Shoshana had joined JROTC in high school. Like Danielle, she had joined the U.S. Army at a time in its gendered and racialized history when African American women were numerically prominent, yet politically unremarked. Like Danielle, Shoshana had been deployed to Iraq and assigned to what was officially categorized as a "non-combat" job. Like Danielle, she was injured in combat.

But Shoshana had enlisted in part to obtain the educational benefits that the army was touting as a reward for enlistment. Unlike Danielle, she already had become a mother before she enlisted. And, unlike Danielle, she had immediate family members who had served in the military before her. "It was also, basically, the family business. My dad did 20 years. My sister did 11 years. Aunts, uncles, cousins have served in the military."[28]

After they each had left the army, Shoshana Johnson and Jessica Lynch continued to see themselves as bound together. Shoshana did not blame Jessica for the celebrity status thrust upon her. Most of the American media chose to treat the white woman as the wartime hero, as the "story." Thus, when the two women came together to attend a memorial event in Arizona honoring their comrade Lori Ann Piestewa, the first Native American woman to be killed in combat while serving in the U.S. military, photographers present at the event edited their photographs so that only Lynch was in the frame: "It hurts, you know," Shoshana explained. "I made a contribution to my government and to my country, and it's hard when your contribution is ignored."[29]

Danielle left Walter Reed Hospital as soon as the doctors and therapists would allow, in part to get away from the media gaze, to get on with her life. She was a civilian Chicagoan when it came time to vote in the 2008 presidential election. We don't know how Danielle cast her vote—as a member

FIGURE 6.   Danielle, having returned to civilian life, spoke to a Chicago high
school audience in April 2005. (Photo: Peter Thompson/for the *New York Times*/
Redux)

of the post–civil rights era African American generation, as a woman, as an
Iraq War veteran, as a person needing expensive medical care, as an education professional, as a Chicagoan. Even so, we do know from exit poll results
that black women turned out to vote on November 4, 2008 in even higher
proportions than did black men, and that across the country between 90 and
100 percent (100 percent in North Carolina, 95 percent in Ohio, 90 percent in
Indiana) of black women voted for Barak Obama.[30]

> I think my goal is just to live life to the fullest. When I was younger, I
> thought the glass was half empty. Now it is a glass half full all the time.[31]

Danielle had returned to Chicago, received a medical discharge from
the military, and resumed her married life with Willie Byrd. As Danielle
Green-Byrd, she became an amateur runner. She initially took a job with the
Sports Department of the Chicago Board of Education. Then she decided to
take a new career path, entering graduate school to earn a master's degree in

educational counseling, a challenge: "It was tough. Can you imagine typing 20-page papers with one hand?" she told a reporter.[32]

She received her master's degree in May 2008 and began to plan for a second master's degree, this time in educational leadership.

The Defense Department sought her out. Danielle's status as one of the first American women soldier amputees, combined with her determination to make a productive life after her wartime injury made a good story—not only to encourage other severely wounded soldiers, but to persuade an increasingly skeptical American public that, even having made such a sacrifice, a former soldier could be upbeat about her prospects.

However, Danielle was not simply a poster girl for the military. She saw herself as essentially a civilian. When asked by the Defense Department's "Wounded Warrior Diaries" journalist whether the army and her wartime experience defined her, Danielle replied, "I tell people I only lost my arm. . . . The Army didn't define who I was. I was 26 years old when I came in, and I was pretty confident who I was as a person. I discovered that person at Notre Dame."[33]

CHAPTER EIGHT

Kim

"I'm in a Way Fighting My Own War"

Kim Gorski was in her early thirties when the Bush administration decided to launch a military invasion of Iraq. She was a white American woman married to Mike Gorski, a white American man. They were making their young married lives in Hayward, California, part of the sprawling, racially diverse San Francisco Bay Area. They had a house and a mortgage. The couple didn't yet have children, just two dogs, Chesty and Bosco. Kim was training to become a real estate broker.[1]

The San Francisco Bay Area was an expensive part of the country in which to live in the early twenty-first century. A two-income household would make that life economically sustainable. Houses were selling and property values were still soaring, so real estate looked like a promising career. No one yet was talking about the housing "bubble."

Kim's husband Mike was also at an early stage in his civilian career. He was a junior executive at a Bay Area bank, working his way up the company ladder. In 2002, banking still looked like a solid profession.

Mike previously had been in the active-duty Marine Corps but chose not to reenlist. He left the marines in the early 1990s, still in his twenties. He didn't leave the military entirely, however. Mike joined the California National Guard. He thought that by joining the National Guard he could continue to contribute to society patriotically, while getting on with his civilian life. He and Kim married, and he joined the bank. Mike imagined that he would be doing what members of the state National Guard traditionally had done, attend weekend trainings and occasionally be called up by California's governor to serve close to home for classic state National Guard operations such as postearthquake rescues. Among those in Mike's 870th Military Police Company of the California National Guard were "teachers, bankers, mortgage brokers, telecommunications experts, police officers and copy machine repairmen."[2] Many had children and mortgages; many of their households depended on two incomes.

During the Vietnam War, when the United States mobilized most of its soldiers through male conscription—the draft—the National Guard was seen by many American young men as a safe haven. It wasn't easy, but if a young man could manage to get into the National Guard, he could fulfill his military service obligations and yet avoid being deployed to a deadly war zone in Southeast Asia. As a result, during the 1960s and 1970s the National Guard acquired a reputation for being the site of relative privilege in a wartime America marked by racialized and classed inequalities.

In the early 2000s, however, the National Guard no longer filled this safe haven role for well-connected young men. The draft had been ended, the ranks of the active-duty forces were filled by men and women who had volunteered, and the active-duty forces had become stretched so thin by the government's expansive global assignments that National Guard soldiers were being deployed overseas. Prior to September 2001, nonetheless, many American men and women who enlisted in their home state's National Guard continued to take at face value the National Guard's alluring message: they could remain essentially civilians, still earning some extra money and standing ready to help their fellow citizens in times of emergency. As late as June 2008, after more than five years of multiple National Guard deployments to Iraq, after scores of deaths and injuries endured by National Guard members while serving in war zones, the Army National Guard published a full-page recruitment advertisement still describing the National Guard's mission in these terms: "Whether it's a hurricane, tornado, earthquake, fire, flood, or blizzard, a civil disturbance or even a terrorist attack, you can count on the

Citizen-Soldiers and -Airmen of your National Guard to provide comfort and security, establish order, and ease suffering."[3]

The reality was quite different. To cope with the American military's expanding missions, the Pentagon's personnel planners had been crafting a new model for the twenty-first-century U.S. military. It would almost erase the comforting line between the career active-duty soldier and civilian part-time soldier. These officials integrated the National Guard's troops—as well as members of the Reserves, likewise made up of part-time soldiers leading civilianized daily lives—into their worldwide security strategies. On paper, National Guard units still answered to their state governors and could be nationalized by the president only in exceptional circumstances. In practice, governors and the president had become rivals for the services of the National Guard. The president usually won. The states' ability to fight forest fires and respond to hurricanes, earthquakes, and floods might drop. It thus helps to think of hurricane Katrina, which required thousands of National Guard troops to cope with its devastation along the Louisiana, Mississippi, and Alabama coasts, as a wartime hurricane.

A shift in priorities and strategies began during the 1990–91 Gulf War and reached its peak during the Iraq War. By 2003, Pentagon planners were assuming that the overseas deployment of Mike Gorski and other National Guard members from California to Massachusetts would take an essential part in U.S. war waging. The change would bring the Iraq War close to home. Hometown newspapers and the metro news sections of national papers would all cover the deployment, leaves, and the return of local National Guard units from Iraq and Afghanistan as local news.

The award-winning documentary *The War Tapes* captured on film the local character of so many troops deployed to Iraq.[4] The film was shot with handheld cameras given by the director to five of the men in the New Hampshire National Guard. The tightly edited final film showed not only the American men interacting with each other, with their Iraqi interpreters, and with the Iraqis whose houses they raided but also with their wives and girlfriends back in New Hampshire. The film's final segment showed deceptively peaceful scenes. The National Guard men were back home, dressed in plaid shirts and blue jeans, going to work, doing home repairs, playing with their children. There were no sudden explosions, the hillsides were green. But underneath all was not well. Their wives and girlfriends were finding the men changed, often silent, on edge. The American hometown life had been profoundly changed by this war.

The Defense Department's conceptual and strategic transformation of the part-time soldier into a full-time soldier would have serious implications for the women married to the soldiers of the National Guard. Of course Mike's overseas full-time soldiering would have an impact on Kim. But now the U.S. government would rely on Kim to help its military wage its war in Iraq. Kim was taken aback. She had not seen herself as a "military wife." She had not imagined that she was on the Pentagon's institutional mind.

For generations, women who married active-duty, full-time American soldiers had been socialized to perform the demanding role of "the military wife." Their socialization had been intense. Often the chief agents of this socialization were other military wives. They welcomed the newly wed woman into the military fold; they provided advice, support, and warnings; they wrote guidebooks for other military wives. These experienced military wives, along with the military's chaplains, senior officers, social workers, and the full-time male soldier she had married, taught the young woman how to support her husband, how to help him win promotions, how to contribute to the smooth running of the military base community. They taught the new military wife how to pack, unpack, and repack. They taught her when to socialize and when to keep silent.[5]

In both peacetime and wartime, the U.S. military has counted on those women married to its male full-time soldiers to support their husbands in ways that simultaneously supported the military's mission. Crucial to this institutional effort has been persuading women that they were good wives *insofar as* they worked to support the military's institutional mission. Each woman needed to be persuaded that she was most helpful and loyal to her own husband if she organized her labor and emotions in a way that enhanced the military *as a whole*. That is, "the good wife" and "the good military wife" should come to be seen as one and the same, not only in the institution's eyes, but in the eyes of each woman married to an active-duty male soldier. No daylight should shine between the two.

It had taken decades of thinking, researching, and experimenting to refine this official effort—to craft a discourse of the "military family," to build more day care centers on military bases, to extend appealing base shopping discount privileges, to construct comfortably familiar suburban neighborhoods on overseas bases, and to improve military family counseling services. All this effort notwithstanding, the government's persuasion had not always been successful.[6]

The more obvious indicators of less than total success in socializing women to become good military wives have been the divorces among American soldiers. Between the start of the Afghanistan War and the fourth year of the Iraq War, divorces among American enlisted (nonofficer) soldiers had increased by 28 percent.[7] Less obvious signals were patterns of mental health problems among women married to soldiers and incidences of domestic violence perpetrated by male soldiers against the women and children within their military families.

During the 1990s, in the aftermath of the Gulf War, the Pentagon became increasingly explicit and sophisticated in its efforts to address those underlying pressures on military wives that were producing each of what the Defense Department saw as negative patterns. The U.S. military's stakes in producing at least a moderately contented wife of an active-duty male soldier had been raised by the ending of male conscription in 1973. Once the military depended on volunteers, it not only needed to persuade young men and women to enlist; it also needed to keep those soldiers over the long run—to persuade them to reenlist after their first contracted tour of duty had ended.

Training a contemporary American soldier is costly. A modern military would become unviable if its branches were to lose too many of those expensively trained soldiers after just one or even two tours. By the early twenty-first century, the U.S. active-duty military was becoming a force of married men; and so, military strategists quickly realized, few soldiers reached the decision—reenlist or leave the service—entirely in isolation. Reenlistment rates thus joined rates of divorce and domestic violence on the list of indicators showing whether military wives were being effectively socialized to accept and even find satisfaction in their demanding roles.

By the time of the Iraq War, the more experienced military wives had become acutely aware of the Defense Department's reliance on them to persuade their husbands to reenlist. By the third year of the war, as the army's failure to fulfill its monthly recruitment goals was making headlines, some activist military wives realized that they might have leverage. They were not above publicly reminding senior Pentagon officials that the military could not simply continue to pile extra home front burdens onto the shoulders of civilian, unpaid military wives and yet count on those same women to continue to back their soldier/husbands' reenlistments.[8]

The 15 percent of the active-duty U.S. force that was female drew less concern from these Pentagon officials, not only because their numbers were a relatively small—though crucial—proportion of the total, but also because so many of the careerist active-duty women were not married. Furthermore, there was a far lower official expectation that a husband of an active-duty woman soldier could be transformed into an institutionalized dependent. Consequently, going into the Iraq War, the "military husband" did not provoke as much official anxiety as the "military wife."[9]

Kim Gorski would pose an even greater challenge for the Pentagon. She had married Mike after he left active duty as a marine. Nor was Kim the wife of a full-time active-duty soldier. She and Mike were making their married lives together as civilians in a San Francisco civilian suburb. Mike's soldiering was supposed to be only a sideline. Socializing Kim to act like a good military wife would be harder. Kim didn't see herself as part of the big military family. She didn't live on a military base. Her friends were not other military wives. She didn't shop at a post exchange. She didn't volunteer in base organizations. Kim hadn't expected that her married life would entail long separations from her husband. She didn't imagine that Mike's career success would depend on her performing the duties of a military wife. The National Guard wife was a different political creature.

The Defense Department began to get a taste of the National Guard's and Reserve's soldiers' wives' greater autonomy and political resources early in the Iraq War. In October 2003 the Pentagon, already feeling the pinch of inadequate numbers of military personnel, cancelled the upcoming leaves scheduled for the soldiers of New England's Army Reserve 368th Engineer Battalion. Women as reservists' wives and mothers, women who did not identify chiefly as military wives, went into political action. They had made elaborate plans for their husbands' and sons' leaves. They felt betrayed by the Defense Department. Maria LaMonica, of Revere, Massachusetts, defended her husband's patriotism. He was a policeman in his civilian life; he already had been deployed to Kosovo, where he had been injured. But this cancelled leave for her husband's unit deployed in Iraq politicized her. Maria was not a full-time military wife. She hadn't been socialized into silent compliance. She and other women in their region wrote letters to their congressional representatives and to the president. They voiced their complaints openly to journalists. Maria predicted that her husband would not reenlist in the National Guard: "(He) wants out as soon as he gets home."[10]

> I don't know what day it is. I wake up and there are phone calls that need to be made, meetings need to be planned, people need help or if they don't have questions they need to be consoled. I have to tell them everything is going to be O.K.[11]

Kim was describing her daily life in the sixth month of the Iraq War. Mike and his California National Guard unit had been deployed for months, first for training up in Fort Lewis, Washington, then on to Karbala in southern Iraq.

The Pentagon expected a lot of Kim Gorski. Of the 124 soldiers in Mike's National Guard 870th Military Police Company, the overwhelming majority—118—were men. Only six were women.[12]

By the time of the Iraq War, the U.S. Army's National Guard had become 13 percent women, but this was not reflected in the makeup of Mike's more fully masculinized company.[13] Thus it was chiefly men deployed and women in their families left to sustain the home front. Kim was supposed to dispel the frustrations of other wives when deployments in Iraq were suddenly extended. The Defense Department announced a new "stop-loss" policy. It prevented soldiers whose contracted tours of duty had ended from leaving the military. Instead, they had to stay in the service so long as the rest of their unit still was deployed. "Stop-loss" made news when it was imposed on active-duty soldiers in 2004; but the policy had been imposed on National Guard and Reserve soldiers two years earlier.[14] This policy did little to ease Kim's job of sustaining morale among the families of Mike's soldiers.

In addition, Kim needed to calm other wives' fears when the evening news carried reports from Iraq of combat injuries and deaths. The government counted on her to help National Guard wives struggling with economic hardship and the trials of single parenting. Kim should prevent them from passing along their worries to their soldier/husbands. This was before the 2008–9 economic crisis would make sustaining American households even more difficult. No matter what the financial and emotional stresses being dealt with at home, husbands were supposed to stay focused on their war-waging missions. Wives should not be distractions.

To fulfill the military's expectations, Kim had gone into debt. By September 2003, she had put $11,000 on her credit card. She was charging the costs of phone bills, overseas postage for care packages, purchases of food for the family-support meetings she was running. These charges would not appear in any Washington war-waging budget. Kim summed up her long days of wartime unpaid work: "I'm in a way fighting my own war on the home front."[15]

Mike's superior, Major General Paul Monroe, commander of the California National Guard, had called upon Kim, as Mike's wife, as the wife of a staff sergeant in the National Guard, to head what the Defense Department called the police company's "family readiness group." "Family readiness" was one of the concepts that had been honed by Defense Department officials during the 1990s, especially in the wake of the Gulf War. Family readiness had ambiguous objectives. It was first applied by women's advocates inside government and military wives' support groups outside the Pentagon to justify and organize expanded programs to support military families. If calls for anti-violence programs or better housing could be framed in terms

FIGURE 7. Kim at home in September 2003, wearing her husband's military dog tags, talking about her tasks as a civilian married to a soldier. (Photo: Randi Lynn Beach/pixchannel.com)

of a concept Pentagon decision makers understood—"force readiness"—
then those calls, advocates calculated, had a better chance of being heard,
perhaps even answered. On the other hand, family readiness could be and
was used during the early 2000s to enable the government to mobilize wives
to help it wage war in Iraq. A "ready" family, in the Pentagon's militarized
understanding, was a U.S. soldier's family whose members were willing and
equipped to handle—uncomplainingly—the stresses of sudden, repeated,
and long dangerous deployments.

"Readiness" had become a central concept in Defense Department planning during the late 1980s. By the time of the Iraq War this concept had
become elaborated and ever more sophisticated as it shaped and justified the
Pentagon's mobilization of the wives and children of both its full-time and
part-time soldiers. If Kim had been married to a National Guardsman in
the 1970s, she might never have been called upon to provide counseling, to
organize volunteers, to create phone trees, to double-check news of extended
deployments, and to plan repeated wives' meetings during wartime. In mid-
2003, Kim's phone trees were deemed by American war strategists to be integral to waging war in Iraq. Kim thereby became part of the marital history
of American warfare.

Marriage is political. Wartime politics are marital politics.

Behind the family readiness concept was also the presumption that
women married to American soldiers would relate to each other in a ranking hierarchy that paralleled the pyramid that determined the relationships
between the country's soldiers. Thus those civilian women married to officers and sergeants would be called upon to take responsibility for providing emotional and material support to the wives of their officer/husbands'
military subordinates. Previously, this had meant that women married to
officers in the active-duty military—wives of sergeants, captains, majors,
generals, admirals—would take on a virtual ranking responsibility in their
relationships to those women married to specialists, privates, and seamen.
During the Iraq and Afghanistan wars this hierarchical model was expanded
to cover the National Guard as well. Consequently, Kim Gorski, as the wife
of Staff Sergeant Mike Gorski, was expected by the Pentagon to encourage,

provide practical advice to, create support networks among, and calm the women married to the lower-ranking men under Mike's command in the 870th Military Police Company.

The Defense Department was worried about marital dynamics. Its officials knew that by deploying to Iraq so many thousands of National Guard members and reservists, it imposed a heavy burden on their wives, husbands, and children. On the other hand, it was in the interests of the principal war-waging strategists not to do a full tally of those burdens. Just as the Bush administration had made the decision to omit the costs of the Iraq War from the annual budgets it submitted to Congress during 2003–8, so too it had an institutional stake in underestimating the emotional and financial tolls the war would take, tolls that Kim Gorski in her family readiness work could see all too clearly.

In this sense, then, Kim Gorski was an eyes-wide-open wartime accountant. She could keep track on a daily basis of the true costs of this war. She told the *New York Times* reporter Sarah Kershaw that already, by September 2003, during its first war zone deployment, Mike's unit and its four allied California National Guard units and their families had endured "five divorces, two attempted suicides, several bankruptcies and a lot of depression among soldiers and their spouses."[16]

And this was just September 2003. Kim couldn't know it then, but the Iraq War and the Afghanistan War each were in only their early stages. Yet even at this point Kim was worried that she wouldn't be able to hold back the emotional and financial floods. She hoped she could do whatever possible to ensure that no one in Mike's company and its members' families "dies on my watch, nobody ends up in the loony bin, that all heads stay above water."[17]

A federal law, the Uniformed Services Employment and Reemployment Rights Act, required that a civilian employer guarantee that a reservist or National Guard member called up for duty would have his or her job still there waiting when they returned from a tour, though the deployed employee nonetheless might miss chances for job training and promotions.[18]

This was Kathy Martin's worry. She was one of the California National Guard wives Kim was supposed to be keeping under her wing. Although

Kathy herself was working full-time as a mortgage broker in the San Francisco Bay area and caring for her and her National Guard husband Joe's five children, she feared that Joe, a police officer in the Hayward Police Department, would miss opportunities for promotion in the police because he was away for months.[19] Job promotion anxieties weren't just about status or responsibilities; they were about take-home pay.

The federal law's obligations for employers of National Guard and Reserve soldiers did not require that the civilian employer continue to pay that mobilized soldier's salary while on duty. Mike and Kim Gorski were among the lucky ones. Mike's bank voluntarily continued to pay him his salary while he was at Fort Lewis and in Iraq. Many of the employers of men in Mike's military police unit, however, halted their salaries, leaving their wives to cope with drastically reduced military pay, often in desperate financial straights.

Signing up and qualifying for Food Stamps, the federal food subsidy program for low-income and poor Americans, was not uncommon among military wives—those married to active-duty soldiers and those married to National Guard and Reserve soldiers—during the Iraq War. Journalist Karen Houppert provides a graphic account of a woman named Crystal, married to an active-duty soldier named Richard, who tried during the Iraq War to piece together their precarious family finances while living at Fort Drum, one of the major army bases in upstate New York. The process went on for months. It often seemed excruciating. Her mother offered useful advice about federal poverty programs for which Crystal or her children might qualify. She didn't qualify for Head Start, but she did qualify for WIC, the Women and Infant Children food program for low-income and nursing women and their infant children.[20] The government's Food Stamps and WIC expenditures, however, were not figured into the government's official costs of the Iraq War or the Afghanistan War.

The gendered political economy of the Iraq War had another twist. Even though Kim had enlisted both her own mother's and Mike's mother's help to fulfill all her new family readiness responsibilities, she was exhausted. She found she had no time or energy in those wartime days to continue with her own real estate studies. As Kim described it, when she even managed to glance at her real estate course books, they "might as well be in Swahili."[21] Kim Gorski's delayed entry into the paid labor force also would be omitted from any official accounting of the war's costs.

Another woman for whom Kim Gorski was newly responsible was Gale Tompkins-Beschel. Gale was the mother of two small children and married to Dave, a National Guard soldier who in his civilian life worked as a route salesman for a bottled water company. Gale spoke for many National Guard wives: "If we were career military, I think I'd have to take more in stride. . . . But we're not. And we were not prepared for this. Nobody was."[22]

In the Iraq War personal communications between the U.S. soldiers in a war zone and their wives, husbands, girlfriends, mothers, and fathers on the home front were faster and more frequent than in earlier U.S. wars. Mail still mattered, packages of snacks and magazines and even body armor from family members to soldiers still mattered. Telephone calls were still deemed precious. But Internet e-mail access meant that there was a more instantaneous flow of messages. It also meant that the emotional stakes were higher: the wife in San Francisco and the husband in Karbala each expected to hear regularly from each other, sometimes daily, and were tempted to read meanings into any prolonged pauses in e-mails. With the constant flows of e-mail there was also a heightened questioning of what to tell and what not to tell. Each decision left the other partner wondering what was being left out: was their child really recovering from that bad cough? Was the home refinancing really going through? Were the news reports of combat in the soldier's area understated or overblown? Were the soldier's spirits really as upbeat as the husband's e-mail messages claimed?

Then there was the sheer length of this war. By 2008, the Iraq War had gone on longer than the U.S. involvement in World War II. Coupled with its unpredicted length was the Bush administration's initial war plan that turned out to gravely underestimate the numbers of troops that would be needed to not just topple the Saddam Hussein regime but to bring security and reconstruction to a country the size and complexity of Iraq. For military wives this translated into husbands' repeated deployments. One's husband came home, began to reintegrate into the family, restore his friendships and his own personal sense of priorities, then, just a year later he would receive orders to redeploy. This second or third deployment was not, however, simply a repeat of the first. In the meantime, family dynamics might have become more frayed, household finances more precarious; children might find a parent's second deployment harder to cope with than the first. The soldier/husband's mental health problems, mild after the first tour, might deepen during the second or third tour. Marital relationships, even in peacetime among civilians, are no more static than are political relationships; they each continue to evolve, sometimes in surprising ways. The ideas, tolerances, aspirations, and political ideas of American wives of American soldiers might evolve in ways that did not match either the soldier/husbands' expectations or the Pentagon's model of military wives in wartime. The gap between a soldier/husband's expectations of marriage and his girlfriend's or wife's expectations could become so wide as to become cavernous.

Domestic violence within military families became more visible in the Iraq War than it had been in previous U.S. wars. There were reasons for this. First and foremost, the American women's movement of the 1970s–90s had succeeded in turning men's violence against women as wives and girlfriends—and against former wives and former girlfriends—into a national political issue. First termed "wife battering" by feminist activists in the 1970s, men's violence against their women partners had traveled the rocky political road from denial to official acknowledgement. American police, hospital workers, social workers, prosecutors, judges, and state legislators had been compelled by women's activism to rethink their assumptions and professional practices. By 2008, women advocating for military families inside the Defense Department had framed violence prevention inside military families as a matter of "military readiness." They argued, with some success during the 1990s, that soldiers who abused their wives or children were unreliable soldiers—that they jeopardized military readiness. Moreover, advocates contended, a military wife who endured violence at the hands of her husband/soldier was unlikely to encourage him to reenlist and might even file for divorce, and high divorce rates lowered military morale.

Yet there remained deeply ingrained incentives for twenty-first-century American military commanders and their civilian superiors not to take domestic violence within soldiers' families seriously. The incentives were similar to ones that fostered commanders' dismissive attitude toward women soldiers who reported sexual abuse by fellow soldiers: admitting that a male soldier was abusive of women would require the officer taking deliberate action to investigate and perhaps even to punish the violence-wielding soldier (or sailor or airman). This would deflect commanders from what they had been trained to consider their top priority: waging war. Taking seriously reports of domestic violence might also result in losing a trained soldier in whom the military had invested years and a lot of money.

The first contest of the Iraq War between these two opposing forces came nine months before the start of the U.S. invasion of Iraq, but it is useful to think of it as part and parcel of the Iraq War because it raised questions and mobilized actors central to the preparation for waging war in Iraq and sustaining popular American support for that war waging.

It was early summer 2002. The U.S.-led war in Afghanistan was in its first year. Planning for invading Iraq was under way behind the scenes in the White House and the Defense Department, though not yet garnering much attention from the American press or the general public. The first anniversary of 9/11 was still weeks away. The setting was Fort Bragg, North Carolina, one of the army's premier bases for stationing and training combat troops. Fort Bragg and its nearby town of Fayetteville together had been the focus of anthropologist Catherine Lutz's ground-breaking ethnography of a U.S. military base town.[23]

> Marilyn Griffin was stabbed seventy times and her trailer set on fire. Teresa Nieves and Andrea Floyd were shot in the head, and Jennifer Wright was strangled . . . two of the men shot themselves after killing their wives.[24]

All the women were wives of American soldiers. The men who killed themselves were American soldier/husbands. Two of the surviving murder suspects were members of the army's elite, highly masculinized special forces. Both had recently returned from combat missions in Afghanistan. In their initial responses, military sources were defensive. They dismissed any suggestion that combat training, postcombat stress, or the military's more generalized masculine culture might have contributed to the men's murders of the four women. Women working at the Fayetteville domestic violence shelter and feminists across the country were skeptical of such dismissive attitudes. They had heard them expressed too many times before. The incidences of reported domestic violence by American military men against their intimate partners had been tracked by feminist activists for over a decade. Among the suspected culprits were not only male soldiers, but the entire military's masculinized culture.[25]

During the months leading up to the U.S. invasion of Iraq, when the temperature of American political life rose, most of the American media were reluctant to pursue stories of domestic violence against women within military families. Perhaps editors and publishers were afraid that exposing male soldiers' violent behavior toward their wives and girlfriends would be interpreted by readers and viewers as an implicit critique of the entire American military. In wartime such reporting was deemed too great a business risk. This same American media neglect—a decision to treat American male soldiers' acts of domestic violence as a nonissue—continued throughout the early years of the Iraq War.

There was a notable exception, however. During 2003, the first year of the Iraq War, editors and journalists of Colorado's *Denver Post* invested time, money, and print space in a detailed investigation of incidents of military domestic violence. They allowed their reporters to investigate not just official accounts; they also encouraged the reporters to interview the women who had been beaten by their soldier/husbands and to chart the responses by local civilian prosecutors and military commanders. The *Denver Post* entitled its multipart series "Betrayal in the Ranks," strongly suggesting that the loyalty and labor contributed by military wives to their country's security were not being fairly repaid by the military.[26]

The *Denver Post* reporters discovered that, despite clear warning signs and previous military sexual abuse scandals involving all four services and women both as spouses and as uniformed personnel, many women still were being beaten by their husband/soldiers and then ignored or pressured into silence by their husbands' military superiors. The journalists came to a conclusion similar to that reached by many feminist analysts: one had to look *simultaneously* at male soldiers' violence against women as fellow soldiers and at male soldiers' violence against wives and girlfriends. While domestic violence in military families and sexual assault within the ranks might be filed in two separate categories, that conceptualization would prevent uncovering a meaningful, useful explanation. The explanation at the root of both, the *Denver Post* reporters and many feminist analysts concluded, was the dominant culture shaping the twenty-first-century U.S. military. It was, they each found, an institutional culture that privileged a certain kind of combative masculinity, a culture that denied the mental health consequences of waging war, a culture that prioritized fighting a war and treated women as minor players at best, as a subverting distraction at worst.[27]

Whatever reforms had been put into place by the Defense Department after each of the military's 1990s scandals turned out to be tokenist. "We have a war to fight," and "Our highly trained soldiers are too valuable to lose," remained the military's core mantras. Each served to justify trivializing a uniformed woman's report of rape or a civilian military wife's charge of physical abuse by a male soldier, whether in his role as comrade or as husband. According to Dorothy Mackey, a retired air force captain who had become an advocate for women raped by American male military personnel, when she was interviewed by the journalists: "The system is grossly tainted.... It's a Trojan horse—it really looks good, but it's not what it appears to be."[28]

Moreover, the journalists found, members of Congress had been complicit in the ongoing militarized abuse. During the Iraq War, the congressional leadership had refused to hold committee hearings on military domestic violence, to make the military publicly accountable. Congressional inaction had sent the implicit message to the Defense Department's civilian and uniformed decision makers: the system as it had been operating was fine; carry on.[29]

This revealing series was published in late 2003. It circulated among advocates of women soldiers and military wives across the country. Yet it was not until five years later, in 2008, that the more influential national mainstream media began to devote reporters' energies and headline space to American military wives' experiences of domestic violence. By 2008, the Iraq War was losing support among the American public and members of Congress. Editors and publishers at that point in the war may have come to feel less exposed when they criticized any aspect of the military. Consequently, in this later stage of the Iraq War, the American media's militarized gender slide rule was recalibrated.

In November 2008, the *New York Times* printed a feature story about Adriana Renteria, a military wife. "On Christmas Day two years ago, Sgt. Carlos Renteria, recently back from his first tour in Iraq, got drunk and, during an argument, began to choke his wife, Adriana. He body-slammed her onto the couch, grabbed a cushion and smothered her again and again."[30] What happened next retraced the well-worn footsteps along the path mapped earlier by the *Denver Post's* reporters. The local police were called to the couple's home and arrested the husband/soldier on charges of abuse. The police released him, however, when the army intervened, promising the civilian prosecutor that the army would handle the case. This was not the first incident when her husband had turned violent, but the army reassured the accused batterer's wife. "I was told it would be taken care of . . . by the Army. . . . That they would help me. And I believed them."[31]

Adriana Renteria, however, was not passive. For two years, she sent letters and e-mails to her husband's commanders, to military lawyers, and to the domestic violence office on his base. The army, however, did not pursue the assault charges brought by Adriana. Nor did it direct her husband to receive psychological counseling. Instead, the sergeant's superiors first awarded him a promotion and then deployed him on a second tour to Iraq. Adriana's husband's immediate superior, a major, summed up the army's wartime gendered thinking that justified redeploying him to a combat zone: "We are in the business of fighting a war, and we let very little interfere with that."[32]

In January 2009, a week after the American presidential inauguration of a critic of the Iraq War, CBS News televised its prime-time news anchor, Katie Couric, interviewing Jessica Patton, a military wife. Like Adriana, Jessica was married to a member of one of the military's elite combat groups, the Army Rangers. Katie Couric introduced the program: "Since 2001, thousands of wives and girlfriends have been assaulted at the hands of the soldiers they loved. . . . A growing crisis in the U.S. military: the staggering numbers of military wives who have been beaten, raped, or even killed since the wars in Iraq and Afghanistan began."[33]

> COURIC: How did he change after Iraq?
>
> PATTON: He hardly ever slept. . . . He didn't want to be around me . . . didn't like [the baby's] crying. . . . It was always about the Rangers. . . . He said I paid too much attention to our infant daughter. . . . We talked to the chaplain. . . . I came home and [the baby] had a bloody lip. . . . [Five months later] he attacked me. He tackled me in our back yard. I yelled again he would kill me. . . . I went to the Rangers and they said they'd washed their hands of him. Spouses don't get enough attention. . . . They need to listen to wives . . . instead of just being shrugged off.[34]

As the Iraq War grew longer, not only active-duty soldiers, but 220,000 allegedly part-time National Guard soldiers were sent on repeated overseas tours; the number of U.S. soldiers killed in Iraq had climbed to over 4,000; American women who had become war widows had begun to organize; increasing numbers of civilian parents and wives were coping with mental health problems among returning soldiers, and becoming more visible to a worried general public; and the American press was starting to ask questions about the rising tide of soldier suicides (the number of active-duty soldiers who had committed suicide had grown to ninety-three by late 2008).[35] Simultaneously, and owing in part to these trends, the general public was becoming more open to debates about the rightfulness of the Iraq War.

During this period late in the war some American wives of military personnel began tentatively to speak out publicly not just about the physical abuse they were enduring at the hands of their soldier/husbands, not just about the shortage of Defense Department recognition of the burdens they were shouldering, but about the misgivings they had about the very policy of going to war. These women's challenge was to find the words and actions that would allow them to express two sentiments simultaneously: their criticisms of the Iraq War *and* their loyalty to their own military husbands. If mothers of U.S. soldiers found this politicized familial terrain difficult to carve out, wives of soldiers found it even trickier.

For the double message from a military wife critical of the war to be audible depended on her American listeners. To many American civilians, regardless of their own growing skepticism toward the war, a wife critiquing the mission on which her soldier/husband was deployed sounded like a wife being "disloyal." The politics of marriage once again would determine what members of the public—and media—were willing to hear when a military wife took issue with her husband's superiors.

Given how tightly interwoven marital loyalties and national loyalties had become in American culture during the years of the Iraq War, it may not be surprising that women married to National Guard and Reserve soldiers, more than women married to active-duty soldiers, seemed to be the ones who could carve out this discursive terrain. Thus in a collection of interviews of American women and men who had a family member in the military and deployed to Iraq and yet were critical of the war, most of the women willing to be included were mothers. Only a few in the collection were wives, and they were wives of National Guard and Reserve part-time soldiers. None were the wives of full-time active-duty soldiers.[36]

A war does not end for a military wife when a soldier comes home. When Mike Gorski and his National Guard 870th Military Police Company returned to California from duty in Iraq in mid-2004, he was greeted with questions about what exactly his military police unit did there. Evidence of American soldiers physically and psychologically abusing Iraqi detainees in a prison called Abu Ghraib was making front-page and prime-time news. Mike Gorski's unit had been one of those stationed at Abu Ghraib. Almost as soon as they landed, they were asked by journalists and fellow citizens: Were they part of the system of prisoner abuse at the Abu Ghraib prison?

As their sergeant, Mike told reporters, "We had a really good relationship with our inmates." His troops, he contended, were not part of what had become Abu Ghraib. Referring to the National Guard soldiers whose photographs were turning prisoner torture into a national scandal, Mike continued, "You're only talking about 10 soldiers of 140,000 (American troops) in Iraq. The positive much outweighed the bad." He noted, for instance, that he had developed a friendship with the Iraqi man who had served as his Arabic translator in Karbala. The two men still were in touch via e-mail.[37] Despite Mike's reassurances, another member of the 870th told Reuters, "I saw beatings all the time.... A lot of people had so much pent-up anger, so much aggression.... It was not just these six people."[38]

Abu Ghraib was not the only story attaching itself to Mike Gorski's National Guard unit. Its captain, Leo Merck, thirty-two, had resigned from the National Guard after facing a possible court martial on charges that he photographed female soldiers while they were taking showers at the prison. Mike Gorski said he found the accusations hard to believe: "I still don't believe it. I worked with Capt. Merck for five years."[39]

Some of the military wives who were there to greet the 870th on its return described the months of separation as hard. Susanna Crooks, whose husband Jim had been wounded when he was hit during a mortar attack, also worried about the silences that might deepen now that her husband and the other soldiers were back home: "We're so proud of Jim and all these guys.... But it's a bit difficult for Jim. He can't say he was in Abu Ghraib and be proud of it. Instead, he just says he was in Baghdad."[40]

Mike Gorski left the National Guard and returned to being a full-time civilian. Kim Gorski was no longer the object of the Defense Department's anxiety; she no longer was expected to create phone trees among military wives for the sake of waging its war. By February 2009, when the Iraq War was slipping off the front page of American newspapers, Kim was working as a marketing consultant. She and Mike had become a two-income family with a small son, Luke. Both had joined other parents in volunteering at Hayward's Montessori school.[41]

On the surface, at least, the Iraq War seemed over for Kim Gorski.

CHAPTER NINE

Charlene

Picking Up the Pieces

Charlene Cain worried about her son. Michael had played sports in the local high school and had graduated with decent grades, but he seemed to be floundering. The teenager had passions—the Green Bay Packers memorabilia and Harley Davidson motorcycle accessories. Neither easily translated into an adequate income, much less a career. He had lost interest in going to college. So after graduating from high school in 1999, Michael, like many young men and women from American small towns, had taken a job at Wal-Mart. He had been assigned the job of stocking shelves. He continued to live at home, cared for by Charlene. When he wasn't at his job, Michael stayed in his room playing PlayStation2.[1]

The Cain family's home was a rented converted schoolhouse surrounded by farmland on the outskirts of Berlin, Wisconsin. Charlene knew that Berlin wasn't an easy place in twenty-first-century America for a young person to make a living. In the early 2000s, Berlin's population, overwhelmingly white, was only five thousand, three hundred people. The town had an attractive early twentieth-century small downtown lined with red brick two- and three-story buildings, but it struggled to support its shops and schools. On the eve of the Iraq War, small-town and rural America lacked civilian economic opportunities. That was one of the reasons the military's recruiters paid an unusual amount of attention to young people in small towns such as Berlin.

Charlene carried a lot of the responsibility for sustaining her three-gener-ational household. She didn't appear in the government's census as a "female head of household," because her husband was still alive and remained an integral part of Cain family life. Charlene's husband, Kenneth, however, had suffered a back injury on the job and depended on Social Security benefits. He tried to help out at home. Charlene's daughter, Michael's sister, had men-tal health problems, making it difficult for her to hold down a job. She had become pregnant and given birth to a little girl. Charlene had taken in both her daughter and granddaughter. The entire extended family depended on the income Charlene earned as a clerk at the Winnebago County mental health clinic, a forty-five-minute drive away in Oshkosh. This was exactly the sort of public service agency that would come under intense budgetary pressure in the later years of the Iraq War.

So it was with mixed emotions that Charlene first heard Michael's news in 2000. He had taken the initiative to drive to the Oshkosh City Center shop-ping mall where the army recruiters had their store front office.

Michael by then was nineteen years old. Legally, the army did not require his parents' approval in order to accept him as an enlistee. By the early 2000s, the U.S. military's recruitment command had learned, nonetheless, that to achieve its overall personnel goals, winning the approval of young enlistees' mothers and fathers was important. Thus the army recruiter drove over to Berlin to talk with Charlene and Michael in the family's kitchen. Charlene took the opportunity to make sure that her son knew what he was getting himself in for. In 2000, American soldiers were not engaged in a major over-seas conflict, but Charlene had other concerns. "You hate having people tell you what to do," she reminded her son.[2] And with the army recruiter sitting between them in the homey cluttered kitchen, Charlene repeatedly asked Michael, "Are you sure you want to do this?"[3]

What the recruiter offered the nineteen-year-old, small-town Wal-Mart male employee was appealing: an income with benefits, a wider horizon than that offered by Berlin, a chance to learn a trade, and perhaps a cause worth fighting for. Michael enlisted and left home for army boot camp.

Charlene expressed pleasure, as well as surprise, that Michael seemed to thrive on the military's discipline. "The unity of purpose, the clarity of authority, and the hard physical work all gave him hope of becoming the man he wanted to be—serious, competent, respected."[4] He was trained to drive a thirty-eight-thousand-pound military truck. That seemed as manly as playing football or riding a Harley Davidson motorcycle.

Michael had joined the army before 9/11, before the U.S.-led invasion of Afghanistan, before the U.S.-led invasion of Iraq. Thus his first overseas deployment wasn't to a war zone. It was to Vicenza, Italy, one of the many military bases that the United States had maintained in southern Europe even after the cold war. Charlene did not have to expend much maternal worry on a soldier/son deployed to peacetime Italy.

But in the wake of the U.S. invasion of Iraq in March 2003, the military needed truck drivers in its new war zone. Michael and his 299th Engineer Battalion were among the U.S. troops to be deployed to Iraq in the months following the invasion. At first, Michael found soldiering in Iraq to be invigorating. He continued to gain promotions, rising to the rank of sergeant. He loved driving his mammoth transport down the Iraqi highways. Civilian vehicles had to move aside, even off the road. The American convoys, with their armed guards and driving at top speed, gave no quarter. The military convoys' modus operandi gave new meaning to "aggressive driving."

As reporters Chris Hedges and Laila Al-Arian discovered when they interviewed both the American soldiers who drove and guarded military convoy trucks and the Iraqis who were forced to give way to them, "The convoys are a potent symbol of the disparity in power and wealth between the occupation forces and Iraqis. They are a constant reminder to Iraqis that the main concern of the American occupation is to protect and indulge American troops."[5]

Waging a war and sustaining an occupation required a steady stream of materiel. The Iraq War turned into a war conducted on highways. In one sense, it was a truckers' war. Michael does not seem to have thought much about Iraqis' impressions. Some American soldiers, however, did. One American sergeant ruminated:

All these Iraqis are just seeing this vast amount of housing units, vast amount of convoys going by with this aggressive protection. And they're probably thinking, "How does this help us? They're just helping themselves stay here longer." ... We're just using these vulnerable, vulnerable convoys, which probably piss off more Iraqis than it actually helps in our relationship with them ... just so we can have comfort and air-conditioning and sodas—great—and PlayStations and camping chairs and greeting cards and stupid T-shirts that say, "Who's Your Baghdaddy?"[6]

In past American wars, military truck drivers had not caught the public's attention. It had been fighter pilots, submarine crews, tank corpsmen, infantrymen in trenches and jungles, special forces behind enemy lines, marines on beachheads, and, occasionally, battlefront nurses who had inspired American popular admiration—and novelists and movie directors—back home. Driving an olive drab truck didn't seem the stuff of story making. The Iraq War, however, was different.

Iraq is a large country. Towns such as Baghdad, Basra, Falluja, Mosul, Kirkuk, and Haditha are separated by miles of open road. To keep the multitude of U.S. military bases supplied, truck convoys had to travel exposed roadways day and night. As the Iraq War moved into its second phase, Iraqi insurgents, just as outgunned and outmanned insurgents have done everywhere, began to compensate for their material disadvantages by concentrating on the opposing military's vulnerabilities. Thus roads became a principal battleground in the Iraq War. The insurgents' weapon of choice was the improvised explosive device, the IED. An insurgent could plant an IED inside an innocent-looking rubber tire or a cardboard box, or just under the soil, and then, at a safe distance, set off the deadly explosive when a targeted vehicle passed by.

American soldiers such as young Michael Cain were not the only war-waging drivers on Iraq's roads. Large private contractors, such as Kellogg Brown and Root (KBR), then a subsidiary of the even larger contractor, Halliburton, relied on the same roads to ferry supplies from Kuwait to American installations all over Iraq. Most of the employees whom the private contractors hired to drive their trucks were men from poor countries, such as Bangladesh, India, and Pakistan. Many of these men took these dangerous war zone jobs in order to send money home to mothers, fathers, wives, sons, and daughters.

The snaking lines of private contractors' trucks, in turn, were protected by American military convoys—military drivers and infantry. Some American soldiers expressed sympathy for the Asian civilian foreign drivers, who were assigned to drive KBR trucks lacking even basic protective armament. These soldiers simultaneously voiced unhappiness at the risks they, as soldiers, were being ordered to endure for the sake of getting frozen pizzas, bottled water, and shaving cream from one place to another and for the sake, as they saw it, of lining the pockets of private contractors.[7]

On August 10, 2003, Michael was "riding shotgun" with a partner at the wheel of a large army truck on a routine run near his unit's base in Tikrit. Their truck hit an IED. Michael was seriously injured. Thanks to the improved U.S. military evacuation system in place for the Iraq War, Michael survived, but he lost his right leg below the knee.

Michael's commander at Fort Hood, Texas, kept Charlene and Kenneth informed regularly of each step along Michael's medical journey, from Iraq to Germany to Washington. In the decades since World War II, the military had created a system that fostered parents' and spouses' communication after a soldier had incurred a serious physical injury. At Walter Reed Army Medical Center in Washington, DC, Michael's medical team believed that soldiers who were enduring the shock of amputation, the traumas of repeated operations, and painful rehabilitation sessions did much better if their spouses or parents could be with them at the hospital during the first weeks of recovery. Mothers were deemed especially helpful. Thus the doctors asked Charlene and her husband to come from Wisconsin to Washington to become active members of Michael's medical team. The army flew Charlene and Kenneth at its own expense to Washington. It was Charlene who would tell her until-then heavily sedated son that his leg was gone.

Amputation rates among American soldiers had risen sharply with the launching of the Iraq War, and especially as the Iraqi insurgency gained momentum. At the same time, the U.S. military's capacity to save the lives of its grievously injured soldiers had been vastly expanded. The result would become especially clear during the later years of the Iraq War: thousands of soldiers would survive who in earlier wars would have died, but their lasting disabilities would make it necessary for them to have the assistance of long-term caretakers. Many of those caretakers would be civilian women, the mothers and the wives of surviving soldiers.[8]

As eager as Charlene had been to answer the doctors' call from Washington, taking several weeks off work would prove very difficult financially. After all, Charlene, like so many other women in wartime America, was the principal income earner in her household. Three generations of family members depended on the modest salary she earned. Moreover, Charlene lived the reality of the stubbornly persisting gender gaps between women's and men's pay in early twenty-first-century America. In 2008, the gap between full-time, year-round male and female workers was 22.2 percent. That category is notable. It does not take into account the accompanying fact that in the U.S. economic system, women were far less likely than men to have full-time, year-round jobs. Thus while the 22.2 percent gender gap in pay was significant, it underestimated the full extent of economic inequality. Moreover, the 22.2 percent was between women of all races and men of all races. African American women and Latina women looked across an much wider chasm than did white women in America. Despite thirty years of women's activist efforts to shrink the inequality between women and men in the paid labor force, and their success on many fronts—legislation passed, labor union consciousness raised, women workers' own elevated expectations—the gender pay inequality remained, in part due to the ongoing channeling of women workers into feminized—"pink-collar"—job sectors, sectors such as clerical work that were relatively low paid.[9]

This gap had made the prospect of Charlene taking an unpaid leave to care for Michael in Washington all the more daunting. And unlike the U.S. law passed to guarantee that employers would keep National Guard and Reserve soldiers' civilian jobs waiting for them if they were deployed, there was no legal requirement that an employer save the job of a woman pulled

away to care for a wounded soldier/son or daughter. Nonetheless, by the
Iraq War, the U.S. government's war-waging strategy had come to depend
in part not only on its sophisticated military medevac system but on civilian
mothers and fathers devising their own ways to do the unpaid, often excruciating work of caring for those of its soldiers who returned home severely
wounded.

It was Charlene's workmates at the Winnebago County mental health
clinic who provided the solution. A group of women at the clinic got together.
They took on extra work hours and divvied up Charlene's job responsibilities among themselves. Charlene still would get her weekly paycheck even
though she was away, at Michael's bedside. Friendship among civilian women
thereby played its part in enabling the government's war strategists to sustain their war. We don't know what each of these Wisconsin women thought
about the Iraq War or about soldiering. To make feminist sense of the Iraq
War, we should. These women might well have been motivated not by any
particular view of war or soldiering, but rather by a shared sense of what any
mother must do and by what workplace friendships are about.

At Walter Reed, Charlene found Michael deeply depressed. He expressed
no interest in his recuperation, his physical therapy. He was a young athletic
man with multiple injuries and now only one leg. It was unlikely he would be
driving another large military truck, speeding down an open road. He still
was in the army, but he wasn't doing what soldiers do. Only his Green Bay
Packers and Harley Davidson paraphernalia aroused any spark of interest
in him.

Thus one of Charlene's chief tasks was to pull Michael out of his depressed
state. She worked on this daily, spending hours at the hospital, encouraging Michael to reengage with life, to find the stamina to invest energy in
the often grueling physical therapy sessions. No one thought to record how
many mothers, fathers, wives, and girlfriends were there in the corridors
and patients' rooms of Walter Reed on any given day assisting the military
doctors, nurses, and physical therapists in caring for the Iraq War's and
Afghanistan War's wounded. Just trying to imagine all these women calls
to mind the U.S. Civil War one hundred and fifty years before, when other

civilian women traveled to field hospitals to lend their energies and skills to the care of wounded soldiers.[10]

Slowly, Michael recovered to the point that he could be released from Walter Reed. He and Charlene and Kenneth returned to Berlin, Wisconsin. Charlene went back to her job. Still, her care for a wounded soldier had not ended. There would be more operations for Michael to endure and recover from; there would be drug prescriptions to fill and daily regimens to organize.

The government's care—and neglect—of wounded soldiers became a major political issue in American politics in the middle stages of the Iraq War, as the war dragged on, as individual soldiers' deployments multiplied, as the distinctive forms of bodily damage done by IEDs to brains and limbs became more visible and as the sheer numbers of severely injured American soldiers multiplied. The first major story to break was by journalists Dana Priest and Ann Hall of the *Washington Post.* In February 2007 the paper published its investigation of Walter Reed on the front page. While the amputee wards received positive mention, Priest's and Hall's investigation revealed that in other sections of the hospital—especially the outpatient section, Building 18—male and female soldiers were being left unattended for days.[11]

The hardships faced by soldiers and by their familial caregivers do not ever automatically become a political issue salient to senior policy officials. As always, one has to ask why does one condition become an "issue," while another does not. In the instance of Walter Reed, it was the *Washington Post,* which members of Congress, the civil service, armed services, and White House treated as their local paper, that broke the story. It was Walter Reed, the country's premier military hospital, where the alleged neglect was occurring, the hospital that presidents, secretaries of defense, and congressional representatives visited to demonstrate their gratitude and concern for "our men and women in uniform." The revelation, furthermore, came at a moment in the course of the war—as perceived and experienced by Americans—when there was growing public disillusionment with the Iraq War, and when journalists and their editors, perhaps as a result, were rediscovering their critical voices. It was possible to frame the Walter Reed issue in a way that its promoters could position themselves as supporters of soldiers and their families without having to take a policy stance on the war itself, much less on militarism more generally. It was 2007, moreover, when the Republicans no longer controlled both the presidency and congressional majorities. And, finally, it was the male injured soldiers, the "fallen warriors," whose neglect could be foregrounded by those trying to turn the conditions at Walter Reed into an issue.

Together, the revelations were shocking enough to many Americans to amount to a "scandal." Congressional committees held special hearings to dig deeper, generals and civilian officials of the Bush administration were called to testify and explain how this could have happened. Mothers, fathers, and wives appeared as well, to describe the endless frustrations they and their sons, daughters, husbands, and wives were facing as they were trapped in what appeared to be bureaucratic limbo. At a hearing convened at Walter Reed itself by the House of Representatives' Committee on Oversight and Government Reform, two of the witnesses called were injured service personnel. They appeared at the hearing in uniform. But one of the three witnesses was a civilian, Annette L. McLeod. Her husband Wendell had returned from Iraq suffering from a head injury. She told the members of Congress what it was like trying to get her husband the treatment he required:

> My life was ripped apart the day my husband was injured, and having to live through the mess we've had to live through at Walter Reed has been worse than anything I've had to sacrifice in my life.[12]

Increasingly, there grew a popular sense among Americans that the Bush war plan had been inadequate not only on the ground in Iraq, with too few personnel, trucks ill-equipped to withstand roadside bombs, and no preinvasion plan for grappling with Iraq's complex and fluid politics, but inadequate also in planning for American soldiers who would return home suffering from myriad aftereffects of performing their duties in Iraq.

The scandalous conditions in the outer wards of Walter Reed turned out to be only the tip of the iceberg. Journalists and elected representatives began to look further afield. They offered an opening to many women who had been privatizing their frustrations with the military's medical system. At this juncture in the war, they could speak out with less risk of being labeled merely disloyal complainers. At this point in the war, too, they were also more likely to be heard. When, in 2004, Charlene allowed a reporter to follow her to Washington and back home to Berlin, she was not the story. Michael was the story. By 2007, American civilian women's frustrations and efforts to care for wounded soldiers and veterans were becoming, belatedly, if not *the* "story," at least a "story."

Congress, in response to public pressure—including intense lobbying by a proliferating number of new veterans' groups—created a commission to study the problem of injured soldiers' and veterans' care. It was co-chaired by the former secretary of health and human services Donna Shalala, a Democrat, and former Republican Senator Robert Dole, himself a disabled veteran of World War II. The commission found that thousands of wounded soldiers' "friends or family gave up a job to be with them or act as their caregiver."[13]

As the stories unfolded and the issue developed, it was not only the Defense Department that was subjected to scrutiny in its care for the wounded, it was also the Veterans Administration. The VA too was found to be unprepared for what by 2007 had become a mounting stream of Iraq War veterans suffering from the sorts of injuries that would require exceptional medical care and long-term assistance. One of the most common charges was that the Defense Department treated wounded soldiers as if they were potential cheats, as if they were trying to get more government-financed care than they deserved.[14] On top of this issue was the sheer volume of paperwork that a wounded soldier or veteran had to fill out in order to be declared qualified for medical care. The father of one wounded soldier, who had quit his job so that he could be a full-time advocate and caretaker for his wounded soldier/son, found that VA medical facilities were understaffed and underequipped. He advised researcher Aaron Glantz: "Get to know the system. . . . You have to do lots of research. Understand what the VA and the Department of Defense are all about. Information empowers you and gives you options. Don't wait for things to come to you. If you don't, in many cases things are a long time coming."[15]

By the early 2000s, many American health care activists were giving similar advice to ordinary civilians. The emerging crisis in Iraq War veterans' health care was coming at a moment in the gendered history of American medicine when many women rethought their relationships to the medical establishment and to their health in general. The origins lay in the 1970s–80s American women's health movement, pioneered by such grassroots women's efforts as the one that created *Our Bodies, Ourselves*.[16] The movement encouraged women to take charge of their bodies, to participate in the crafting of health care appropriate to women, and generally to stop being passive in their dealings with the male-dominated medical profession. Women diagnosed with cancer or with reproductive problems had started doing their own research on alternative medical procedures and made themselves informed on the ins and outs of the fragmented American health system. Even if he may not have realized it, this wounded soldier's father's advice was built upon a foundation of this new feminist activist approach to health care.

Granted, during the years of the Iraq War the neglect of wounded veterans' health care needs had far greater political saliency in American society than the health care needs of ordinary civilian women. A soldier injured while on duty had made a sacrifice for his/her country that was popularly acknowledged. There was even the presumption in many instances that the soldier had been injured while acting heroically. That sacrifice was memorialized in public monuments and recognized annually on special holidays. There also was an unwritten but no less potent public understanding that the government would stand by the soldier when he/she suffered bodily harm in carrying out the government's orders. Moreover, in early twenty-first-century American culture, the soldier was held up as the model citizen. Civilians might not be worthy of publicly financed medical care, but soldiers were.

While the injuries endured by amputees such as Danielle and Michael might have been those most visible to public officials and other civilians, the signature American injury of the Iraq War was traumatic brain injury. It became so widespread among military personnel—especially soldiers and marines—returning from Iraq that it acquired its own acronym, TBI. It was not an injury for which the U.S. military medical system was well prepared. Traumatic brain injuries were caused by explosions, and explosive devices had become Iraqi insurgents' weapon of choice. Because the damage suffered was internal, often the injury's extent and character went undetected in the first hours, even days of medical treatment. Traumatic brain injury typically so disabled its survivors that they would require extensive care for the rest of their lives. Many soldiers who survived brain injury were denied the Purple Heart. The U.S. military's outdated presumption persisted; "there had to be blood" to qualify for the Purple Heart. Surviving traumatic brain injury was a prospect that depressed many veterans and daunted many wives and mothers and fathers. Gail Ulerie was the mother of Sergeant Shurvon Phillip. The sergeant communicated with her by moving his eyebrows. Gail, a Trinidadian American, faced a future of caring for her almost entirely paralyzed grown son.

> The first time I gave my son a bath . . . I cried. It took me a good while to get used to cleaning him up. In the morning if we have to go somewhere, everything that a mom with a baby has to walk with—wipes and every-thing in a bag—I have to walk with. . . . Nobody wants anyone else to clean them. . . . He's this grown man, but he just can't do it.[17]

The mother of a soldier harmed in Iraq who attracted more media and public attention than either Charlene or Gail was Cindy Sheehan. Her son, Casey, was one of the more than four thousand American soldiers who did not survive, who died of his injuries in Iraq in April 2004. His mother did not confine her criticisms of the military to its treatment of soldiers. Cindy Sheehan criticized the policies behind the war. And she took very public action. She first attracted journalists' attention when she traveled from her home in California to President George W. Bush's ranch near Crawford, Texas. It was summertime and the president was vacationing at his ranch. Cindy Sheehan said that her initial desire was simply to have Mr. Bush personally apologize to her for having sent her son to his death. As the days went on with no apology and no presidential appearance, three things seemed to happen. First, her tent on the outskirts of the Texas ranch attracted the attention of journalists and film crews, who otherwise had little that was newsworthy to report on in Crawford. Second, this civilian mother of a dead soldier became radicalized by the lack of engagement with her by the president, prompting her to speak not just about her son but about oil. Third, as the media brought Cindy Sheehan's modest encampment to the pages of newspapers and the screens of Americans' television sets, she became the magnet for both anti-war activists, such as those in Code Pink, and those who continued to think that the war in Iraq was justified and that the American soldiers deployed to fight that war were patriots sacrificing for a worthy cause.[18]

Following her Crawford encampment, Cindy Sheehan was in demand to speak at anti-war events around the country. To make her point that a mother could cherish the memory of her dead soldier/son and yet be opposed to the war he was sent to fight, Cindy Sheehan founded Gold Star Mothers Against the War to mobilize American women who had lost sons or daughters fighting in the Iraq War and yet had decided to publicly oppose the government's war policies. Unlike the Gold Star Mothers and Blue Star Mothers, the Gold Star Mothers Against the War received no support or recognition from the federal government. The Iraq War, among other things, became a war over American militarized motherhood.[19]

While many mothers, fathers, and wives were trying to make sense of their wartime politics, and some of them were pressuring the Defense Department and the Veterans Administration to recognize their sons' and daughters' and husbands' traumatic brain injuries, another wartime injury was gaining prominence as the Iraq War continued: mental health illness.

The American military was loath to acknowledge the mental health consequences of war for its soldiers. Witnessing a friend's violent death, seeing body parts scattered on the street in the aftermath of an explosion, constantly being on edge, having to be prepared for sudden outbursts of violence, killing another person, often a person who turned out to be an innocent bystander—these were the soldier's everyday experiences in a combat zone. If they were treated as the cause of mental disabilities, how could any government wage a war? This dilemma would prove especially acute for U.S. officials during the Iraq War because of the military's limited personnel, which required soldiers to be deployed to war zones not just once, not just twice, but sometimes three or four times. Every soldier officially diagnosed with a mental disorder was a soldier whom the Defense Department could not redeploy.

More than that, to acknowledge the mental-health consequences of soldiering would tarnish the glory of soldiering. The prospect of glory, especially manly glory, was one of the most prized resources in any military recruiter's toolbox. Thus it was not surprising that many civilian and uniformed war strategists did not want to hear the findings of Theodore Nadelson, a psychiatrist who had spent years treating American veterans for their postwar mental health problems:

> For many returned veterans, the heroic myths of fabled wars erode
> under the onslaught of visions of exploding bodies, of carnage, and of
> devastation. Strive as they might to retain the 'echoes and re-echoes' of
> duty, honor, and country, the many sorry souls who cannot are doomed
> to remember an eternity of war's horror.[20]

As many drill sergeants around the world could testify, carrying out killings without remorse and becoming accustomed to being the target of killing turn out to be not natural for men or women; in many cases, they were not teachable.[21]

Charlene Cain's first job at Walter Reed was to pull Michael out of his depression. Depression would be an anticipated result of severe bodily injuries. And while that might have been the sole source of Michael's mental problems, depression among soldiers became the object of increasing concern as more and more soldiers returned from Iraq exhibiting its debilitating effects. As early in the war as December 2004—less than two years after the invasion—a U.S. Army study revealed that "one in six soldiers in Iraq report symptoms of major depression, serious anxiety or post-traumatic stress disorder."[22] Mental health professionals began questioning how the unprepared military medical system and Veterans Administration would provide adequate services for the estimated 100,000 American military personnel who would come home with mental health problems.[23]

It was not merely the senior military commanders and their civilian superiors who were reluctant to acknowledge the mental health costs of waging the Iraq War. Many soldiers, especially male soldiers, resisted admitting that they were suffering from mental ill health. In 2005, the Public Broadcasting Service aired a documentary film, *The Soldier's Heart,* following one group of male marines returning to their hometowns, families, and girlfriends. The men talked about not wanting to admit they had depression or nightmares and not accepting any help from mental health professionals. To do either would lower their status among their fellow marines. They would be admitting they were not "man enough" to stomach war, that they were less than "real marines." Some of the men's officers reinforced this message: real men don't get depressed; real marines don't go to therapists.[24]

Four years and many deployments later, some American soldiers told military medical officers that they would rather be diagnosed with traumatic brain injury than with PTSD. At least the former diagnosis would leave them, they believed, with their masculinity in tact.[25]

Militarized notions of manliness added to the burdens shouldered by the civilians in these marines' lives. As crimes of violence perpetrated by Iraq veterans, particularly male veterans, mounted, civilian police, prosecutors, and judges became disturbed, wanting both to make allowances for the wartime roots of many of these men's crimes and to hold accountable the individuals accused of the crimes and their former military superiors alike.[26]

Most often the family members of returning military personnel were left to diagnose the veterans' problems, belatedly, and to cope with them as best they could. The Rand Corporation, a major Defense Department research contractor, admitted this (though did not pursue it) in its 2008 report "Invisible Wounds of War."[27] Mothers, fathers, wives, and girlfriends became the American military mental health system's backup service. These civilians' lives became militarized, no matter what were their own views of this war or of soldiering, insofar as all found themselves immersed in coping with an individual soldier's ongoing flashbacks, nightmares, alienation, violent outbursts, and depression.

Joyce and Kevin Lucey were among the parents who spoke publicly about their frustrating, and ultimately tragic, efforts to understand and respond effectively to their soldier/son Jeffrey's postdeployment mental health problems.[28]

JOYCE: He wrote, "The reality of the war has hit us." He crossed into Iraq very early on.... He wrote his girlfriend in mid-April that he felt he had done immoral things; he wanted to erase that last month of his life.[29]

KEVIN: His letters to us were really sanitized. He'd say, "Don't watch the news." Little did he know, Joyce had three TVs and watched all the news programs. She paid the price. She had a stroke three weeks before Jeffrey came home....

KEVIN: He came back early in July 03 to the States. He was very tan, had lost weight, not that he had much to lose, and he looked fantastic. The Marines told us to expect a lot of adjustment. They never mentioned PTSD....

JOYCE: He had nightmares. He'd yell out. I heard him say, "They were coming after me in an alleyway." I could kick myself now. Why didn't I ask him more about it? What was I thinking? I should have noticed this. Part of why we come out to talk now, is, maybe now someone will do that for their kid....

JOYCE: The real crash came the week of spring break. He just sat in the living room, in melancholy. He talked low-key, a hopeless tone in his voice. We encouraged him to see our internist. We were starting to think of PTSD. He begged us not to tell his unit. He was afraid he'd get Section Eight [medical discharge]; he didn't want it to follow him through life.

Joyce and Kevin became more and more alarmed as Jeffrey's drinking intensified and he scarcely left his room. Efforts to get the local VA hospital to admit him failed. Jeffrey continued to fear that admission to any PTSD program would "destroy my future."

KEVIN: In April [2004], we were all hurting. We were all tense, focused on Jeff and Jeff's needs. I think families can have a form of PTSD. I'm not saying we suffer anything like what soldiers suffer. But dealing with the changed essence of a person, the whole family suffers the impact tremendously. We were worn down, isolating ourselves.

On June 22, 2004, Lance Corporal Jeffrey Lucey hanged himself in his parents' home.

The number of both attempted and completed suicides among American military personnel rose steadily during the Iraq War. In 2006, the number of suicides by army personnel was 102. The following year, the number rose to 140.[30] No one could accurately count the number of attempted and completed suicides among soldiers after they left the military and returned to civilian life.

With Charlene's maternal support, Michael Cain's interest in life, including his girlfriend, slowly returned. After multiple operations and drug prescriptions, his prosthetic leg began to function well. The Defense Department's athletic program for veteran amputees engaged him. He began running and playing ice hockey. He married his longtime girlfriend and together they moved out of Charlene and Kenneth's house to a place of their own in her home state of North Dakota. He and his wife were soon to be parents.[31] Michael's seemed to be a hopeful story, a counterweight to the rising number of reports and journalistic accounts of the war's mental and physical health tolls.

How did Michael manage to recover? Perhaps it was the fact that his army job did not involve killing that helped reduce the mental health impacts. Maybe it was his having been injured in his first tour so severely and so physically that he could not be redeployed. Also worth considering is the type of injury Michael suffered: an injury that necessitated amputation, one of the medical procedures that the U.S. military establishment appeared best equipped to handle and about which it was least ambivalent. Some credit certainly must also go to Michael's own rediscovered stamina.

Where was Charlene in this? Charlene was "the family rock.... She absorbs blow after blow without appearing to crack. Michael's injury is her project."[32] After returning home with Michael from Walter Reed, Charlene went back to her civilian job, but she rose at four-thirty in the morning and worked into the evening to ensure that Michael got all the care he needed. She kept tabs of his medications. She made appointments for him to see a physician in Milwaukee if there were signs of infection. And it was Charlene who did all the paperwork. Michael's postwar recovery took stacks of military paperwork. Charlene would spend hours sitting at the kitchen table filling out her soldier/son's medical forms. The Iraq War was being waged by a Wisconsin mother sitting at her kitchen table.

The Long War

Abu Nawas Street was becoming lively again. It was early 2009. For years the street that wound its way along the banks of the Tigris in central Baghdad had been famous for its nightclubs. Then came Saddam Hussein's post–Gulf War efforts to woo religious conservatives, followed, after 2003, by the rise of sectarian militias with their campaign against alcohol—as well as the loss of reliable water and electricity—that forced owners to shutter their nightclubs along Abu Nawas Street.

Now conditions were looking promising for the club owners. Iraq's prime minister, trying to demonstrate his secular credentials to skeptical city voters, had allowed at least a few alcohol-serving establishments to reopen. The American soldiers and Iraq's expanded security forces recently had driven out—or at least driven underground—many of the armed insurgents and sectarian militias who had terrorized Baghdad's small business owners during the recent years. The U.S. government had distributed funds to businesses, and a few nightclub owners were among the recipients. Some young Iraqi men appeared to have sources of income again, enough to afford a club's $45 entrance fee and to buy its imported beer.[1]

The photographs that appeared in the *Washington Post* on February 28, 2009, accompanying the article by reporter Sundaran Raghaven, were as surprising as the story he wrote. One photograph showed a U.S. male soldier, attired in camouflage fatigues and wearing a helmet fitted with night vision equipment, dancing with the nightclub's customers as they wove around tables littered with empty beer bottles. Lounging at a table nearby was his camouflaged, helmeted colleague, carrying a rifle. The activities seemed incongruous, perhaps illegal. U.S. military personnel had been under orders throughout the war not to leave their bases except on official missions; drinking on duty was prohibited. The Iraqi club owner, though, seemed proud that these and other American soldiers were frequenting his newly reopened club while out on their nighttime patrols. He was glad too that they drank his Tuborg beer: "They buy drinks and pay for them."[2] Their visits seemed to him a sign of Baghdad's new security.

Iraqi civilian men were the nightclub's chief customers. Women were there apparently to entertain. The most noted entertainer in this club was Adeeba, a famous Iraqi singer who recently had returned from exile in Bahrain. "The dark era is over," Adeeba announced. One of her young male admirers agreed: "Listening to her made me feel secure."[3]

Among the women in the newly reopened nightclub on Abu Nawas Street was a dancer in a red dress performing for the young men. Still other women were at the club that evening, women who did not appear to be club patrons, "young Iraqi women who appeared to be prostitutes."[4] Perhaps they had been teenagers when the United States and its allied forces invaded in March 2003: when had they dropped out of school? With whom were they sharing their earnings? But they were not the focus of the journalist's account of the city's newly secure atmosphere. As in the accounts of Haditha massacre, so too here: the American male soldiers were in the spotlight. Thus feminist viewers of the newspaper's photograph were left to puzzle over whether these young Iraqi women shared the view that in early 2009 Iraq's "dark era" was over.

Since the 1980s, Iraqi feminists such as Hanaa Edwar had been keeping a close eye on the rise in prostitution—and the numbers of Iraqi women choosing or being pressured to enter prostitution. So they did not view prostitution's resurfacing in public places in isolation, nor did they treat it sanguinely as a sign that a new postwar security was taking root. They had been monitoring prostitution in Iraq for decades, as one way to chart escalating pressures on women—pressures to make a living in desperate circumstances, pressures to escape intolerable family conditions, pressures to do men's bidding. Edwar and others noted that increasing numbers of Iraqi women had gone into prostitution during the 1990s, as a result of the international economic sanctions' devastation of an already weak postwar Iraq economy, and during the six years of the most recent war, when more and more women had become the sole household income earners supporting their children. Those increases had not been as publicly visible perhaps as they were becoming in the reopened nightclubs. Only now, in 2009, were those prostitution sightings being heralded by some observers as a "return to normalcy."[5]

The supposed cornerstone of the new security was a military agreement. Two months earlier, in November 2008, officials in Washington and Baghdad had signed off on a joint security agreement, called a "status of forces agreement," a SOFA. Senior policy makers pointed not to nightclub reopenings, but to this military agreement, as marking the start of a new era of Iraq security. The SOFA went into effect on January 1, 2009. Washington negotiators had been compelled to make significant concessions in order to gain Iraqi parliamentary ratification of their U.S.-Iraq SOFA. The Americans had had to agree as well not only to the transfer of major responsibilities for security to the Iraqis, but also to their own commanders' shrunken authority. They would have to seek Iraqi officers' and judges' approval for many operations. The joint security agreement, furthermore, eliminated the immunity from Iraqi prosecution previously enjoyed by both private security company personnel and those American soldiers accused of crimes while off duty. While even American officials of the new Obama administration seemed to prefer to keep their options open, the wording of the agreement was clear: all U.S. military personnel would be withdrawn from Iraq by December 31, 2011.[6]

SOFAs, negotiated by American officials with scores of governments around the world, have been notoriously complex. The provisions of some SOFAs have allowed the U.S. military to construct full-blown bases with port facilities large enough to handle aircraft carriers, with runways, firing ranges, housing, shops, and bowling alleys. Other SOFAs have allowed Americans to establish smaller bases in dozens of foreign countries. Still other government-to-government SOFAs promoted by the U.S. government around the world have set the terms whereby American military personnel could use the territories of other countries for rest and recreation, joint maneuvers, training, and repairs. Ordinary citizens of those countries hosting American military operations have had no access to the political processes through which the SOFAs were hammered out or implemented. The negotiations have been classically masculinized affairs, with very few women reaching the senior levels of the United States' or other governments at which they might have a modicum of influence over the fine print of any SOFA. There always has been a lot of fine print in a SOFA, some of it with implications for local women's relationships to public health, to policing, to employment, to military prostitution, and to soldiers' sexual assaults. Nonetheless, the signing of the U.S.-Iraq SOFA was heralded in early 2009 as a principal building block for creating a postwar Iraq that would provide for Iraqi women's and girls' future security.[7]

The signing of the security agreement seemed to set the stage for not only the reopening of nightclubs, but the holding of the countrywide provincial council elections on January 31, 2009. A state-to-state military agreement, the reopening of nightclubs, and the holding of provincial elections—all three were seen as mutually reinforcing in their marking a new stage of the long war, a winding-down stage characterized by increased security. Little gender analysis was done on any of the three markers.

Maha Hashim, widowed when militiamen killed her policeman husband and displaced when she was driven out of her home in Saydia, might have had a hard time casting her ballot in those provincial council elections. One had to be named on one's home neighborhood government food rations list to qualify to vote. But returning home wasn't easy for Maha and the millions of Iraqi women and men who had been exiled and internally displaced by the years of wartime violence.

The 15,000 candidates for the provincial council seats seemed to campaign more openly than they had at the height of violence during 2005–7.

Women made up 28 percent of those provincial council candidates. That translated into almost 4,000 Iraqi women deciding to run for provincial office.[8] In Diyala province, still plagued by sectarian violence, Islam Abbas Faraj decided to run for a seat on the provincial council after her husband, active in Sunni politics, had been taken away by Shiite militiamen. She never heard from him again and was left the sole supporter of their children. She acknowledged being afraid when campaigning in rural villages. She likewise questioned how independent Diyala's women voters would be allowed to be on election day: "Some men will demand that the women of their family vote as they do, but at the end of the day she has the right."[9]

In the southern city of Basra, Zeinab Sadiq Jaafar, a forty-one-year-old lawyer, was one of 325 women among 1,280 candidates running for just thirty-five council seats in her province. She expressed confidence in her candidacy, eschewing any party affiliation. When rumors spread during the campaign that she had been assassinated, she appeared on a local television station. She also hired sound trucks to offer her campaign message in her own voice and to confirm that she was indeed alive.[10] In Baghdad, Sabah al-Tememy campaigned by plastering her posters on buildings. While her platform prioritized increasing public assistance to women, it was allowing the posters to reveal her face and hair that provoked local controversy.[11]

Voter turnout in the provincial elections ranged from 40 percent in some provinces to 60 percent in others. Large numbers of Sunni Arab voters in the northern city of Mosul and Shiite voters in Basra in the south cast their ballots for Dawa, the pro-centralization party of the current prime minister. In young Safah Yunis Salem's turbulent Anbar province, prominent male tribal sheiks charged electoral fraud. These men were heads of the U.S.-backed Awakening Council militias. They had transformed themselves into political party leaders for the provincial council elections. The masculinization of Iraq's political life was not receding; it was taking new forms. The Awakening's tribal leaders threatened violence if the election results were not invalidated. Nonetheless, many of Anbar's unemployed Sunni male former government employees told journalists that they had voted for the National List, a party headed by a secular Shiite, because they believed its candidates cared about their loss of livelihoods. Women's employment was not high on the list of parties' campaign issues.[12]

Nationally, parliamentarian Shatha al-Musawi's commitment to sharia law seemed far less politically salient to Iraqi voters in early 2009 than it had been three years earlier. In interviews, many Iraqi voters going to the polls to vote in January 2009 said they were judging candidates and parties now less on their religious stances than on whether they could deliver jobs and reliable daily supplies of water and electricity.[13] Nimo Din'Kha Skander and her fellow hairdressers were not the only Iraqis who saw delivery of public services as a late-stage major wartime electoral issue.

And yet Article 41 of the constitution still stood. And Iraqi women's rights advocates remained wary. Shatha would have to run for reelection to her parliamentary seat in December 2009. As others charted what they claimed to be increasing security, Shatha had her eyes on the economy and government spending. She had become a member of the legislature's important Finance Committee. To business journalists, she spoke in early 2009 more about budgets than about sharia law. She was monitoring the political impacts of the global recession. While many of her fellow legislators were concentrating on oil price declines and the immediate budgetary short-falls, however, Shatha was urging parliamentary colleagues to keep their eyes on Iraq's long-term reconstruction.[14]

Oil would remain a women's issue. In Iraq, as in most countries, in wartime and peacetime, oil companies' operating cultures are masculinized. Most oil workers are male. How well—or ineptly or corruptly—oil production is managed, and how fairly or unfairly its revenues are distributed determine whether widows receive adequate state subsidies, whether women as well as men gain paying jobs, whether girls' and boys' schools are well staffed, and whether infrastructures are built and maintained in ways that ensure that reliable flows of electricity and clean water to lessen women's household burdens.

While killings of Iraqi civilians continued into 2009, the rate at which Iraqi civilians were dying violent deaths was down. Fewer American soldiers were dying while on duty in Iraq. Shops in Baghdad were back in business.

Some beauty parlor owners were reopening their doors. Political contests were becoming even more intense, as more male tribal leaders were developing stakes in party rivalries. To many observers, these seemed reasonable criteria for measuring the country's level of security.

Nonetheless, as American troops were winding down their operations, ballots cast in the provincial council elections were being tallied, and nightclubs along Abu Nawas were hiring dancers and entertaining American soldiers, Iraq's minister for women's affairs was doing her own security audit. Her conclusion was far less sanguine. On February 8, 2009, with little notice in the international media, Nawal al-Samaraie resigned as Iraq's minister for women's affairs. Explaining her resignation, al-Samaraie cited the failure of the Iraqi male elite—and their American backers—to provide the ministry with meaningful resources. Al-Samaraie appeared to be fulfilling the predictions made by feminist observers in the earlier phase of the American-led war: although the ministry that was mandated to empower and protect women had been launched with fanfare, it had been left hollow:

> I have only an office, not a full ministry, with insufficient resources and limited authority. . . . My mission is very hard, if not impossible, to achieve. . . . My office is inside the Green Zone with no affiliated offices in other provinces and not enough funds to hold conference, invite experts for studies and implement development plans.[15]

The minister singled out as the Iraqi women particularly in need of more serious political attention and more meaningful support those lacking education, those who had become internally displaced, and those who during the war had become widows or victims of domestic violence. "My resignation," al-Samaraie concluded, "is a warning to the government and a protest against its inability to evaluate the needs of women."[16]

What is a gender-informed measure of security? SOFAs, nightclubs, and political party rivalries may not be adequate or realistic measures.

Making feminist sense of any war—during each of its several distinctively gendered phases—requires taking women seriously: their calculations, their analyses, their actions, and, of course, their silences. That, in turn, entails conducting a more energetic kind of analysis, one that does not refer lazily to "families," "children," "parents," "militias," "political candidates," "Sunnis," "Shiites," "Kurds," "Latinos," "whites," "African Americans," "contractors," "activists," "police," "soldiers," "refugees," "tribal leaders," "government employees," "the unemployed," "decision makers," "influencers," or "PTSD sufferers" *as if* women and men related identically to each, *as if* presumptions about masculinities and femininities did not critically shape the actions, worries, goals, and influence of each.

Only when women—in all their diversity and historically dynamic complexity—are taken seriously will men be investigated as men, in all their historicized diversity. Only when women are taken seriously will the full range of powers wielded for the sake of preparing for, launching, and sustaining any specific war be fully charted. Only when women's experiences and actions during each gendered phase of a war are assigned analytical weight will the costs of preparing for, waging, and picking up the pieces after any war be accurately tallied.

Only when women's lives, ideas, and actions are seriously explored and carefully weighed will we gain an understanding of how the privileging of certain forms of masculinity at particular moments in time promotes the ideas that make war waging seem rational and honorable. Only with the resultant sophisticated understanding will we be able to explain how alleged postwar societies remain so nurturing of those stories and those relationships that provide the seedbed for the next militarized enterprise. Peacetime often becomes a prewartime. Only when women's historically situated lives, ideas, and actions are the subjects of sustained curiosity will we be able to assess war preparers' and war wagers' efforts to use women and ideas about femininity. Only then, too, will we be able to weigh the results of particular women's private and public efforts to resist or subvert those militarizing schemes.

That is, if we do not try to make feminist sense of wars, we are unlikely to make reliable sense of any war.

Oxfam, the independent international humanitarian aid organization, with its Iraqi research partner the Al-Amal Association, released a report in early 2009 based on criteria for assessing rises or falls in security that were quite different from those employed by most mainstream commentators and officials. Al-Amal's researchers interviewed Iraqi women about their daily lives. The 1,700 Iraqi women interviewed lived in five provinces: Baghdad, Basra, Kirkuk, Najaf and Nineveh. The report confirmed former minister al-Samaraie's security assessment. Oxfam and Al-Amal entitled their report *In Her Own Words*.[17]

Al-Amal's interviewers talked to women during 2008. At this time in the ongoing Iraq War both U.S. and Iraqi officials, as well as many commentators, were touting the success of the American military's "surge," the deployment to Iraq of thousands of American additional troops designed to confront insurgents and armed militiamen. For many American active-duty and National Guard troops, the deployment policy meant yet another separation from their wives, husbands, sons, daughters, mothers, and fathers. For Iraqis, the intensification of violent military operations was to be endured for the sake of reducing violence. The objective: to reestablish Iraqis' security.

When Al-Amal's interviewers asked Iraqi women whether they assessed their own security as having improved, their answers did not match the male elite's headlined security assessments. Overall, the report stated, "As compared with 2007, 40% felt their security situation was worsening in 2008."[18]

Worsening.

Perhaps even more striking were the surveyed Iraqi women's comparisons of the daily level of security they were experiencing in 2008—at the end of the surge—compared to 2006, when sectarian violence had reached its height, when thousands of Iraqi women lost their homes, livelihoods, and family members. A majority of women's replies should have been a resounding "More secure." But perhaps such an expectation rests on unrealistic security criteria, criteria irrelevant to women's actual needs, hopes, and daily responsibilities. What in fact the Oxfam and Al-Amal researchers heard from Iraqi women was "As compared with 2006, 43% said it was worse, 34% said it was better & 22% said it had not changed."[19]

Iraqi women providing substance to their sense of insecurity in late 2008 described having no permanent housing for themselves and their children, broken local water pipes that mixed sewage with drinking water, detained and kidnapped husbands and fathers whose fates remained uncertain, government pensions denied, injured and mentally disturbed male family members needing constant care, children without the means to return to school, inaccessible medical care, and their own inability to obtain meaningful paid employment. Among the forms of work that Iraqi women respondents of diverse economic backgrounds reported that they were doing in late 2008 in order to provide for their households were

> collecting straw and mud to make clay ovens
>
> cleaning other people's houses
>
> selling bricks picked up at refuse sites
>
> sewing at home (when there is electricity).[20]

At the same time as male leaders and ordinary women were disagreeing about whether Iraqi security was improving, the sense of insecurity among many Americans was deepening. In the United States, the highlight of January 2009 was a historic presidential inauguration. The national mood, at least for a few days, was upbeat. Strangers smiled at one another and exchanged inauguration day stories. And, even if briefly, people around the world seemed to think more kindly of Americans. When the festivities were over, however, most Americans turned back to their domestic worries: home foreclosures were continuing to rise, the value of retirement accounts was plummeting, the unemployment rate climbed to above 8 percent, colleges had stopped hiring, the banks still were tight-fisted with credit, and every day more factories and shops were boarded up. The insecurity on Americans' minds in early 2009 appeared to flow less from overseas wars and more from the actions of homegrown hedge fund managers.

Even when the Iraq War occasionally did make the American headlines in the weeks following the inauguration, it was framed as a nightmare now over. President Barak Obama, as one of his first official acts, signed an order to start the process to close the infamous military prison at Guantánamo Bay. Eric Holder, his appointee for attorney general, declared that waterboarding, the near-drowning interrogation technique used by American interrogators on wartime prisoners, was indeed torture.[21]

Out in California, Kim Gorski was more engaged in early 2009 with her young son's Montessori school than with duties imposed on her by the Pentagon. Danielle Green-Byrd had finished her second master's degree and was immersed in her Chicago school counseling work. Charlene's son had moved out of his parents' house in Berlin, Wisconsin. Emma's older son was still in uniform but outside a war zone. The war was slipping off the front page and beyond popular attention, fast becoming another American war that was "over."

Yet paying attention to four American women's experience of this war shines a bright light on underaccounting the postwar costs of the Iraq War for American society that made few headlines but kept war in women's and men's daily lives: the long-term effects of an officially dismissive attitude to soldiers' divorces, suicides, attempted suicides, and mental ill health; the consequences of the military's failure to follow up on women's charges of domestic violence and of soldier-on-soldier sexual assault by uniformed male soldiers; the implications of so many soldiers returning home with severe injuries requiring weeks, months, and years of unpaid care by wives and mothers. And then there are the postwar silences, silences in public forums, silences within households, between soldier/husbands and their girlfriends and wives. The consequences of militarized gendered silences can ripple on for generations.

From March 2003 to March 2009, between 91,556 and 99,452 Iraqi civilians had been killed by war-related violence, according to the best estimate of independent monitors from the nongovernmental organization Iraq Body Count. This group decided to step in when the U.S. government announced early in the war that it would make no attempt to keep track of Iraqi civilian deaths in the war.[22] To many, these numbers seemed unrealistically low. Numbers matter, but they tend to flatten thick realities. Among the Iraqi dead were Safah's brother, sister, and aunt killed in Haditha and Maha's policeman husband killed in Baghdad's Saydia neighborhood. Three had been killed by a U.S. Marine, the other by an Iraqi sectarian militiaman. Some of the estimated ninety thousand Iraqi men and women, boys and girls who died in the Iraq War had received proper burials. Many others disappeared without a trace or had been dismembered beyond recognition, then dumped in mass graves or left unclaimed in the city morgue because their relatives feared to retrieve their bodies. An Iraqi woman who could not identify the body of her missing husband would not have access to the family's bank account (which usually was in her husband's name), would not be eligible for government aid to widows, and would not be able to remarry. Wartime life is gendered. So is wartime death.[23]

What the U.S. government *had* been willing to count were the deaths of its own military personnel. By the end of January 2009, the government announced, 4,226 American military men and women had died while serving in Iraq. "COTTING, Grant A., 19, Pvt., Army; Corona, California; Fourth Maneuver Enhancement Brigade," read the brief Defense Department announcement published in the *New York Times* on January 28, 2009.[24] Among the American dead were sons of Emma Bedoy-Pina's colleagues in the San Antonio chapter of the Blue Star Mothers. Among the dead also was Lori Ann Piestewa, the Native American comrade of Shoshana Johnson and Jessica Lynch, killed when their supply convoy had been ambushed.

The Bush administration had taken steps to prevent soldiers' flag-draped coffins from being photographed as they were unloaded from military cargo planes in Dover, Delaware. Yet most American male and female soldiers who died in Iraq did receive proper hometown funerals and burials, along with tributes, when their remains were delivered to their families. Local newspapers gave each ceremony prominent coverage. Photographs of stoic or weeping women as new war widows appeared in local newspapers across the country. But the deaths of American soldiers who committed suicide either in uniform or in the months after returning from Iraq went uncounted. Treated with sorrow by their surviving wives, mothers, and fathers, their deaths met ambivalence or denial by Washington.

In February 2009, the new Obama administration lifted the ban on media coverage of military coffins being flown into Dover Air Force Base.[25]

"Over." How long does it take for any war to be over? In the midst of the Iraq War, Drew Gilpin Faust, the distinguished historian, published her nuanced study of dying, death, and memorializing in the American Civil War.[26] She detailed shared nineteenth-century American popular yearnings, people's hopes that each soldier would experience a "good death." Many of Faust's Iraq War-era readers could not help bridging the generations and joining in their predecessors' fervent desire that those soldiers who had died (or had returned home mentally and physically transformed) had not made their sacrifices for an unworthy cause.

In Iraq too, there were, when possible, ceremonies to commemorate the war dead. Yet we know woefully little about how the women expressed their grief or how they gave meaning to their husbands' wartime deaths. We know that some women and children who had endured violent losses sought mental health care at the few clinics equipped to offer it. Mainly, however, we've been left with the photographs of usually nameless Iraqi women grieving.

Women are wartimes' grievers. Those who grieve are not expected to have ideas about the causes, courses, or aftermaths of war. Those whose role it is to grieve—mothers, sisters, and wives of male soldiers killed at Gettysburg or Bull Run, mothers, sisters, or wives of men killed in Falluja or Haditha or on the Baghdad-to-airport highway—are expected not only by their governments, but by many of their fellow citizens to weep in public and private, to honor their fallen male relatives, and to be quiet. For those who share this widespread assumption, widows' wartime and postwar political organizing comes as an unwelcome surprise.[27]

Any war can live on in private rituals, personal pride, and dread, the contents of dreams, seemingly endless trips to the hospital, dozens of little pill bottles on the kitchen counter, medical bills unpaid, daily care taken to not broach certain sensitive topics. For those who are fortunate enough not to lose everything when displaced by war's violence, there are photos on mantelpieces, letters read and reread, bedrooms turned into household shrines, stories handed down to children and grandchildren, awkward silences left unbroken, rank and service dates chiseled into gravestones, flags and flowers replenished at cemeteries, names carved into plaques erected on town squares—these are wartime and postwar practices that continue after news of the war has slipped off the front page and elected officials turn their attentions to banking and oil.

Wars don't end abruptly. Postwar is an era that can last a very long time. Charlene could be worrying about her son for years. Even after her older son has left the air force and her younger son has forgotten the appeals made to him by army recruiters, Emma's sense of public confidence gained through her activities in the Blue Star Mothers might survive. When Safah is eligible to vote for the first time, in Iraq's 2010 parliamentary election, she could bring with her into the Haditha voting booth an understanding of the war forged out of a traumatic wartime girlhood. Even if Danielle would prefer to be seen as a professional educator, she is likely to be perceived by many of her fellow Chicagoans as the basketball ace who lost her arm in war. If Nimo has been able to reopen her beauty parlor, she might be all the more aware that the political space she provides for women is fragile and needs protection.

Postwar is most usefully understood as another phase in the series of gendered phases that structure any war. Even "postwar" can have distinct phases. Soon after a war may be a time when senior civilian officials and military academy instructors construct the recent war's lessons—lessons about how to recruit young men, lessons about how to control women's sexuality, lessons about how to socialize military wives into volunteer work, lessons about how to effectively negotiate with men of another culture. Years later, the origins of those lessons in a particular war may fade from consciousness and become in many policy makers' and professional soldiers' minds simply the "rational" way to wage a war. Likewise, in the early months and years of a postwar era, the economic and emotional stresses imposed on women as war widows and veterans' caregivers might prompt governments, relatives, neighbors, and workmates to provide some modest support. Later, while the burdens may persist, the support may disappear, although images of the loyal military wife, the resourceful refugee woman, the wartime prostitute, the troublesome wartime feminist, the caring veteran's mother each and together will linger, becoming perhaps even more deeply entrenched in the political culture, ready to be called upon for waging the next war.

Nimo, Maha, Safah, Emma, Danielle, Kim and Charlene—they are not just objects of, but also the authors, transmitters, and and archivists of wartime memory. Yet they are not usually commissioned to be the writers of the history textbooks that will frame the war for the next generation of citizens. Nor are they recruited to become the military academy instructors who will tease out the political, strategic, and tactical lessons for the next generation of soldiers. They rarely cast the deciding vote on the design of a public war memorial. And yet these women expend thought and energy in shaping the postwar meanings of the last war, meanings that will help shape the debates about waging the next war.

To ignore women's often localized, unassuming, privatized postwar practices intended to shape the meaning of the last war, to concentrate our attention only on the public rituals and authoritative expressions, is, Gilpin Faust and others wisely remind us, to grossly underestimate how past wars are assigned meaning, meanings that are likely to be mobilized when governments call on citizens to support the next war.

And where are they now? Even as a girl, I loved newspaper features that tracked down individuals once in the headlines but since faded from view. What happened to the radio operator whose skill and perseverance saved the ship's passengers? How did the young woman who won a major court case conduct her life after she no longer made headlines? So it has been hard to end this book. A book ends, but lives go on.

Each of these women, I think, is still alive. If so, she is continuing to think and to make decisions. She still is dealing with family members' and government officials' presumptions about her marital status, about her job aspirations, about her religious, ethnic, or political affiliations. She continues to fashion her own "lessons" garnered from the Iraq War. She goes on making choices about which of her wartime experiences she is willing to talk about and which she prefers to wrap in a blanket of silence.

Nimo, Maha, Safah, Shatha, Emma, Danielle, Kim and Charlene: how have the waves set off by the Iraq War continued to ripple through their distinctive lives? Maybe an enterprising researcher equipped with a feminist curiosity will try to find out. I hope so.

NOTES

CHAPTER ONE. *EIGHT WOMEN, ONE WAR*

1. Lina Vuskovic and Zorica Trifunovic, eds, *Women's Side of War* (Belgrade: Women in Black, Belgrade, 2008). For more on the Belgrade Women in Black, see Cynthia Cockburn, *From Where We Stand: War, Women's Activism and Feminist Analysis* (London: Zed Books, 2007).

CHAPTER TWO. *NIMO*

1. Sabrina Tavernise, "Aftereffects: Rights and Tolerance; Iraqi Women Wary of New Upheavals," *New York Times,* May 5, 2003.

2. Ellen Knickmeyer, "Baghdad Neighborhood's Hopes Dimmed by the Trials of War," *Washington Post,* September 27, 2005, www.washingtonpost.com (accessed September 3, 2008).

3. Tavernise, "Aftereffects."

4. Ibid.

5. Ibid.

6. Mona Domosh and Joni Seager, *Putting Women in Place: Feminist Geographers Make Sense of the World* (New York: Guilford Press, 2001).

7. Susan Ossman, *Three Faces of Beauty: Casablanca, Paris, Cairo* (Durham, NC: Duke University Press, 2002), 54. For insightful investigations of how women's—and men's—hairstyles have become politicized, see Chie Ikeya, "The Modern Burmese

Woman and the Politics of Fashion in Colonial Burma," *Journal of Asian Studies* 67, no. 4 (November 2008): 1277–308; Suzanne G. O'Brien, "Splitting Hairs: History and the Politics of Daily Life in Nineteenth-Century Japan," *Journal of Asian Studies* 67, no. 4 (November 2008): 1309–39.

8. See, for instance, Kathleen M. Jenning, Fafo AIS, Oslo, Norway, "The Political Economy of DDR in Liberia: A Gendered Critique" (paper presented at the International Studies Association annual meeting, San Francisco, March 26–29, 2008).

9. Nadje Al-Ali, *Iraqi Women: Untold Stories from 1948 to the Present* (London: Zed Books, 2007), 86. For the emergence of and ideas crafted by the Egyptian Feminist Union, see Margot Badran, *Feminists, Islam, and the Nation: Gender and the Making of Modern Egypt* (Princeton: Princeton University Press, 1995); Nadje Al-Ali, *Secularism, Gender and the State in the Middle East: The Egyptian Women's Movement* (Cambridge: Cambridge University Press, 2000).

10. On the role of beauty salons in the emergence of the modern girl in 1930s Japanese-ruled Okinawa, see Ruri Ito, "The 'Modern Girl' Question in the Periphery of Empire," in *The Modern Girl Around The World*, ed. Modern Girl Around the World Research Group (Durham, NC: Duke University Press, 2008), 240–62. See also Insook Kwon, "'The New Women's Movement' in 1920s Korea," *Gender and History* 10, no. 3 (November 1998): 381–405; Lila Abu-Lughod, ed., *Remaking Women: Feminism and Modernity in the Middle East* (Princeton: Princeton University Press, 1998). For the early twentieth-century globalization of advertising selling particular images of the New Woman's feminized beauty, see Denise Sutton: *Globalizing Ideal Beauty: How the Women Copywriters of J. Walter Thompson Contributed to a Global Concept of Beauty* (New York: Palgrave Macmillan, 2009).

11. Ossman, *Three Faces of Beauty*, 70–71.

12. See, for instance: Judy Lown, *Women and Industrialization: Gender at Work in Nineteenth-Century England* (Minneapolis: University of Minnesota Press, 1990); Seung-kyung Kim, *Class Struggle or Family Struggle? The Lives of Women Factory Workers in South Korea* (New York: Cambridge University Press, 1997).

13. Quoted in Al-Ali, *Iraqi Women*, 114.

14. Joni Seager, *Penguin Atlas of Women in the World*, 4th ed. (New York: Penguin Books, 2008); see also issues of the journal *Feminist Economics*.

15. Naomi Klein, *The Shock Doctrine* (New York: Metropolitan Books / Henry Holt, 2007), 444.

16. Yasmin Husein Al-Jawaheri, *Women in Iraq: The Gender Impact of International Sanctions* (London: I. B. Tauris, 2008). Regarding the shifting wartime politics of Iraq's male tribal leaders, see Farnaz Fassihi, *Waiting for an Ordinary Day: The Unravelling of Life in Iraq* (New York: Public Affairs, 2008), 87–101.

17. Al-Jawaheri, *Women in Iraq,* 26.

18. Ibid.

19. Ibid., 69–72.

20. Quoted in ibid., 71.

21. Ibid., 36.

22. Ibid., 40.

23. Women's Rights Watch, "Climate of Fear: Sexual Violence and Abduction of Women and Girls in Baghdad," Human Rights Watch (New York), July 16, 2008, http:www.org/reports/2003/iraq0703/1.htm#_Toc45709960 (accessed September 17, 2008). Act Together, the alliance of British and Iraqi women in Britain raising issues of women in Iraq, issued a public letter that assessed the Human Rights Watch report and spelled out Act Together's own demands. Its members called for the British government, the U.S. government's most prominent ally in the Iraq invasion, to take steps to address violence against Iraqi women in the British zone of authority in southern Iraq and especially in the city of Basra, the British forces' headquarters. See Act Together, public letter to Patricia Hewitt, British Secretary for Trade and Industry and Minister for Women and Equality, September 20, 2003, http://www.acttogether.org (accessed September 17, 2008).

24. Marjorie P. Lasky, "Iraqi Women Under Siege" (San Francisco: Global Exchange and Code Pink, 2006), 9.

25. Klein, *Shock Doctrine,* 439–48.

26. Integrated Regional Information Networks (IRIN), "Iraq: Unemployment Forces Female Professionals into Domestic Work," *WLUML Newssheet* 18, no. 3 (2006): 22. WLUML is the highly respected transnational feminist organization Women Living Under Muslim Laws.

27. IRIN, *WLUML Newssheet.*

28. Fassihi, *Waiting for an Ordinary Day,* 69.

29. Ibid.

30. Lasky, "Women Under Siege," 2.

31. Ibid., 103.

32. International Committee of the Red Cross (ICRC), "Iraq: No Let-up in the Humanitarian Crisis," March 2008, http://www.icrc.org/wb/eng/siteengo.nsf/htmlall/$file/ICRC (accessed September 3, 2008).

33. Hannah Fairfield, "Money, Unspent, in Iraq's Pocket," *New York Times,* October 30, 2008, describing a report by the U.S. special inspector general for Iraq reconstruction on the shortfalls in the repairs of Iraq's basic utilities and infrastructure.

34. Seager, *Penguin Atlas of Women,* map 27: "Water," 76–77. Also valuable is a report critiquing the lack of gender-disaggregated data in the work of major international

agencies and the parallel lack of systematic curiosity about water in gender studies done by international organizations: Joni Seager, "The State of Gender-Disaggregated Data on Water and Sanitation: An Overview and Assessment of Major Sources" (report prepared for the Expert Group Meeting on Gender-Disaggregated Data on Water and Sanitation, United Nations, New York, December 2–3, 2008).

35. Riverbend, *Baghdad Burning*, vol. 2, *More Girl Blog from Iraq* (New York: Feminist Press at the City University of New York, 2006), 48.

36. James Glanz and T. Christian Miller, "Official History Spotlights Iraq Rebuilding Blunders," *New York Times*, December 14, 2008; for a detailed account of the Bremer-era U.S. policy making on Iraq electricity restoration, see Rajiv Chandrasekaran, *Imperial Life In the Emerald City: Inside Iraq's Green Zone* (New York: Vintage Books, 2006), 168–77.

37. Charles Dickens, *Great Expectations*, as quoted by Stewart W. Bowen, Jr., in Glanz and Miller, "Official History."

38. For reports on how ideas about women's beauty became both politicized and militarized leading up to and during Rwanda's 1994 genocide and Burma's/Myanmar's protracted armed conflict, see Women's Rights Watch, *Shattered Lives: Sexual Violence During the Rwandan Genocide and Its Aftermath* (New York: Human Rights Watch, 1996); Georgina Holmes, "The Postcolonial Politics of Militarizing Rwandan Women," *Minerva Journal of Women and War* 2, no. 2 (Fall 2008): 44–63; and *Catwalk to the Barracks* (Bangkok: Women and Child Rights Project [southern Burma] in collaboration with Human Rights Foundation of Monland [Burma], 2005), 13–15. For a feminist analysis of the reinforcing nationalist discourses of women's beauty and nuclear weapons as they were wielded in late 1990s and early 2000s India, see Rupal Oza, *The Making of Neoliberal India* (New York: Routledge, 2006).

39. Salam Al-Mahadin, "From Religious Fundamentalism to Pornography?" in *Feminist Interventions in International Communications*, ed. Katharine Sarikakis and Leslie Regan Shade (Lanham, MD: Rowman and Littlefield, 2008), 146–60.

40. Riverbend, *Baghdad Burning: Girl Blog from Iraq* (New York: Feminist Press at CUNY, 2005), 22.

41. Ibid., 23–24.

42. Ariana Eunjung Cha, "The Cost of Liberty," *Washington Post*, June 24, 2004.

43. Ibid.

44. Ibid.

45. Ibid.

46. Knickmeyer, "Baghdad Neighborhood's Hopes."

47. Ibid.

48. Ibid.

49. Lourdes Garcia-Navarro, "Analysis: Power of Iraqi Women," National Public Radio (hereafter, NPR), December 20, 2004, http://www.npr.org (accessed September 13, 2008).

50. Ibid.

51. Lourdes Garcia-Navarro, "Iraqi Army Eases Militias' Grip on Women in Basra," NPR, May 27, 2008, http://www.npr.org (accessed September 13, 2008).

52. Ibid.

53. Duraed Salman and Nasr Khadim, "Beauty Salons Back in Business," http://www.iwpr.net/?p = icr &so = f &o = 345783 &apc_state = henficr345816 (accessed August 20, 2008).

54. Ibid.

55. Dominique Soguel, "In Syrian Refuge, Women Find Barest Survival," *Women's eNews,* August 10, 2008, http://womensenews.com (accessed August 20, 2008).

56. Garcia-Navarro, "Iraqi Army Eases."

57. Salman and Khadhim, "Beauty Salons."

58. Ibid.

59. Mervat F. Hatem, "In the Shadow of the State: Changing Definitions of Arab Women's 'Developmental' Citizenship Rights," *Journal of Middle East Women's Studies* 1, no. 3 (Fall 2005): 36–37.

60. Deborah Rodriguez, *Kabul Beauty School: An American Woman Goes Behind the Veil* (New York: Random House, 2007).

61. Similarly, a women's group in Nigeria, Women for Empowerment, Development, and Gender Reform, created women's health materials designed for rural women and developed an outreach strategy of training 420 village hairdressers to disseminate health information to women clients who visit their salons: Ayesha Chatterjee and Sally Whelan, "Motorcycles and Megaphones: The Evolution of Our Bodies, Ourselves," *Our Bodies Ourselves Newsletter,* Fall 2008, 1. In New York City, police department domestic violence prevention officials together with child services officials turned to beauty parlor workers to reach out to the city's Hispanic women who might be suffering domestic abuse and yet be wary of approaching the police directly. A centerpiece of New York City's Cut It Out program became enlisting the help of Latina beauticians, training them to look out for signs of physical abuse among their female clientele and to provide information regarding support services they could call upon. In 2008, there were four hundred beauty parlors in New York's Washington Heights neighborhood alone. The key to the program's effectiveness was city officials' recognition that, for many women, a beauty parlor was a place where they felt comfortable and safe in talking about the embarrassing or frightening

realities shaping their lives: Leslie Kaufman, "Enlisting the Aid of Hairstylists as Sentinels for Domestic Abuse," *New York Times,* November 20, 2008.

62. Sam Dagher and Muhammed al-Obaidi, "5 Bombs Kill 27 in Iraq and Deepen Safety Fears," *New York Times,* September 29, 2008.

63. Ibid.

64. Campbell Robertson and Stephen Farrell, "Green Zone, Heart of U.S. Occupation, Reverts to Iraqi Control," *New York Times,* January 1, 2009.

CHAPTER THREE. *MAHA*

1. Cara Buckley, "Refugees Risk Coming Home to an Unready Iraq," *New York Times,* December 20, 2007.

2. Ibid.

3. Ali Hamdani and Ilana Ozernoy, "No Forwarding Address," *Atlantic,* March 2007, http://www.theatlantic.com/doc/200703/world-in-numbers (accessed September 3, 2008).

4. See ibid. for this house-by-house information.

5. Michael Comstock, "The Battle for Saydia: An Ongoing Case Study in Militia Based Insurgency," *Small Wars Journal* (2007), http://www.smallwarsjournal.com/mag/docs-tamps/51-comstock.pdf (accessed September 3, 2008).

6. Ibid., 9.

7. Ibid., 10.

8. For an innovative analysis of the local and cross-border political economies that develop within war zones, see Carolyn Nordstrom, *Shadows of War: Violence, Power, and International Profiteering in the Twenty-First Century* (Berkeley: University of California Press, 2004).

9. Comstock, "Battle for Saydia," 9, quoting Lt. Matt Noyes.

10. Feminist researchers and women activists in the Kurdish-dominated northern provinces of Iraq, for instance, have noted that the same patriarchal impetus to ensure collective family and national honor seemed to be increasing and justifying two forms of Kurdish men's violence against Kurdish women: first, armed Kurdish men's 1991–92 murders of Kurdish women thought to be prostitutes; and, second, the escalation of male family members' "honor killings" of daughters, wives, and nieces thought to have violated the strict rules of feminine propriety. See Diane E. King, "The Personal Is Patrilineal: Namus as Sovereignty," *Identities: Global Studies in Culture and Power* 15 (2008): 317–42. For more on violence against Iraq's Kurdish women, see Shahrzad Mojab, "No 'Safe Haven' for Women: Violence Against Women in Iraqi

Kurdistan," in *Sites of Violence: Gender and Conflict Zones,* ed. Wenona Giles and Jennifer Hyndman (Berkeley: University of California Press, 2004), 108–33.

11. Buckley, "Refugees Risk Coming Home ."

12. My own modest effort to explore the experiences and thinking of just one ethnicized militia rapist was a profile of a Bosnian Serbian young man: Cynthia Enloe, "All the Men are in the Militias, All the Women are Victims: The Politics of Masculinity and Femininity in Nationalist Wars," in *The Curious Feminist* (Berkeley: University of California Press, 2004), 99–118.

13. Sabrina Tavernise, "The Struggle for Iraq: A Fresh Pattern of Revenge Fuels Increasingly Personal Baghdad Killings," *New York Times,* November 20, 2006.

14. Kristele Younes and Nir Rosen, "Uprooted and Unstable: Meeting Urgent Humanitarian Needs in Iraq," Refugees International, April 2008, 2, http://refugeesinternational.org/file_unprotectedandunstable.pdf (accessed September 27, 2008).

15. Nadje Al-Ali, *Iraqi Women: Untold Stories from 1948 to the Present* (London: Zed Books, 2007), 263–64. For an innovative discussion of the national and state politics of marriages, see also Kristen Williams and Joyce Kaufman, *Women, the State, and War* (Lanham, MD: Lexington Books, 2007).

16. Sabrina Tavernise, "Iraq Power Shift Widens a Gulf Between Sects," *New York Times,* February 18, 2006.

17. Ibid.

18. Sabrina Tavernise, "Sectarian Toll Includes Scars to Iraq Psyche," *New York Times,* September 17, 2007.

19. Haifa Zangana, *City of Widows: An Iraqi Woman's Account of War and Resistance* (New York: Seven Stories Press, 2007), 133.

20. Al-Ali, *Iraqi Women,* 198; Yasmin Husein Al-Jawaheri, *Women in Iraq: The Gender Impact of International Sanctions* (London: I. B. Tauris, 2008), 104–7.

21. IRIN, "Iraq: Women Forced to Give Up Their Jobs, Marriages," Reuters and *AlterNet,* May 30, 2007, http://www.alternet.org/thenews/newsdesk/IRIN/4a66b6c2d010e2842304ea70ed6e0877.htm (accessed July 6, 2007).

22. Amnesty International, *Iraq: Decades of Suffering, Now Women Deserve Better,* February 22, 2005, 21–24, http://www.amnesty.org/en/library/info/MDE14/001/2005/en/650b14bf-d359–11 (accessed July 30, 2007).

23. World Health Organization and Ministry of Health, Iraq, *Iraq Family Health Survey Report* (Geneva: World Health Organization, 2006–7), http://www.emro.who.int/iraq/pdf/his_report_en.pdf (accessed March 9, 2009).

24. Ibid., 25.

25. Ibid., 23–24.

26. Ibid., 25.

27. Ibid.

28. http://www.refugeesinternational.org/content/article/detail/9679 (accessed September 27, 2008); see also·Kristele Younes, "The World's Fastest Growing Displacement Crisis," Refugees International, March 2007, http://www.refugeesinternational.org/file_iraqreport.pdf (accessed September 27, 2008). See also Patricia Weiss Fagen, *Iraqi Refugees: Seeking Stability in Syria and Jordan* (Washington, DC: Institute for the Study of International Migration and Center for International and Regional Studies, Georgetown University, 2007).

29. http://unhcr.org/publ/PUBL/3cb6ea290.html (accessed October 9, 2008); see also "The Iraqi Displacement Crisis," Refugees International, July 18, 2008, http://www.refugeesinternational.org/content/article/detail/9679 (accessed September 27, 2008).

30. http://unhcr.org/publ/PUBL/3cbea290.htlm.

31. This information on a woman who gave her name only as Sajida is from Gaiutra Bahadur, "Survival Sex: In Syria, Iraqi Refugees Are Snared in Prostitution," *Ms. Magazine*, Summer 2008, 28.

32. Ibid.

33. Rasha Elass, "Iraq Refugee Crisis Engulfs Women Silenced by Rape," *Women's eNews*, April 1, 2007, http://www.womensenews.org/article.cfm/dyn/aid/3116 (accessed August 20, 2008).

34. Bahadur, "Survival Sex."

35. Ibid., 29.

36. Elass, "Iraq Refugee Crisis"; Bahadur, "Survival Sex"; Katherine Zoepf, "Iraqi Refugees, in Desperation Turn to the Sex Trade in Syria," *New York Times*, May 29, 2007; Nihal Hassan, "50,000 Iraqi Refugees Forced into Prostitution," *Independent*, June 24, 2007, http://www.independent.co.uk (accessed August 16, 2008); Lina Sinjab, "Prostitution Ordeal of Iraqi Girls," BBC News, December 3, 2007, http://www.bbc.co.uk/2/hi/middle_east/7119473.stm (accessed August 30, 2008); Dominique Soguel "In Syrian Refuge, Women Find Barest Survival," *Women's eNews*, August 10, 2008, http://www.womensenews.org/article.cfm/dyn/aid (accessed August 20, 2008). I am grateful to Debra McNutt, an independent researcher, for sharing her ongoing work on U.S. military prostitution during the Iraq War.

37. See United Nations High Commission for Refugees (UNHCR), *UNHCR Handbook for the Protection of Women and Girls*, March 6, 2008, http://unhcr.org/protect/PROTECTION/47cfae612.html (accessed November 29, 2008). See also feminist studies of refugees, displaced persons and returnees: Laura C. Hammond, *This Place Will Become Home: Refugee Repatriation to Ethiopia* (Ithaca: Cornell University Press, 2004); Maja Korac, *Remaking Home: Reconstructing Life, Place and Identity in Rome and*

Amsterdam (New York: Berghahn Books, 2009); Giles and Hyndman, *Sites of Violence;* Women's Rights Watch, *Seeking Protection: Addressing Sexual and Domestic Violence in Tanzania's Refugee Camps* (New York: Human Rights Watch, 2000); Kirsti Lattu, *To Complain or Not to Complain: Still the Question; Consultations with Humanitarian Aid Beneficiaries on Their Perceptions of Efforts to Prevent and Respond to Sexual Exploitation and Abuse* (Geneva: Humanitarian Accountability Partnership, 2008), http://hapinter national.org/pool/files/bbc-report-lowres.pdf (accessed February 1, 2009); Slavenka Drakulic, *The Balkan Express* (New York: Harper Perennial, 1993); Inderpal Grewal, "Gendering Refugees: New National/Transnational Subjects," in *Transnational American Feminisms, Diasporas, Neoliberalisms* (Durham, NC: Duke University Press, 2007), 158–95. For a study by medical personnel of women's experiences of sexual assault not only while in a war zone, but then again in refugee camps, see Physicians for Human Rights, "Nowhere to Turn: Failure to Protect, Support, and Assure Justice for Darfuri Women," (Cambridge, MA) May 2009, http://physiciansforhuman rights.org/library/report-2009–05–31.html (accessed June 4, 2009). In addition, see Refugees International, "The Iraqi Displacement Crisis," July 18, 2008, http://www .refugeesinternational.org/content/article/detail/9679 (accessed September 27, 2008).

38. For the full text of SCR 1325, see the Women's International League for Peace and Freedom's (WILPF) Web site devoted to the post-2000 efforts to implement SCR 1325, http://www.peacewomen.org. See also the Web site of the Boston Consortium on Gender, Security, and Human Rights, which reports on the obstacles to implementation of 1325, http://www.genderandsecurity.umb.edu. The UN agency that most attentively monitors the implementation—or failures to implement—SCR 1325 is the United Nations Development Fund for Women, UNIFEM. Its Web site is http://www.womenpeacewar.org. For critical analyses of the continued resistance of international agencies' officials to implementing 1325, see Carol Cohn, "Mainstreaming Gender in UN Security Policy: A Path to Political Transformation?" in *Global Governance: Feminist Perspectives,* ed. Shirin M. Rai and Georgina Waylen (London: Palgrave, 2008), 185–206; Nadine Puechguirbal, "Peacekeeping, Peace Building and Post-conflict Reconstruction," in *Gender Matters,* ed. Laura Shepherd (London: Routledge, 2010). Stephen Lewis, the prominent Canadian former diplomat and UN official, has chastised UN peacekeeping commanders for not taking seriously—i.e., not treating as an operational priority, not devoting sufficient political and material resources to, not defining as their own professional responsibility to halt—the widespread violence against women in the countries, such as Liberia and the Congo, where they have been mandated to keep peace: Stephen Lewis, "Peacekeepers Must Protect Women," AIDS-free World, May 27, 2008, http://www.aids-freeworld.org/ content/view/157/153 (accessed December 19, 2008); the transnational feminist caucus

that monitors the International Crimes Court's (ICC) effective prosecution of war-time systematic rape—referred to within the UN as "gender-based violence"—is the Women's Initiatives for Gender Justice. Its recent report critiquing the ICC's pros-ecutor's operations is "Making a Statement: A Review of Charges and Prosecutions for Gender-based Crimes Before the International Court" (The Hague, June 2008).

39. Nadje Al-Ali and Nicola Pratt, *What Kind of Liberation? Women and the Occupa-tion of Iraq* (Berkeley: University of California Press, 2008), 157–58. See also Nadje Al-Ali and Nicola Pratt, eds., *Women and War in the Middle East* (London: Zed Books, 2009).

40. Women's Rights Watch, "Climate of Fear: Sexual Violence and Abduction of Women and Girls in Baghdad," Human Rights Watch, July 16, 2008, http://www.org/reports/2003/iraq0703/l.htm#_toc45709960 (accessed September 17, 2008). For an account of a rare Iraqi woman who went on the Arabic-language television channel Al Jazeera in 2007 to describe how she had been sexually assaulted by male officers of the Iraqi National Police, see Marc Santora, "Rape Accusation Reinforces Fears in a Divided Iraq," *New York Times*, February 21, 2007.

41. Anna Badkhen, "Rape's Vast Toll in Iraq War Remains Largely Ignored," *Christian Science Monitor*, November 24, 2008, http://www.csmonitor.com/2008/1124/p07s01-wome.html (accessed December 4, 2008).

42. Ibid.

43. Buckley, "Refugees Risk Coming Home."

44. Human Rights Watch, *Shattered Lives: Sexual Violence During the Rwandan Geno-cide and its Aftermath* (New York, 1996); Catherine Newbury and Hannah Baldwin, "Aftermath: Women's Organizations in Postconflict Rwanda" (working paper no. 304, Center for Development Information and Evaluation, U.S. Agency for International Development, Washington, DC, July 2000).

45. The governing party in Gaza, Hamas, concerned about both its male combat-ants' lack of familial ties and the growing number of Palestinian women in Gaza who had lost their husbands in the Palestinian-Israeli violence, arranged marriages between widows and Hamas soldiers and in 2008 sponsored a public wedding and celebration for three hundred couples: Taghreed El-Khodary, "For War Widows, Hamas Recruits Army of Husbands," *New York Times*, October 31, 2008.

46. Joshua Partlow, "Widows Strain Welfare System in Iraq," *Washington Post*, July 23, 2006.

47. Ibid.

48. Ibid.

49. Zangana, *City of Widows*.

50. Amnesty, *Iraq: Decades of Suffering*, 8.

51. Michael Kamber, "Wounded Iraqi Forces Say They've Been Abandoned," *New York Times,* July 1, 2008.

52. International Committee of the Red Cross, *Iraq: No Let-up in the Humanitarian Crisis* (Geneva, March 2008), 7, http://wwwicrc.org/web/eng/siteengo.nsf/htmlall/iraq-report-170308/$file/ICRC (accessed September 3, 2008).

53. IRIN, "Iraq: Women Forced to Give Up Their Jobs, Marriages," IRIN News, May 30, 2007, http://irinnews.org/Report.aspx?ReportId = 72451 (accessed February 3, 2009).

54. Ernesto Londono, "Forged by Loss, War Widows Embrace New Roles," *Boston Globe,* April 27, 2008. See also Anthony Shadid, *Night Draws Near* (New York: Henry Holt, 2005); Edward Wong, "Iraqi Widow Saves Her Home, but Victory Is Brief," *New York Times,* March 30, 2007; Lourdes Garcia-Navarro, "Widows Face Challenges, Tough Conditions in Iraq," *All Things Considered,* NPR, October 1, 2008, http://nl.mewsbank.com/nl-search/we/Archives?p_action = doc &p_docid = 123934A814 (accessed February 3, 2009).

55. ICRC, *Iraq: No Let-up,* 5.

56. Londono, "Forged by Loss."

57. Ibid.

58. Jeffrey Gettleman, "Sectarian Suspicion in Baghdad Fuels a Seller's Market for Guns," *New York Times,* April 3, 2006.

59. Partlow, "Widows Strain Welfare System."

60. Cara Buckley, "Iraq Premier Sees Families Returning to Safer Capital," *New York Times,* November 13, 2007.

61. Ibid.

62. Jamie Tarabay, "Iraq Struggles to Cope with Returning Refugees," NPR, September 3, 2008, http://www.npr.org/templates/story/story.php?storyId = 16855971 (accessed September 3, 2008).

63. Ellen Knickmeyer, "Slowly, Iraq Brings Refugees Home as Security Improves," *Washington Post,* September 8, 2008, available online, http://www.chicagotribune.com/news//nationworld/chi-iraq-security; see also Sabrina Tavernise, "Fear Keeps Iraqi Out of their Baghdad Homes," *New York Times,* August 24, 2008.

64. Timothy Williams, "In Dire Need, War's Widows Struggle in Iraq," *New York Times,* February 23, 2009.

65. Alissa J. Rubin, "More Iraqi Dead Last Month, But Fewer Than Last Year," *New York Times,* December 1, 2008.

66. John Agnew, "Commentary: Baghdad Nights: Evaluating the US Military 'Surge' Using Nighttime Light Signatures," *Environment and Planning A* 40 (2008):

2285–95. See also John Agnew, "Satellite Images and 'the Surge'" *AAG Newsletter,* 43, no. 11 (2008): 13.

CHAPTER FOUR. *SAFAH*

1. Safah Yunis Salem was mentioned by name as one of the survivors of the U.S. Marines' attack on homes in Haditha in June 2007, according to the report on the Haditha killings by the U.S. Naval Criminal Investigative Service: Paul von Zielbauer, "U.S. Inquiry Backs Charges of Killings by Marines in Iraq," *New York Times,* June 7, 2007. For an interview with a nine-year-old girl who also lived through that day, see Tim McQuirk, "Collateral Damage or Civilian Massacre in Haditha?" *Time,* March 19, 2006, www.time.com/time/world/article/0,8599,1174649,000.html (accessed, May 15, 2009).

2. This account of the shootings at Haditha is derived from the following: Thom Shanker, Eric Schmitt, and Richard Oppel, "Military Expected to Report Marines Killed Iraqi Civilians," *New York Times,* May 26, 2006; Carolyn Marshall, "On a Marine Base, Disbelief over Charges," *New York Times,* May 30, 2006; John M. Broder, "Versions Differ Wildly about Haditha Killings," *International Herald Tribune,* June 17–18, 2006; Paul von Zielbauer, "At Least 5 Marines Are Expected to be Charged in Haditha Deaths," *New York Times,* December 6, 2006; Josh White, "Death in Haditha," *Washington Post,* January 6, 2007, http://www.washingtonpost.com/wp-dyn/content/article/2—7/01/05/AR200701050; Paul von Zielbauer, "Propaganda Fear Cited in Account of Iraqi Killings," *New York Times,* May 6, 2007; Benedict Carey, "Stress on Troops Adds to U.S. Hurdles in Iraq," *New York Times,* May 6, 2007; Paul von Zielbauer, "Officer Says Civilian Toll in Haditha Was a Shock," *New York Times,* May 9, 2007; Paul von Zielbauer, "Marine Says His Staff Misled Him on Killings, *New York Times,* May 11, 2007; Paul von Zielbauer, "Lawyers on Haditha Panel Peer into Fog of War," *New York Times,* May 17, 2007; Eric Schmitt and David S. Cloud, "Military Inquiry Is Said to Oppose Account of Raid," *New York Times,* May 31, 2007; Paul von Zielbauer, "Forensic Experts Testify That 4 Iraqis Killed by Marines Were Shot From a Few Feet Away," *New York Times,* June 15, 2007; Paul von Zielbauer, "A Marine Tutorial on Media 'Spin'," *New York Times,* June 24, 2007; Anna Badkhen, "Two Portraits of Local Marine Awaiting Trial," *Boston Globe,* July 15, 2007; Paul von Zielbauer, "Marines' Trials in Iraq Killings Are Withering," *New York Times,* August 30, 2007; Paul von Zielbauer, "General and 2 Colonels Censured for Poor Investigation into Haditha Killings," *New York Times,* September 6, 2007; Tony Perry, "Marine to Stand Trial in Haditha Killings," *Los Angeles Times,* January 1, 2008, http://articles.latimes.com/2008/jan01/world/fg-haditha1 (accessed December

4, 2008). See also the documentary film by Arun Rath, writer and director, *Rules of Engagement* (Frontline and Yellow River Productions, Public Broadcasting Service [hereafter, PBS], 2008). The full texts of all the Geneva Conventions, which most governments and human rights investigators today use as the bases for assessing their own and other militaries' adherence to rules of warfare, can be found on the ICRC's Web site, http://www.icrc.org/ihl.nsf/CONVPRES.

3. An especially thoughtful exploration of American soldiers' evolving cultural assumptions about, and behaviors toward civilians in Iraq is Chris Hodges and Laila Al-Arian, *Collateral Damage: America's War Against Iraqi Civilians* (New York: Nation Books, 2008). See also Bob Herbert, "Abusing Iraqi Civilians," *New York Times,* July 10, 2007; Reuters, "Not All Troops Would Report Iraq Abuse, Study Says," *New York Times,* May 5, 2007. The Pentagon report referred to in the last article revealed that only 40 percent of American marines and 55 percent of American army personnel serving in Iraq would report a comrade who killed or injured an innocent Iraqi. The report was made available on the Web, http://armymedicine.army.mil.

4. Paul von Zielbauer, "Case Against U.S. Marine Dismissed," *New York Times,* March 29, 2008, http://www.nytimes.com/2008/03/29/world/middleeast/29haditha. html?_r = 1 (accessed December 4, 2008).

5. For more on the Tailhook sexual harassment case, see Cynthia Enloe, *The Morning After: Sexual Politics at the End of the Cold War* (Berkeley: University of California Press, 1993), 195–96, 212–14.

6. Paul von Zielbauer, "Killings of Afghan Civilians Recall Haditha," *New York Times,* April 20, 2007; see also Paul von Zielbauer, "Military Cites 'Negligence' in Aftermath of Iraq Killings," *New York Times,* April 22, 2007. Two years later, the pattern of U.S. military's and other NATO militaries' killings of Afghan civilians had become so prominent that it jeopardized the entire alliance between the Afghan government and NATO; it especially undermined the Afghan-U.S. relationship at the start of the Obama administration, since the U.S. military, its ground troops and its air force, was blamed for the most serious incidents of civilian deaths: for specific numbers of Afghan civilian deaths, see Helene Cooper, "Putting Stamp on Afghan War, Obama Will Send 17,000 Troops," *New York Times,* February 18, 2009.

7. For firsthand accounts of young people's experiences of war, see Zlata Filipovic and Melanie Challenger, eds., *Stolen Voices: Young People's War Diaries, from World War I to Iraq* (New York: Penguin Books, 2006).

8. Zielbauer, "U.S. Inquiry Backs Charges"; see also Rath's film *Rules of Engagement.* The other Iraqi teenage girl whose experience of American military violence made the news headlines—in both the United States and Iraq—was Abeer Qassim Hamza al-Janabi. Abeer was fourteen years old in March 2006 living with her family

in the town of Mahmudiya, 20 miles south of Baghdad, when four American soldiers, whose unit recently had endured heavy combat losses, saw her while they were staffing a military checkpoint. Changing into civilian clothes, the four men broke into her home, murdered her parents and sister, raped her, and then shot her. No survivors lived to tell her story. As the result of a military investigation, three of the American men were tried in a U.S. military court, found guilty, and sentenced to varying lengths of prison time. The fourth soldier and alleged ringleader, Steven D. Green, already had been discharged from the army on grounds of psychological disorder and, consequently, was tried in an American civilian court in Kentucky. Members of the jury found Green guilty but, since they could not come to an agreement about whether or not to advise the death sentence, he received a sentence of life imprisonment without parole. Upon hearing the verdict and sentencing, many Iraqis, especially male leaders of Abeer's own Janabi tribe, expressed outrage, both that Green had not received the death penalty and that the trial had not been conducted in an Iraqi court: James Dao, "Ex-Soldier Gets Life for Killings in Iraq," *New York Times,* May 23, 2009; Marc Santora and Suadad N. Al-Salhy, "Iraq Tribes Are Upset by Sentence Given to G.I.," *New York Times,* May 23, 2009.

9. "Investigating Officer's Report (of Charges Under Article 32 UCMJ 405 Manual for Courts Martial)," http://64.233.169.132/search?q = cache:1asDBS2Wr6UJ: warchronicle (accessed December 10, 2008). See also http://warchronicle.com/TheyAreNotKillers/SSgtWuterich/Art_32_Report_ICO_Wuterich.pdf.

10. Deborah Scranton, director, *The War Tapes* (Senart Films and Scranton/Lacy Films, 2007).

11. Riverbend, *Baghdad Burning,* vol. 2, *More Girl Blog from Iraq* (New York: Feminist Press at CUNY, 2006), 170–76.

12. Ibid., 173.

13. Quoted in ibid., 172.

14. Ibid., 173.

15. Ibid., 174.

16. Ibid.

17. Ibid., 175.

18. Ibid.

19. Campbell Robertson, "New Rules in Iraq Add Police Work to Troops' Jobs," *New York Times,* December 31, 2008.

20. Lourdes Garcia-Navarro," Treating Iraqi Children for PTSD," *The Impact of War,* NPR, Morning Edition, August 26, 2008, http://www.npr.org (accessed October 28, 2008).

21. Ibid.

22. Erica Goode, "War That Traumatizes Iraqis Take Toll on Hospital That Treats Them," *New York Times,* May 20, 2008.

23. Ibid.

24. Ibid.

25. Dyan Mazurana and Susan McKay, *Where Are the Girls? Girls in Fighting Forces in Northern Uganda, Sierra Leone and Mozambique: Their Lives During and After War* (Montreal: Rights and Democracy; International Centre for Human Rights and Democratic Development, 2004); Dyan Mazurana and Khristopher Carlson, "The Girl Child and Armed Conflict: Recognizing and Addressing Grave Violations of Girls' Human Rights" (Division for the Advancement of Women, United Nations, New York, September 2006); Helen Brocklehurst, *Who's Afraid of Children? Children in International Relations* (London: Ashgate, 2006); Joni Seager, *Penguin Atlas of Women in the World,* 4th ed. (New York: Penguin Books, 2008), for disaggregated data revealing the particular conditions of girls, country by country; UNICEF, *A World Fit For Children, Statistical Review,* 2007 (New York: United Nations, 2007); International Plan, "Because I am a Girl," May 2007, http://www.plan-international.org/reseources/publications/childrights/becauseiamagirl/ (accessed December 8, 2008). Regarding Eritrean girls' empowering experiences as members of an insurgent fighting force and their later disappointing experiences as demobilized fighters in postwar society, see Elise Fredrikke Barthe, *Peace as Disappointment: The Reintegration of Female Soldiers in Post-Conflict Societies* (Oslo: International Peace Research Organization, 2002). I am grateful to three colleagues in particular who have helped me think explicitly about girlhood, Wendy Luttrell, Jessi Willis, and Mikaela Luttrell-Rowland.

26. Seager, *Penguin Atlas of Women;* Mazurana and McKay, *Where Are the Girls?;* Mazurana and Carlson, "Girl Child and Armed Conflict." See also Grace Akallo and Faith J. H. McDonnell, *Girl Soldier: A Story of Hope for Northern Uganda's Children* (Grand Rapids, MI: Chosen Books, Baker Publishing Group, 2007); Kirsti Lattu, *To Complain or Not to Complain: Still the Question; Consultations with Humanitarian Aid Beneficiaries on Their Perceptions of Efforts to Prevent and Respond to Sexual-Exploitation and Abuse* (Geneva: Humanitarian Accountability Partnership, 2008), http://hapinternational.org/pool/files/bbc-report-lowres.pdf (accessed February 1, 2009).

27. Alisa Tang, "Lives on the Line," *Ms. Magazine,* Winter 2009, 53.

28. Dexter Filkins, "Afghan Girls, Scarred by Acid, Defy Terror, Embracing School," *New York Times,* January 14, 2009.

29. UNESCO, "UNESCO and Education IRAQ Fact Sheet (28 March 2003)," http://portal.unesco.org/en/ev.php-URL_ID = 11216 &URL_DO = DO (accessed December 21, 2008).

30. At the early 2009 meeting in Davos, Switzerland, of economic, political, and

philanthropic elites a session on girls was held for the first time in the history of the annual gathering. It was reportedly one of the most heavily attended: Don Tapscott, "The Girl Effect," *Businessweek,* January 31, 2009, http://www.com/careers/management/archives/2009/01/the_girl_effect.html (accessed February 4, 2009).

31. Rajiv Chandrasekaran, *Imperial Life in the Emerald City: Inside Iraq's Green Zone* (New York: Vintage Books, 2006), 66–69.

32. Joni Seager and Ann Olson, *Women in the World: An International Atlas* (New York: Simon and Schuster, 1986), map 22.

33. Ibid.

34. Ibid., "Country Table."

35. UNESCO, "Beyond 20/20 WDS—Report Folders: Time Series Data: Secondary education/enrollment" (Paris, 2005), http://stats.uis.unesco.org/unesco/ReportFolders/ReportFolders.aspx (accessed December 21, 2008).

36. Somini Sengupta, "For Iraqi Girls, Changing Land Narrows Lives," *New York Times,* June 27, 2004.

37. Ibid.

38. Ibid.

39. Ibid.

40. Ibid.

41. IRIN, "Iraq: Number of Girls Attending School Dropping, Say Analysts," Reuters and *AlterNet,* October 29, 2007, http://www.alternet.org/thenews/newsdesk/IRIN/378f4f07e8919edb3 (accessed December 26, 2008).

42. Ibid.

43. Ibid.

44. Gordon Dillow, "Dillow in Iraq: Haditha Prospers as 'Massacre' Fades," *Orange Country Register,* September 26, 2008, http://ocregister.com/articles/iraq-haditha-american-2171633-ye (accessed December 15, 2008).

45. Steven Lee Myers and Sam Dagher, "After Orderly Elections in Iraq, the Next Big Test Is Acceptance," *New York Times,* February 10, 2009.

CHAPTER FIVE. *SHATHA*

1. Damien Cave, "Shiite's Tale: How Gulf With Sunnis Widened," *New York Times,* August 31, 2007.

2. Ibid.

3. Ibid.

4. Lina Abood, Sawsan Al-Barak, Ala Talabani, and Maha Muna, "Women Organizing in Iraq" (conference, sponsored by the Boston Consortium on Gender,

Security, and Human Rights, Tufts University, Medford, MA, November 8, 2003). I am grateful to Carol Cohn, the consortium's director, for making this transcription available.

5. Abood et al., "Women Organizing," 4.

6. One of the most engaging and valuable close studies of women in wartime becoming politically active focuses on the women who created the Grandmothers of the Plaza de Mayo: Rita Arditti, *Searching for Life: The Grandmothers of the Plaza de Mayo and the Disappeared Children of Argentina* (Berkeley: University of California Press, 1999). British feminist researcher Cynthia Cockburn has written three books based on her participant observations of and extensive interviews with women wartime activists: *The Space Between Us: Negotiating Gender and National Identities in Conflict* (London: Zed Books, 1998); *The Line: Women, Partition and the Gender Order in Cyprus* (London: Zed Books, 2004); and *From Where We Stand: War, Women's Activism and Feminist Analysis* (London: Zed Books, 2007).

7. Haifa Zangana, *City of Widows: An Iraqi Woman's Account of War and Resistance* (New York: Seven Stories Press, 2007), 34.

8. Quoted in ibid., 35.

9. The classic cross-national comparative study of how women activists weighed these questions—and how those who expressed skepticism of male leaders' assurances that women's rights would follow automatically from anti-colonial and revolutionary success met censure and ridicule—is Kumari Jaywaradena, *Feminism and Nationalism in the Third World* (London: Zed Books, 1986). See also Margot Badran, *Feminists, Islam, and the Nation: Gender and the Making of Modern Egypt* (Princeton: Princeton University Press, 1995); Hue-Tam Ho Tai, *Radicalism and the Origins of the Vietnamese Revolution* (Cambridge, MA: Harvard University Press, 1992); Cynthia Enloe, *Bananas, Beaches, and Bases: Making Feminist Sense of International Politics*, 2nd ed. (Berkeley: University of California Press, 2000).

10. Nadje Al-Ali, *Iraqi Women: Untold Stories from 1948 to the Present* (London: Zed Books, 2007), 87. After the 1958 revolution the group was renamed Rabitat al-Mara' al-Iraqiya, the Iraqi Women's League.

11. For a comparative investigation of personal status laws and family codes, see Lynn Welchman, *Women and Muslim Family Laws in Arab States: A Comparative Overview of Textual Development and Advocacy* (Amsterdam: Amsterdam University Press, 2007).

12. Al-Ali, *Iraqi Women*, 90.

13. Zangana, *City of Widows*, 63.

14. Al-Ali, *Iraqi Women*, 140.

15. Ibid.

16. Sabrina Tavernise, "Shielding Women From a Renewal of Domestic Vio-

lence," *New York Times,* October 14, 2004. See also Linda Marshall, "Yanar Moham-med Talks about the Impact of the U.S. Occupation," *Off Our Backs,* July-August 2004, 14–15; Bay Fang, "The Talibanization of Iraq," *Ms. Magazine,* Spring 2007, 46–51.

17. Quoted in Fang, "Talibanization," 50.

18. Nadje-Al-Ali and Nicola Pratt, *What Kind of Liberation? Women and the Occupa-tion of Iraq* (Berkeley: University of California Press, 2008), 129–30.

19. See, for instance, Dana Frank, *Bananeras: Women Transforming the Banana Unions of Latin America* (Boston: South End Press, 2005). I am indebted to my Clark Uni-versity colleague Valerie Sperling, whose research has explored Russian feminists' post-Soviet organizing, for alerting me to some of the pitfalls local women activists face when seeking foreign assistance, see, for instance, Valerie Sperling, *Organizing Women in Contemporary Russia* (Cambridge: Cambridge University Press, 1999).

20. For a detailed description of Americans' lives inside the Green Zone in 2003–4, see Rajiv Chandrasekaran, *Imperial Life In the Emerald City: Inside Iraq's Green Zone* (New York: Vintage Books, 2006).

21. Jim Lobe, "Administration Chooses Anti-Feminist Group to Train Iraqi Women," *Commondreams.org,* February 28, 2004, http://www.commondreams.org/headlines04/1005–05.htm (accessed September 14, 2008).

22. Al-Ali and Pratt, *What Kind of Liberation?* 84.

23. Lourdes Garcia-Navarro, "Analysis: Power of Iraqi Women," NPR, Decem-ber 20, 2004, http://www.npr.org (accessed September 13, 2008).

24. See, for example, Teresa Sacchet, "Beyond Numbers: The Impact of Gender Quotas in Latin America," *International Feminist Journal of Politics* 10, no. 3 (2008): 369–90; Susan Franceschet and Jennifer M. Piscopo, "Gender Quotas and Women's Substantive Representation: Lessons from Argentina," *Politics and Gender* 4, no. 3 (September 2008): 393–425; Jane Mansbridge, "Quota Problems: Combating the Dangers of Essentialism," *Politics and Gender* 1, no, 4 (December 2005): 622–38; Lisa Baldez, "The Pros and Cons of Gender Quotas," *Politics and Gender* 2, no. 2 (March 2006): 102–9.

25. Thanassis Cambanis, "Iraq's Female Candidates Raise Voices Before Vote," *Boston Globe,* January 26, 2005.

26. A valuable source of regularly updated country-by-country data on women in national legislatures is "Women in National Parliaments," a report compiled by the Inter-Parliamentary Union, http://www.ipu.org/wmn-e/world.html.

27. Sam Dagher, "Defying Hurdles, Thousands of Iraqi Women Vie for Votes and Taste of Power," *New York Times,* January 29, 2009. Nadje Al-Ali, a London-based Iraqi feminist scholar, voiced this same concern, while also supporting electoral quotas, which, she said, helped several Iraqi feminist candidates win seats in the

parliament: Sara Wajid, "The Battle Against Brutality," *Guardian* (London), January 28, 2009.

28. "Guide to Iraqi Political Parties," BBC News, January 20, 2006, http://news .bbc.co.uk/2/hi/middle_east/4511450.stm (accessed January 7, 2009).

29. Sam Dagher, "Gunmen Kill Iraqi Cleric Campaigning for Council," *New York Times*, January 17, 2009.

30. Alissa Rubin and Sam Dagher, "Election Quotas for Iraqi Women Are Weakened, Provoking Anger as Vote Nears," *New York Times*, January 14, 2009.

31. Dagher, "Defying Hurdles."

32. "Voices of Iraq," September 23, 2007, http://warnewstoday.blogs.pot.com/2007_09_01_ocrdian.html (accessed December 30, 2008). Safiya al-Shuail also is quoted in Dagher, "Defying Hurdles."

33. Al-Ali and Pratt, *What Kind of Liberation?* underscores this point.

34. Ibid.

35. I am grateful to former ambassador Swanee Hunt, who has brought together women from a dozen countries active in postconflict police and judiciary reform, to Jennifer Klott, a UN consultant and director of the Social Science Research Council project on women in postconflict areas, and to Nadine Peuchguirbal, a former gender advisor to the UN's peacekeeping mission in Haiti, for tutoring me on women's efforts to transform police forces during international peacekeeping missions. For a case study of local women activists' efforts to undo the masculinization of the East Timor police force during that small country's UN peacekeeping operation, see Vijaya Joshi, "Building Opportunities: Women's Organizing, Militarism and the United Nations Transitional Administration in East Timor" (PhD diss., Clark University, Worcester, MA, 2005).

36. Aseel Kami, "Iraq's Policewomen Struggle to Change Perceptions," Reuters, reprinted in *Spare Change News*, April 23–May 6, 2009; Thom Shanker, "New Lessons for the Army," *New York Times*, February 19, 2009.

37. Michael R. Gordon, "For Training Iraq's Police, the Main Problem Was Time," *New York Times*, October 21, 2004; Associated Press, "First Iraqi Women Police Force Set for Work," Gulfnews.com, July 15, 2008, http://www.gulfnews.com/region/Iraq/10228891.html (accessed September 28, 2008); Anna Johnson, "Iraqi Women as Police Officers," *Seattle Times*, September 13, 2008, http://seattletimes.newsource.com/html/nationworld/2008176795_iraqwomen13.ht (accessed September 19, 2008); "Graduation Day in Iraq," *Boston Globe*, January 27, 2009; Steven Lee Myers, "Woman Held by Iraq Is Accused of Recruiting Suicide Bombers," *New York Times*, February 4, 2009.

38. For an enlightening discussion of British male colonial officials' similar strategies of allying with Iraq's male tribal sheikhs during the 1920s, see Toby Dodge,

Inventing Iraq: The Failure of Nation Building and a History Denied (New York: Columbia University Press, 2005). For a detailed account of how, during the U.S. occupation, these armed, sheikh-led Sunni Awakening Councils and their militias became intensely masculinized electoral rivals in the campaigning for provincial council seats in January 2009, and how some voters in the Sunni-dominated province of Anbar saw them chiefly as vehicles for corruption, see Sam Dagher, "Tribal Rivalries Persist as Iraqis Seek Local Posts," *New York Times,* January 20, 2009.

39. Alissa J. Rubin, "Militants Show a New Boldness in Cities in Iraq," *New York Times,* April 1, 2009; Alissa J. Rubin and Rod Nordland, "U.S. Military Expresses Concern About Perception of an Iraqi Crackdown on Sunnis," *New York Times,* April 16, 2009. One of the most valuable recent books on the diverse ways in which exploring masculinities can shed a brighter light on international politics is Jane L. Parpart and Marysia Zalewski, eds., *Rethinking the Man Question: Sex, Gender and Violence in International Relations* (London: Zed Books, 2008). I am especially grateful to Terrell Carver, theorist of masculinity and professor of politics at Bristol University, for nudging me to keep an alert eye on the myriad politics of masculinity.

40. See the Web site of the United Nations branch of WILF for ongoing reports monitoring the implementation of 1325, http://www.peacewomen.org. The full text of SCR 1325 on Women, Peace, and Security, with further information and links, is available at http://www.peacewomen.org/un/sc/1325.html.

41. I am particularly indebted to my friends and colleagues Carol Cohn, Dyan Mazurana, Felicity Hill, Angela Raven-Roberts, Nadine Peuchguirbal, and Swanee Hunt for introducing me to the feminist history and continuing politics of SCR 1325. Carol Cohn is a professor of women's studies at University of Massachusetts, Boston, and the director of the Boston Consortium on Gender, Security, and Human Rights, which specializes in bringing together policy makers, activists, and scholars to assess and explain the implementation of—and obstacles to the genuine implementation of—1325. Its Web site is one of the prime sources for discussions by researchers, activists, and practitioners of women's involvement in—or exclusion from—UN and other international peacekeeping missions, women's groups' activities in war zones, and the issues women both face and analyze in postwar eras, http://www.gender andsecurity.org. A case study of an early attempt by an alliance of transnational and local women activists to implement 1325 in one postconflict case, Timor-Leste— the former Portuguese colony of Portugal that was subsequently forcibly occupied by Indonesia—is Nina Hall and Jacqui True, "Gender Mainstreaming in a Post-Conflict State," in *Gender and Global Politics in the Asia-Pacific,* ed. Bina D'Costa and Katrina Lee-Koo (New York: Palgrave-Macmillan, 2009), 159–74.

42. Joni Seager, *Penguin Atlas of Women in the World,* 4th ed. (New York: Penguin Books, 2008), 97.

43. Al-Ali and Pratt, *What Kind of Liberation?* 93. See also "Iraqi Governing Council Initiates Shari'a—Iraqi Women Protest," *Peacework,* February 2004, 17.

44. Robert F. Worth, "In Jeans or Veils, Iraqi Women Are Split on New Political Power," *New York Times,* April 13, 2005. For a valuable exploration of the transnational discussion going on among women from diverse Muslim communities about the relationships of particular feminist experiences to diverse Islamic interpretations, traditions and trends, see Elora Halim Chowdhury, Leila Farsakh, and Rajini Srikanth, eds., "Feminisms, Religiosities and Self-Determinations." Special issue, *International Feminist Journal of Politics* 10, no. 4 (2008). For continuing cross-national coverage of debates about the role of sharia law, see the Web site and publications of the transnational feminist group Women Living Under Muslim Laws, http://www.wluml.org.

45. Edward Wong, "On the Air, On Their Own: Iraqi Women Find a Forum," *New York Times,* September 4, 2005.

46. Edward Wong, "Draft for New Iraqi Constitution Includes Curbs to Women's Rights," *New York Times,* July 20, 2005. See also an article by Houzan Mahmoud, activist in the Organization of Women's Freedom in Iraq, a group calling for a secular constitution: Houzan Mahmoud, "Secular Resistance Movement in Iraq," *Peacework,* June 2006, 13.

47. Wong, "Draft."

48. Ibid.

49. James Glanz, "Some Fear Iraq's Charter Will Erode Women's Rights," *New York Times,* August 8, 2005.

50. "Post-election Iraq: What's Next for Women" (conference, Middle East Program, Woodrow Wilson International Center for Scholars, Washington, DC, January 19, 2006), http://www.wilsoncenter.org/index.cfm?topic_id = 1426 &fuseaction+t (accessed January 6, 2009). For a perhaps more sanguine analysis, see Isobel Coleman, "Women, Islam, and the New Iraq," *Foreign Affairs* 85, no. 1 (January–February 2006): 24–38.

51. Women Living Under Muslim Laws, "Iraq: Women's Rights Under Attack—Occupation, Constitution, and Fundamentalisms," Act Together, occasional paper 15 (London:, December 2006). For more on Act Together, see its Web site, http://www.acttogether.org (accessed December 20, 2008).

52. Al-Ali and Pratt, *What Kind of Liberation?* 140–41.

53. Quoted in Sharene Azimi and Cyrille Cartier, "Constitutions Give Slow

Birth to Female Blocs," *Women's eNews,* October 21 2005, http://www.womensenews
.org/article.cfm/dyn/aid/2498 (accessed January 9, 2009).

54. Damien Cave, "Iraqi Premier Stirs Discontent, Yet Hangs On," *New York Times,* August 19, 2007, http://www.iranfocus.com/en/iran-world-press/iraqi-premier-stirs -dissent (accessed December 30, 2008).

55. "Iraqi MP Challenges Speaker of Parliament," http://www.govtube.com/ watch?v=qq1x2kvhp2o (accessed December 30, 2008).

56. Marie Colvin, "Ticking Bomb of Iraq's Forgotten Refugee Children," *Sunday Times,* March 16, 2008, http://www.timesonline.co.uk/tol/news/world/iraq/ article3559422.ece (accessed December 30, 2008).

57. Shatha al-Musawi, quoted in ibid.

CHAPTER SIX. *EMMA AND THE RECRUITERS*

1. Damien Cave, "San Antonio Proudly Lines Up Behind the Military Recruiter," *New York Times,* October 7, 2005.

2. Ibid.

3. So far, we have only one detailed account of the experiences, values, and relationships among civilians and military personnel in a military base town in the United States, Catherine Lutz's deeply observed study of Fayetteville, North Carolina, home of Fort Bragg. Catherine Lutz, *Homefront: A Military City and the American Twentieth Century* (Boston: Beacon Press, 2001).

4. Peter S. Canellos, "National Perspective: Military Culture Rooted in Geography," *Boston Globe,* May 11, 2005. Many army, navy, and air force bases located in the North and Northeast had been closed in the decades since the end of the cold war, although their congressional representatives had pressed hard to keep them open, arguing that each base was crucial for the health of the local civilian economy. By the time of the Iraq War, nonetheless, American regionalism and militarism appeared ever more coterminous.

5. They were followed, in ranking, by Alabama, Maine, Montana, Oklahoma, South Carolina, Alaska, and Virginia. The lowest yielding states—the states either where the army made the least effort to recruit young men and women or where their recruiting efforts met with the least wartime success in fiscal year 2004—were Rhode Island, Connecticut, and Vermont; just above them in the bottom-most rankings were Utah, New Jersey, Massachusetts, Minnesota, and Michigan. Data for U.S.-controlled territories of the U.S. Virgin Islands, Guam, American Samoa, the Marshall Islands, and the Northern Marianas were not included in these recruitment rankings. Still, local analysts and periodic Defense Department casualty reports

together suggested that these impoverished and militarized territories—especially those in the South Pacific—yielded disproportionately high numbers of young enlistees into the U.S. military's several branches. These per capita state rankings were based on the army's own enlistment data and U.S. Bureau of the Census data as compiled and published by: Suzanne M. Smith and Sam Diener, "Recruiters Target DC, Hawai'i, Rest of Country," *Peacework,* June-July 2005, 6. I am indebted to Teresa Teaiwa, a specialist on gender and militarization in the South Pacific and professor at Victoria University of Wellington, New Zealand, for alerting me to the efforts of both the U.S. and the British militaries to acquire recruits in the territories and countries of the South Pacific. See Teresia K. Teaiwa, "Globalizing and Gendered Forces: Contemporary Militarization of Pacific/Oceania," in *Gender and Globalization in Asia and the Pacific,* ed. Kathy Ferguson and Monique Mironesco (Honolulu: University of Hawaii Press, 2008), 318–32.

6. Emma Bedoy-Pina, e-mail to the author, January 21, 2009.

7. Cave, "San Antonio Proudly Lines Up."

8. See, for example, a brochure containing interviews with Native American, African American, Latina, Asian American, and white women military veterans, along with government data on women military personnel's experiences of PTSD and of sexual assault: "What Every Girl Should Know About the U.S. Military: Consider This—Before You Enlist," written and distributed jointly by two American anti-militarism groups, the War Resisters League, http://warresisters.org, and the Oakland, California-based Women of Color Resource Center, http://www.coloredgirls.org, 2008.

9. Damien Cave, "Growing Problem for Military Recruiters: Parents," *New York Times,* June 3, 2005. See also Tamar, "Drafted at 19, Opposing Military Recruiters at 61," *New York Times,* May 10, 2009. Outside school, the Explorer Scouts, an affiliate of the Boy Scouts of America, began in the early 2000s to train its teenage boys and girls, some as young as thirteen, and all wearing camouflage uniforms, in what its adult leaders, with the support of the U.S. Border Patrol, considered anti-terrorism, anti-drug smuggling, and anti-illegal immigration tactics. The training included maneuvers involving the use of dummy guns. The adult leaders of the Explorer Scouts said that their intent was to encourage teenagers to later join the Border Patrol: Jennifer Steinhauer, "For Explorer Scouts, Good Deeds Have Whole New Meaning," *New York Times,* May 14, 2009.

10. Among the sources that critique or respond to the military's efforts in American public schools during the Iraq War years are Youth and Militarism Program, American Friends Service Committee, "No Child Left Behind Act: Recruiting in the Schools," 2003, http://www.afsc.org/youthmil/no-child.htm (accessed October

12, 2003); Rick Jahnkow, "Youth Targets of Military Recruitment: National Counter-Recruitment Movement Enters a New Stage," *Resist Newsletter,* December 2004, 6–7; Committee for Conscientious Objectors, "Joining the Military Is Hazardous to Your Education Recruitment," http://www.objector.org/before-you-enlist/gi-bill.html (accessed September 18, 2004); Oskar Castro, "Exposing Recruitment Fraud: Youth Counter-Militarism Activism on the Rise," *Resist Newsletter,* May–June 2005, 1–2; Mark Sanchez and Dan Kelly, "San Francisco Votes to Replace JROTC: First City to Eject High School Military Program," *Peacework,* December 2006–January 2007, 13; Sam Diener, "Military Recruiting Test Ensnares Over 600,000 Students a Year," *Peacework,* February 2007, 24; Rick Jahnkow, "How Peace Activists Can Win Access to Schools Equal to That of Military Recruiters," *Peacework,* March 2008, 5; Tzili Mor, "WILPF Challenges U.S. Army Central Tactics," *Peace and Freedom,* Spring 2008, 4–5; Sam Diener, "Countering Military Recruitment in Schools," *Peacework,* September 2008, 15. *Peacework* is the publication of the American Friends Service Committee (AFSC). The AFSC has a youth and militarism program that specifically works with boys and girls and young men and young women on questions and practices of militarism in American society. *Peace and Freedom* is the newsletter of the U.S. branch of the Women's International League for Peace and Freedom (WILPF). In February 2009, a network of groups from around the country organized a national counter-recruitment and demilitarization conference in Chicago. Among the organizers' concerns for discussion was the new Obama administration's pledge to increase the U.S. military by 92,000 soldiers. The Web site of the National Network Opposing the Militarization of Youth is http://www.nnomy.org.

    11. Cave, "Growing Problem for Military Recruiters."

    12. Ibid.

    13. Cave, "San Antonio Proudly Lines Up."

    14. Ibid.

    15. I have delved into the cross-national and historicized militarized politics of mothering in several earlier books, especially Cynthia Enloe, *Maneuvers: The International Politics of Militarizing Women's Lives* (Berkeley: University of California Press, 2000), and, most recently, Cynthia Enloe, "Feminism and War: Stopping Militarism, Critiquing War," in *Feminism and War: Confronting U.S. Imperialism,* ed. Robin L. Riley, Chandra Talpade Mohanty, and Minnie Bruce Pratt (London: Zed Books, 2008), 258–63. I am grateful to Israeli researcher and peace activist Rela Mazali for sharing with me her insights into the politics of militarizing and demilitarizing mothering.

    16. http://goarmy.com/for_parents/hughes01.jsp (accessed January 22, 2009).

    17. Ibid.

    18. I am grateful to Tyler Wall of Arizona State University for sharing his insights

into the sophisticated interpersonal strategies of American military recruiters, based on his ethnographic research in one Midwest public school during 2007–8. He presented part of his ongoing research as a paper: "'School Ownership Is the Goal': Public Schools, Military Recruiting and the Fronts of War" (paper presented at the Association of American Geographers annual meeting, Boston, April 17, 2008). See also Karen Houppert, "I Want You! The 3 R's: Reading, 'Riting, and Recruiting," in *Security Disarmed: Critical Perspectives on Gender, Race, and Militarization,* ed. Barbara Sutton, Sandra Morgen, and Julie Novkov, 213–22 (New Brunswick, NJ: Rutgers University Press, 2008).

19. Lizette Alvarez, "More Americans Joining Military as Jobs Dwindle," *New York Times,* January 19, 2009.

20. James Brooke, "On Farthest U.S. Shores, Iraq Is a Way to a Dream," *New York Times,* July 31, 2005.

21. Damien Cave, "For Army Recruiters, a Day of Rules, and Little Else," *New York Times,* May 21, 2005.

22. Denise Sutton: *Globalizing Ideal Beauty: How the Women Copywriters of J. Walter Thompson Contributed to a Global Concept of Beauty* (New York: Palgrave Macmillan, 2009).

23. Brian MacQuarrie, "Army Scouting NASCAR Circuit," *Boston Globe,* August 28, 2005.

24. Quoted from the bilingual brochure by Department of the Army, U.S. Department of Defense, May 2002.

25. Sam Roberts, "A Generation Away, Minorities May Become the Majority in U.S.," *New York Times,* August 14, 2008.

26. http://www.census.gov/acs/www/Products/Profiles/Single/2003/ACS/Tab (accessed January 22, 2009).

27. Joseph Williams and Kevin Baron, "Military Sees Big Decline in Black Enlistees," *Boston Globe,* October 7, 2007.

28. U.S. Department of Defense, Office of the Under Secretary of Defense, Personnel, and Readiness, *2006 Population Representation in the Military Services,* January 2008, http://defenselink.mil/prhome/PopRep_FY06/summary_print.html (accessed January 24, 2009).

29. Williams and Baron, "Military Sees."

30. For more on the history of Latinos in World War II, see, for instance, Richard Griswold del Castillo, ed., *World War II and Mexican American Civil Rights* (Austin: University of Texas Press, 2007). Also see studies of California Latinos' youth culture and resistance—especially as symbolized by the urban Mexican American male "zoot suit"—and white soldiers' and white authorities' reactions to this Mexican

American culture during World War II: Eduardo Obregón Pagán, *Murder at the Sleepy Lagoon: Zoot Suits, Race, and Riot in Wartime L.A.* (Chapel Hill: University of North Carolina Press, 2003); Luis Alvarez, *The Power of the Zoot* (Berkeley: University of California Press, 2008). While most of these studies have focused on the Mexican American men who adopted the zoot suit and its cultural expressions, new feminist historical research is revealing the significant roles that Mexican American women played in the zoot suit culture and in the racialized conflicts that that erupted in wartime Los Angeles: Catherine S. Ramirez, *The Woman in the Zoot Suit: Gender, Nationalism, and the Cultural Politics of Memory* (Durham, NC: Duke University Press, 2009). Regarding Latino anti-war politics during the 1960s-70s United States, see Lorena Oropeza, *¡Raza sí! ¡Guerra no! Chicano Protest and Patriotism During the Viet Nam War Era* (Berkeley: University of California Press, 2005).

31. Ken Burns and Lynn Novick, directors and producers, *The War* (PBS, 2007). The film features the 1940–45 experiences of African American, white, and Japanese American men and women from Waterbury, Connecticut, Mobile, Alabama, Sacramento, California, and Laverne, Minnesota at home and on the battlefronts in Europe, the Pacific, and Asia.

32. David Montgomery, "After the War, a Struggle for Equality," *Washington Post*, September 22, 2007.

33. I have tried to explore the ethnic and racial politics of militaries—and police forces—in a dozen countries in Cynthia Enloe, *Ethnic Soldiers: State Security in Divided Societies* (London: Penguin Books, 1980). I am ashamed to admit, however, that when I was writing *Ethnic Soldiers,* in the late 1970s, I had not yet developed a feminist curiosity. Readers will be quick to notice its glaring absence. During the Iraq War, the British military personnel was 6.3 percent black and Asian, with the British army having the highest percentage, at 8.8 percent, while its Royal Navy had only 2.1 percent Asian and black uniformed personnel and its Royal Air Force had a mere 1.8 percent. British critics noted, however, that even these low numbers were deceptive because a significant proportion of the black and Asian British military personnel had been recruited by the Ministry of Defense (the MoD) from overseas, especially from Britain's former colonies, such as Fiji. As of April 2009, the British Ministry of Defense had enlisted 2,000 Fijians, particularly into the army, to fight in Iraq and Afghanistan. Eight Fijian soldiers had been killed, more had been seriously wounded, often provoking expressions of resentment by their mothers and wives: Don McDougall, "To Hell and Back," *Observer Magazine*, April 26, 2009, http://www.guardina.co.uk/uk/2009/apr/26/fijians-british-army-iraq (accessed April 27, 2009). I am grateful to Vron Ware for sharing this article and her insights with me. See also Audrey Gillan, "Diversity in Forces Slow to Improve," *Guardian,* January 13, 2009; Matthew Taylor

and Shane Croucher, "MoD Investigates Race Hate on Web," *Guardian*, January 19, 2009. During the years of the Iraq War, black and Asian Britons—a majority of them Britain-born—together made up approximately 7 percent of the total population of Great Britain. Once again, I am grateful to British researcher and writer Vron Ware for sharing with me her findings from her current research into the ethnic and racial dynamics inside the early twenty-first-century British military. Seira Tamang, Nepali feminist scholar, and Teresia Teaiwa, Fijian feminist scholar, have alerted me to the practice of the British army during the Iraq War years sending recruiters to Nepal and to Fiji to enlist Nepali and Fijian men—and a handful of women—into the British forces.

34. Eduardo Porter, "Advertising: Army's Hispanic-Recruitment Ads Cater to Mom," *Wall Street Journal*, May 24, 2002. See also Roberto Lovato, "The War for Latinos," *Nation*, October 3, 2005, http://thenation.com/doc/20051003/lovato (accessed October 1, 2005).

35. Office of the Under Secretary of Defense. Throughout the 1980s and 1990s, the Defense Department listed "Hispanics" under its racial categories. In the early 2000s, it began, instead, to list "Hispanics/Latinos" under its ethnic categories in order to include all those who identified themselves as "Hispanic/Latino," regardless of their skin color.

36. See, for instance, Kathleen Staudt, *Violence and Activism at the Border: Gender, Fear and Everyday Life in Ciudad Juárez* (Austin: University of Texas Press, 2008); Lynn Stephen, "Los Nuevos Desaparecidos y Muertos: Immigration, Militarization, Death and Disappearance on Mexico's Borders," in Sutton, Morgen, and Novkov, *Security Disarmed*, 79–100.

37. Jorge Mariscal, "Homeland Security, Militarism, and the Future of Latinos and Latinas in the United States," *Radical History Review*, no. 93 (Fall 2005): 46.

38. Quoted in Porter, "Advertising."

39. Ibid.

40. Kim Geron, *Latino Political Power: Latinos, Exploring Diversity and Change* (Boulder, CO: Lynne Rienner, 2005).

41. See for instance, Gloria Anzaldúa, *Borderlands = La Frontera, the New Mestiza*, 3rd ed. (San Francisco: Aunt Lute Books, 2007); Latina Feminist Group, *Telling to Live: Latina Feminist Testimonios* (Durham, NC: Duke University Press, 2001); "The Chicana Studies Issue," special issue, *Feminist Studies* 34, nos. 1–2 (Spring–Summer 2008); Oropeza, *¡Raza sí! ¡Guerra no!*

42. Among African Americans in the 2004 Congress, 11 were women, 26 were men; among Asian American members of Congress, none were women, 5 were men. All of these figures come from Carol Hardy-Fanta, Pei-te Lien, Dianne Pinder-

hughes, and Christine Marie Sierra, "Gender, Race and Descriptive Representation in the US," *Journal of Women, Politics and Policy* 28, nos. 3–4 (2006): 15.

43. Matt A. Barreto, Luis R. Fraga, Sylvia Manzano, Valerie Martinez-Ebers, and Gary M. Segura, "'Should They Dance with the One Who Brung 'Em?' Latinos and the 2008 Presidential Election," *PS: Political Science and Politics* 41, no. 4 (October 2008): 753–60.

44. Institute for Women's Policy Research, "Women's Vote Clinches Election Victory: 8 Million More Women Than Men Voted for Obama," *News*, November 6, 2008.

45. Ibid.

46. CNN November 4, 2008, exit polling data, as analyzed by Sharon Krefetz, feminist political scientist, specialist in American women and politics, and chair, Department of Government, Clark University. Over our more than three decades as department colleagues, Sharon Krefetz generously has taught me how to make reliable sense of polling and electoral data. For an analysis of Republican presidential candidates' ability to garner Hispanic/Latino votes—only Ronald Reagan and George W. Bush were able to win a majority of Hispanic/Latino votes between 1980 and 2008—see Charles M. Blow, "Back to the Future," op. ed., *New York Times*, November 15, 2008.

47. Emma Bedoy-Pina, e-mail to the author, January 21, 2009.

48. Bryan Bender, "Down Economy Boosts Military," *Boston Globe*, March 1, 2009. See also Alvarez, "More Americans Joining the Military."

49. Bender, "Down Economy."

50. In most countries that rely on volunteers rather than on conscripts to fill their military's ranks, civilian unemployment is good news to recruiters. In China, for instance, the newspaper of the People's Liberation Army reported that in 2008, as the global economic slowdown caused thousands of factories producing goods for export to close and as anxiety intensified among even those students at the most prestigious universities, "10,000 college students joined the military, a much higher number than in previous years." Edward Wong, "Job Pinch Trickles Up in China as Economy Slumps," *New York Times*, January 25, 2009.

51. The group's national Web site is http://bluestarmothers.org (accessed February 10, 2009).

52. Melissa Gorley, "San Antonio Chapter of 'Blue Star Mothers' Gathers Support for Soldiers' Families," *Today's Catholic*, February 16, 2007, http://www.satodays catholic.com/021607_Blue StarMoms.aspx (accessed January 10, 2009).

53. Emma Bedoy-Pina, e-mail to the author, January 21, 2009.

54. "Saddam's Execution Brings Satisfaction, Unease," *San Antonio Express-News'*

online feature *My SA News,* December 29, 2006, http://www.mysanantonio.com/news/MYSA123006_11A_saddams_dead (accessed January 10, 2009).

55. Emma Bedoy-Pina, "Comments," http://.mysanantonio.com/weblogs/blue star/2007/12/what_is_.

56. "77 Women to Support Justin Rodriguez for District 7," the Walker Report, April 02, 2007, http://walkerreport.blogspot.com/2007/04/77-women-to-support-justin (accessed January 10, 2009).

CHAPTER SEVEN. *DANIELLE*

1. The details of Danielle Green's growing up and her army experiences come from two interview-based profiles of her, a year apart, by *New York Times* reporters, after she had returned, injured, from Iraq: Ira Berkow, "A Star Athlete, a Soldier, and a Challenge," *New York Times,* June 3, 2004; Juliet Macur, "Two Women Bound by Sports, War and Injuries," *New York Times,* April 10, 2005.

2. Hasbro's Web site provides a history of the popular toy, describing "G.I. Joe" as "the single greatest brand in the history of boys' toys." http://www.hasbro.com/gijoe/default.cfm?page+History (accessed February 6, 2009). The toy also has inspired scores of additional Web sites created by G.I. Joe collectors and enthusiasts. The popular girls' toy "Barbie" also has had a wartime history. In the wake of the September 11, 2001, attacks on New York and Washington, consumer commentators noticed an increasing demand amongst American girls and their parents for the models of the Barbie doll dressed in the military uniforms of the U.S. Air Force, Navy, and Marines. Mattel, the maker of Barbie, had discontinued these military Barbies in the 1990s, but the sales of used military Barbies via Internet sellers spiked upward: Michelle Slatella, "Online Shopper: Home Front? Combat? A Mission for Barbie," *New York Times,* October 19, 2001.

3. Matthew Hickley, "He's Back: MoD Launches Own 'Action Man' Range of Toys to Boost Profile of Armed Forces," *Mail Online,* January 14, 2009, http://dailymail.co.uk/news/article-1115462/Hes-MoD-launches-ActionMan (accessed January 14, 2009). I have tried to reflect on my own childhood war games in Cynthia Enloe, *The Curious Feminist: Searching for Women in a New Age of Empire* (Berkeley: University of California Press, 2004).

4. Catherine Lutz and Lesley Bartlett, *Making Soldiers in the Public Schools: An Analysis of the Army ROTC Curriculum* (Philadelphia: American Friends Service Committee, 1995); Mark Sanchez and Dan Kelly, "San Francisco Votes to Replace JROTC: First City to Eject High School Military Program," *Peacework,* December 2006–January 2007, 13. It was Harold Jordan, then director of the AFSC's Youth and

Militarism Program, who first encouraged me to pay close attention to local debates over JROTC in American high schools. See Harold Jordan, "Making Student Soldiers: JROTC Academies," *On Watch: Newsletter of the National Lawyers Guild Military Task Force* 16, nos. 2–3 (November 1995). See also Youth and Militarism Program, *Is JROTC a Wise Use of Class Time?* (Philadelphia: American Friends Service Committee, 1998).

5. Project on the Status and Education of Women, *What Constitutes Equality for Women in Sport? Federal Law Puts Women in the Running* (Washington, DC: Association of American Colleges, 1975); Project on the Status and Education of Women, *Update on Title IX and Sports, no. 3* (Washington, DC: Association of American Colleges, 1980); Ying Wushanley, *Playing Nice and Losing: The Struggle for Control of Women's Intercollegiate Athletics, 1960–2000* (Syracuse: Syracuse University Press, 2001).

6. Michelle Morkert, of Concordia College in Illinois, has interviewed women who have self-identified as "soccer moms" as part of her investigation of white Protestant middle-class midwestern women's attitudes toward the Iraq War and toward militarized patriotism more generally: Michelle Morkert, "Securing the Heartland: The Militarization of American Women's Lives in One Small Midwestern Town During the Iraqi and Afghanistan Wars, 2003–2006" (PhD diss., Clark University, Worcester, MA, 2007).

7. Danielle Green, quoted in Berkow, "A Star Athlete."

8. Ibid.

9. Danielle Green, quoted in Macur, "Two Women Bound."

10. Lory Manning, *Women in the Military: Where They Stand,* 5th ed. (Arlington, VA: Women's Research and Education Institute, 2005), 32, and 6th ed. (2008), 34. See also Sabina Frustuck, *Uneasy Warriors: Gender, Memory, and Popular Culture in the Japanese Army* (Berkeley: University of California Press, 2007); Jennifer G. Mathers, "Russia's Women Soldiers in the Twenty-first Century," *Minerva Journal of Women and War* 1, no. 1 (Spring 2007): 8–18. For more on the workings of and political activism by both women and men around conscientious objection to military service in countries such as Turkey, Israel, and Germany, see Ozgur Heval Cinar and Coskun Usterci, eds., *Conscientious Objection: Resisting Militarized Society* (London: Zed Books, 2009). For an insightful feminist analysis of the Australian government's 2001–7 manipulations of policies regarding women for the sake of pursuing its militarized version of national security, see Bronwyn Winter, "Presumptive Fridge Magnets and Other Weapons of Masculinist Destruction: The Rhetoric and Reality of 'Safeguarding Australia'," in "War and Terror II: Raced-Gendered Logics and Effects Beyond Conflict Zones," ed. Mary Hawkesworth and Karen Alexander, special issue, *Signs* 33, no. 1 (Autumn 2007): 25–52.

11. I have explored the history and politics of women—and the racialized politics of women—in the United States' and other countries' militaries more fully in several books. See especially Cynthia Enloe, *Maneuvers: The International Politics of Militarizing Women's Lives* (Berkeley: University of California Press, 2000), and Cynthia Enloe, *Globalization and Militarism: Feminists Make the Link* (Lanham, MD: Rowman and Littlefield, 2007). For each, I benefited from a rich literature created by feminist historians and political analysts of wars and militaries. Their works are included in both books' extensive bibliographies.

12. Enloe, *Maneuvers*; Enloe, *Globalization and Militarism*.

13. Manning, *Women in the Military*, 6th ed. (2008), 4.

14. Ann Scott Tyson, "Bid to Limit Women in Combat Withdrawn," *Washington Post*, May 26, 2005, http://www.washingtonpost.com/wp_dyn/cpntent/ article/2005/05/2 (accessed November 8, 2008).

15. Historians of women in the U.S. military have found no other women military amputees in any previous American wars: Donna St. George, "Limbs Lost to Enemy Fire, Women Forge New Reality," *Washington Post*, April 18, 2006.

16. For more on Tailhook, the sexual harassment incidents that occurred during the convention of U.S. Navy aircraft carrier pilots in Las Vegas in September 1991, see Cynthia Enloe, *The Morning After: Sexual Politics at the End of the Cold War* (Berkeley: University of California Press, 1993); U.S. Department of Defense, Office of Inspector General, *Tailhook 1991*, pt. 1, *Review of the Navy Investigations* (Washington, DC, September 1992).

17. For instance, in fiscal year 2007, "women accounted for 14% of the army's active duty force while making up 46% of DADT discharges.... Similarly, FY 2007 data from the Air Force show women were 20% of the force but made up 49% of the DADT discharges": "Women in Uniform Disproportionately Affected by 'Don't Ask, Don't Tell' Law," newsroom, Servicemembers Legal Defense Network, June 23, 2008, http://www.sldn.org (accessed July 3, 2008). See also Nathaniel Frank, *Unfriendly Fire: How the Gay Ban Undermines the Military and Weakens America* (New York: St. Martin's Press, 2009). I am indebted to Aaron Belkin for sharing with me his research findings, which have challenged the basic presumptions undergirding the government's anti-gay/lesbian "don't ask, don't tell" policy. Aaron Belkin is a professor of political science at the University of California, Santa Barbara, and founder of the university's Palm Center, a research center devoted to investigating the politics of sexuality inside militaries. Nathaniel Frank is also a researcher at the Palm Center.

18. Among the American nongovernmental feminist organizations that have been the most assiduous in all of these activities on behalf of women in the military has been the Washington, DC-based Women's Research and Education Institute

(WREI). Though small and modestly funded, WREI's Women in the Military Project has published reports, appeared before congressional committees, and become a source of reliable information for journalists. I am indebted to all the women who have headed WREI's program, especially, in its early days, Carolyn Becraft, who was later chosen by President Bill Clinton for a senior post in the Defense Department, and, while writing this book, Lory Manning, the project's current director and herself a retired navy captain. See http://www.wrei.org. Some of the earliest research and biographical articles on women in the U.S. military—and comparisons with women in other countries' militaries—were published in the journal *Minerva,* founded in 1983 by historian Linda Grant DePauw. (*Minerva* was recently relaunched as a more explicitly academic journal, *Minerva Journal of Women and War.*)

19. Manning, *Women in the Military* 6th ed. (2008), 2.

20. Ibid., 11. Manning and WREI derive all of their enlistment figures from the U.S. Defense Department's own data. The U.S. Defense Department annually collects and publishes demographic data on military personnel by both gender and race.

21. Janice Karpinski, *One Woman's Army: The Commanding General of Abu Ghraib Tells Her Story* (New York: Hyperion, 2005).

22. *On Point,* NPR/WBUR, November 11, 2008.

23. Helen Benedict, "The Scandal of Military Rape," *Ms. Magazine,* Fall 2008, 41–45; Helen Benedict, *The Lonely Soldier: The Private War of Women Serving in Iraq* (Boston: Beacon Press, 2009); Miles Foundation, "Follow-up: Compassionate Care of Military Servicewomen/Defense Authorization," e-mail from the Miles Foundation, May 18, 2007; the Miles Foundation's Web site is http://www.hometown.aol.com/milesfdn. See also Elizabeth Hillman, " Front and Center: Sexual Violence in the U.S. Military Law," *Politics and Society* 37, no. 1 (2009): 101–29. This special issue of the journal devoted to analyses of militarized rape is edited by Elizabeth Wood. See in addition Jessica Pupovic, "Silence in the Barracks," *In These Times,* March 2008, 25; Celina R. De Leon, "For Female Soldiers, Sexual Assault Remains a Danger," *AlterNet,* January 5, 2007, http://www.alternet.com (accessed January 30, 2007); Sara Corbett, "The Women's War," *New York Times Magazine,* March 18, 2007, 40–72; (Representative) Jane Harman, "Finally, Some Progress in Combating Rape and Assault in the Military," September 10, 2008, http://www.huffingtonpost.com/rep-jane-harman/finally-some-progress-in-b-12 (accessed October 31, 2008); Ann Wright, "Sexual Assault in the Military: A DoD Cover-up?" *Truthdig,* August 1, 2008, http://www.truthdig.com/report/item/20080801_sexual_assault_in_the_military (accessed September 25, 2008). Ann Wright is a retired U.S. military officer and also a retired U.S. foreign service officer, who co-edited a book of firsthand accounts by American government officials in the foreign policy establishment, among them Ann Wright herself, who resigned from

their civil service posts in explicit protest against the Bush administration's invasion of Iraq: Ann Wright and Susan Dixon, eds., *Dissent—Voices of Conscience: Government Insiders Speak Out Against the War in Iraq* (Kihei, HI: Koa Books, 2008). During this same period, there has been a growing awareness of sexual harassment endured by women staff members inside of international humanitarian aid organizations; see, for instance, Relief from Relief, "'Go Tell your Manager': Sexual Harassment in Aid Agencies," Humanitarian Relief, February 2, 2009, http://humanitarianrelief.change. org/blog/view/go_tell_your_manager_sexual_-harassment (accessed February 23, 2009). I'm grateful to sociologist Dan Brook for sharing this with me. For a careful analysis of why it is so difficult to turn wartime and militarized sexual assault against civilian women into a viable political issue, see Katherine Moon, "Military Prostitution and the U.S. Military in Asia," *Asia-Pacific Journal: Japan Focus,* 2009, http://www .japanfocus.org/_Katherine_H_S__Moon-Military_Prostitution_and_the_U.S.__ Military_in_Asia (accessed January 19, 2009).

24. Jane Harman, "Rapists in the Ranks," *Los Angeles Times,* April 2, 2008.

25. Manning, *Women in the Military,* 4th ed. (2003), 14. In 2000, African American men were 18.2 percent of all men in the active-duty military; they were 23.5 percent of all men in the U.S. Army: ibid., 3rd ed. (2000), 14. Over the years, the most energetic, steady chronicler of African American women in the U.S. military has been Brenda Moore, professor of sociology at SUNY, Buffalo. See, for instance, Brenda Moore, *To Serve My Country, to Serve My Race* (New York: State University of New York Press, 1995). For the history of African American women as military nurses, see also Darlene Clark Hine, *Hine Sight: Black Women and the Re-Construction of American History* (Bloomington: Indiana University Press, 1994), 163–202. While he was head of the Institute of Political Studies' project on African Americans in the military, Edwin Dorn was one of the few Washington policy analysts who raised questions about African American women's experiences of military service. I am grateful to both Brenda Moore and Edwin Dorn for having kept me attentive to the ongoing developments of black women in the U.S. military.

26. Manning, *Women in the Military,* 6th ed. (2008), 16.

27. See, for instance, Jennifer K. Lobasz, "Women in Peril and the Ruined Woman: Representations of Female Soldiers in the Iraq War," *Journal of Women, Politics and Policy* 29, no. 3 (2008): 305–34. My own attempt to think through the politics of femininities and masculinities that set the stage for the American abuse of Iraqi male detainees held in the Abu Ghraib prison is Cynthia Enloe, "Wielding Masculinity Inside Abu Ghraib and Guantanamo: The Globalized Dynamics," in *Globalization and Militarism,* 93–116.

28. Shoshana Johnson, quoted in an interview with Michel Martin, in "Shoshana

Johnson on Life After Iraq," *Tell Me More,* NPR, May 28, 2007, http://nl.newsbank .com/nl-search/we/Archives?p_action = doc &pdocid = 11970AB45 (accessed February 3, 2009).

29. Shoshana Johnson, quoted in ibid. For a revealing interview with another Native American woman soldier, Eli Painted Crow, who served in the Iraq War and, after returning home, left the military and became a feminist peace activist, see Setsu Shigematsu, with Anuradha Kristina Bhagwati and Eli Painted Crow, "Women of Color Veterans on War, Militarism and Feminism," in *Feminism and War: Confronting U.S. Imperialism,* ed. Robin L. Riley, Chandra Talpade Mohanty, and Minnie Bruce Pratt (London: Zed Books, 2008), 93–102.

30. Institute for Women's Policy Research, "Women's Vote Clinches Election Victory: 8 Million More Women Than Men Voted for Obama," *News,* November 6, 2008. Regarding the significant role played by African American women voters in the 2008 election campaign, see Gwen Ifill, *The Break-through: Politics and Race in the Age of Obama* (New York: Doubleday, 2009).

31. Danielle Green-Byrd, quoted in Jennifer Craig, "How Life Lessons from the Inner City to the Sands of Iraq Shaped an Iraqi Veteran," *Wounded Warrior Diaries,* January 12, 2009, http://defenselink.mil/home/features/2008/0908_wwd/Green-B (accessed February 2, 2009).

32. Ibid.

33. Ibid.

CHAPTER EIGHT. *KIM*

1. This information about Kim Gorski is drawn from Sarah Kershaw, "For Citizen Soldiers, an Unexpected Burden," *New York Times,* September 15, 2003.

2. Ibid.

3. The National Guard, advertisement, *New York Times,* June 11, 2008. Early in the Obama administration, there were indications that, in trying to fulfill its pledge to send more American military personnel to engage in reconstruction efforts in Afghanistan, the U.S. government would have to rely on National Guard soldiers. Although the initial presumption had been that these additional reconstruction personnel would be civilian staff members of civilian agencies, in practice it proved both hard to persuade these staff people to accept positions in such a dangerous area and to come up with the civilian agency funds to support their work. Thus, increasingly, reconstruction assignments were transferred to the National Guard, whose personnel could not refuse such deployments: Thom Shanker, "G.I.s Filling Civilian Gap To Rebuild Afghanistan," *New York Times,* April 23, 2009.

4. *The War Tapes,* directed by Deborah Scranton (Senart Films and Scranton/ Lacy Films, 2007). Another documentary film directed by Deborah Scranton follows another National Guard company, one responsible for truck convoy protection, during its Iraq deployment: *Bad Voodoo's War,* directed by Deborah Scranton for *Frontline* (PBS, WGBH Educational Foundation, Boston, 2008).

5. Among the valuable sources on American women as pre-Iraq War military wives married to active-duty male soldiers are Donna Alva, *Unofficial Ambassadors: Military Families Overseas and the Cold War* (New York: New York University Press, 2007); Laurie Lee Weinstein and Christie C. White, eds., *Wives and Warriors: Women and the Military in the United States and Canada* (Westport, CT, Greenwood Press, 1997); Francine D'Amico and Laurie Lee Weinstein, eds., *Gender Camouflage: Women and the U.S. Military* (New York: New York University Press, 1999); Elizabeth Brown, "Did Americans Care About Wives of American Servicemen in Vietnam?" *Minerva: Quarterly Report on Women and the Military* 18, no. 1 (Spring 2000): 34–49. Regarding women married to male soldiers in other countries' militaries, see Chis-lin Pao-Tao and Xueliang Wang, " Military Wives in China, 1127–1279," *Minerva: Quarterly Report on Women and the Military* 18, no. (Spring 2000): 7–33; Myna Trustram, *Women of the Regiment: Marriage and the Victorian Army* (Cambridge: Cambridge University Press, 1984); Deborah Harrison and Lucie LaLiberte, *No Life Like It: Military Wives in Canada* (Toronto: James Lorimer, 1994). I have written at greater length about the militarization of women married to male soldiers in Cynthia Enloe, *Maneuvers: The International Politics of Militarizing Women's Lives* (Berkeley: University of California Press, 2000).

6. A fascinating account of the deliberate incorporation of post–World War II suburbia into U.S. overseas military base design is Mark L. Gillem, *America Town: Building the Outposts of Empire* (Minneapolis: University of Minnesota Press, 2007). Since 1996, the Defense Department had moved to privatize the construction of housing for military families, awarding contracts to several well-known architectural firms associated with a school of middle class housing referred to as "New Urbanism," including California-based Calthorpe Associates and Pennsylvania-based Urban Design Associates: William Hamilton, "New Urbanism: It's in the Army Now," *New York Times,* June 8, 2006. The most thorough investigation of a single U.S. military base and its surrounding town within the United States is Catherine Lutz, *Homefront: A Military City and the American Twentieth Century* (Boston: Beacon Press, 2001).

7. Kristen Henderson, "Your Money at War," op. ed., *New York Times,* February 9, 2007. Henderson was the author of a book on U.S. military families and was herself married to a navy chaplain.

8. Tanya Biank, "The Home Fires are Burning Out," op. ed., *New York Times,* March 13, 2006.

9. I am indebted to Carolyn Becraft, the wife of a senior officer, an outspoken and effective advocate for military wives, a former director of WREI's Women and the Military Program, and a senior civilian Defense Department official during the Clinton administration, for sharing her many political insights and experiences with me over several decades.

10. Pam Belluck, "Far From Home, and Staying There," *New York Times,* October 3, 2003. One of the few studies thus far to focus on the members of families of men and women in the U.S. Army Reserve during the Iraq War is Michael Musheno and Susan M. Ross, *Deployed: How Reservists Bear the Burden of Iraq* (Ann Arbor: University of Michigan Press, 2008). Richelle M. Bernazzoli, a geographer at the University of Illinois, compared two towns near the large Fort Campbell with the town of Portage, Pennsylvania, the latter having a long tradition of hosting a Reserve company and supplying it with local recruits and taking pride in those units' veterans. She found that a small civilian community that strongly identifies with the Reserve or National Guard, residents seeing it as a local institution, can become as culturally militarized as a town hosting a large active-duty base: Richelle M. Bernazzoli, "Bases and Places: The Cultural Hegemony of Militarism in American Society" (paper presented at the Association of American Geographers annual meeting, Boston, April 2008).

11. Kim Gorski, quoted in Kershaw, "For Citizen Soldiers."

12. Janine DeFao, "Prison Scandal Mars Return for Veterans," *San Francisco Chronicle,* July 25, 2004, http://www.sfgate.com/c/a/2004/07/25/BAGCF7SP391.DTL (accessed February 2, 2009).

13. Lory Manning, *Women in the Military: Where They Stand,* 6th ed. (Arlington, VA: Women's Research and Education Institute, 2008), 24. The Army Reserve stood out, by contrast for its high proportion of women—23.4 percent in 2007—higher than the proportion of women in the army's active-duty force.

14. Randal C. Archibold, "Soldiers and Their Families Have Mixed Feelings on Policy that Extends Active Duty," *New York Times,* June 4, 2004.

15. Kim Gorski, quoted in Kershaw, "For Citizen Soldiers."

16. Ibid.

17. Ibid.

18. In 2008, a federal court ruled in favor of Michael Serricchio, a member of the Air Force Reserve, who charged that his employer, Prudential Securities in Stamford, Connecticut, had violated the law when it rehired Serricchio after his tour of duty, but assigned him to a lower-paying job: Pam Belluck, "After Duty, New Chance for Old Job," *New York Times,* June 21, 2008.

19. Kershaw, "For Citizen Soldiers."

20. Karen Houppert, *Home Fires Burning: Married to the Military—For Better or Worse* (New York: Ballantine Books, 2005), 88–9.

21. Quoted in Kershaw, "For Citizen Soldiers."

22. Quoted in ibid. For accounts of women married to active-duty army soldiers during the Iraq War, see Houppert, *Home Fires Burning;* Martha Raddatz, *The Long Road Home: The Story of War and Family* (New York: Berkeley Books, 2008; Alex Witchel, "Confessions of a Military Wife," *New York Times Magazine*, November 6, 2005, 62–68; Denise M. Horn, "Boots and Bedsheets: Constructing the Military Support System in a Time of War," in *Gender, War, and Militarism: Feminist Perspectives*, ed. Laura Sjoberg and Sandra Via (forthcoming). Military wife Melissa Seligman wrote an op. ed. piece for the *New York Times* detailing the hardships of having her husband sent on repeated deployments to Afghanistan and Iraq, particularly on how difficult it proved to speak to each other via Webcam, each trying to hide their emotions, each fearing that the other wasn't sharing their real thoughts and emotions. After several months and deployments, as the strain almost unraveled their marriage, they found that written letters proved far more satisfying, less loaded than instant communication: Melissa Seligman, "One Husband, Two Kids, Three Deployments," *New York Times*, May 25, 2009.

23. Lutz, *Homefront*.

24. Catherine Lutz, "Living Room Terrorists," *Women's Review of Books*, February 2004; this article is reprinted in Sutton, Morgen, and Novkov, *Security Disarmed*, 223–27.

25. Lutz, "Living Room Terrorists."

26. The *Denver Post's* series, entitled "Betrayal in the Ranks: Military Response to Rapes, Domestic Abuse Falls Short," ran November 16–18, 2003. The principal reporters were Miles Moffeit and Amy Herdy. The series is available on the Web, http://www.denverpost.com/Stories/0,0,36%257E30137%257E1773329,00.html (accessed May 23, 2004).

27. Thus not only did these *Denver Post* journalists trace the causal links between both sites of male soldiers' violence against women in their 2003 "Betrayal in the Ranks" series, they were lead reporters in two follow-up investigatory articles on female soldiers' charges of sexual assault by fellow male soldiers and on the Defense Department's inadequate responses: Miles Moffeit and Amy Herdy, "Female GIs Report Rapes in Iraq War," *Denver Post*, January 25, 2004, http://www.denverpost .com/Stories/0,1413.36%257E27059%257E1913069,00.html (accessed May 23, 2004); Miles Moffeit, "Rumsfeld Draws Fire on Military Sex Assaults," *Denver Post*, April 16,

2004, http://www.denverpost.com/Stories/0,1413,36~30137~2087145,00.html (accessed May 23, 2004).

28. Quoted in Moffeit and Herdy, "Betrayal.".

29. Ibid.

30. Lizette Alvarez, "Despite Assurances from Army, An Assault Case Founders," *New York Times,* November 23, 2008.

31. Quoted in ibid.

32. Ibid.

33. Quoted in *Katie Couric Investigates,* January 28, 2009, http://www.cbs.news.com/blogs/2009/01/28/couricandco/entry4760522.shtml (accessed January 29, 2009).

34. http://video.aol.com/video-detail/abused-military-wife-speaks-out/2432912069 (accessed January 29, 2009).

35. American soldiers' suicide numbers were reported by the Army Medical Command and included in Charles P. Pierce, "The Forgotten War," *Boston Globe Magazine,* November 2, 2008, 24. Regarding the women who created the American Widow Project, see Tim Arango, "Helping War Widows on Road Ahead," *New York Times,* August 25, 2008. The group's YouTube site: americanwidowproject.org. On families and soldiers coping with postwar mental health problems, see Scott Anderson, "When You Can't Quite Find Your Way Home," *New York Times Magazine,* May 28, 2006, 36–56. Regarding the number and implications of National Guard soldiers deployed to Iraq and Afghanistan by mid-2008, see *The Bill Moyers Journal,* PBS, September 5, 2008, http://www.pbs.org/moyers/journal/09052008/transcript2.html (accessed September 6, 2008).

36. Jane Collins, ed., *For Love of a Soldier: Interviews with Military Families Taking Action Against the Iraq War* (Lanham, MD: Lexington Books, 2008); Kristin Henderson, *While They're at War: The True Story of American Families on the Homefront* (Boston: Houghton Mifflin, 2006).

37. Mike Gorski, quoted in DeFao, "Prison Scandal Mars Return."

38. Sgt. Mike Sindar, quoted in Adam Tanner, "Soldiers Back in U.S. Tell More of Iraqi Abuses," Reuters, May 7, 2004, http://www.commondreams.org/headlines04/0507-02.htm (accessed March 8, 2009).

39. Quoted in DeFao, "Prison Scandal Mars Return."

40. Ibid.

41. Golden Oak Montessori, "Charter Founding Members," August 4, 2008, http://www.goldenoackmontessori.org/?p = 111 (accessed February 2, 2009).

CHAPTER NINE. *CHARLENE*

1. Information on Charlene Cain and her son Michael is drawn from Dan Baum, "The Casualty: An American Soldier Comes Home from Iraq," *New Yorker,* March 8, 2004, 64–73.

2. Quoted in ibid., 64.

3. Ibid.

4. Ibid.

5. Chris Hodges and Laila Al-Arian, *Collateral Damage: America's War Against Iraqi Civilians* (New York: Nation Books, 2008), 10.

6. Quoted in ibid..

7. See Steve Fainaru, *Big Boy Rules: America's Mercenaries Fighting in Iraq* (Philadelphia: Da Capo Press, 2008); Deborah Scranton, director, *Bad Voodoo's War,*" for *Frontline* (PBS, WGBH Educational Foundation, Boston, 2008).

8. Johnny Dwyer, "The Wounded," *New York Times Magazine,* March 27, 2005, 26–27.

9. Institute for Women's Policy Research, "The Gender Wage Gap: 2008," *Fact Sheet,* April 2009. See also Randy Albelda, "Up With Women in the Downturn," *Ms. Magazine,* Spring 2009, 35–37.

10. Drew Gilpin Faust has given us a remarkably detailed and gender-sensitive account of the multiple roles that both southern and northern women played in the caring for the wounded and memorializing the dead during and after the Civil War: *This Republic of Suffering: Death and the American Civil War* (New York: Alfred A. Knopf, 2008).

11. Dana Priest and Ann Hall, "Soldiers Face Neglect, Frustration at Top Army's Medical Failings," *Washington Post,* February 18, 2007.

12. Annette L. McLeod, quoted in Michael Luo, "Soldiers Testify Over Poor Care at Walter Reed," *New York Times,* March 6, 2007.

13. The Dole-Shalala commission, quoted in Aaron Glantz, *The War Comes Home: Washington's Battle Against America's Veterans* (Berkeley: University of California Press, 2009), 61.

14. See, for instance, Joshua Koss, "How the VA Abandons Our Vets," *Nation,* September 15, 2008, 15–20.

15. Glantz, *War Comes Home,* 61–62.

16. *Our Bodies, Ourselves* was launched in the 1970s by a group of fourteen women in Boston, who became the Boston Women's Health Book Collective. First distributed in mimeographed form via feminist bookstores, the book was taken up by a mainstream publisher in 1984 and over the next twenty years was translated and produced

in culturally relevant revised editions by local feminist health groups around the world. See, for instance, the Boston Women's Health Book Collective, *Our Bodies, Ourselves For the New Century* (New York: Simon and Schuster, 1998).

17. Gail Ulerie, quoted in Daniel Bergner, "The Sergeant Lost Within," *New York Times Magazine,* May 25, 2008, 45. See also Lizette Alvarez," Home From War, Veterans Say Head Injuries Go Unrecognized," *New York Times,* August 26, 2008.

18. For Cindy Sheehan's views about her son's military experience, see Cindy Sheehan, introduction, and "You May Be Killed" in *Ten Excellent Reasons Not to Join the Military,* ed. Elizabeth Weill-Greenberg (New York: New Press, 2006), 1–5, 7–17.

19. See, for instance, the essays by American mothers of sons and daughters in the U.S. military who came to oppose the Iraq War in Jane Collins, ed., *For Love of a Soldier: Interviews with Military Families Taking Action Against the Iraq War* (Lanham, MD: Lexington Books, 2008).

20. Theodore Nadelson, *Trained to Kill: Soldiers at War* (Baltimore, MD: Johns Hopkins University Press, 2005), 103.

21. David Grossman, *On Killing: The Psychological Cost of Learning to Kill in War and Society* (New York: Cambridge University Press, 1995).

22. Scott Shane, "A Deluge of Troubled Soldiers Is in the Offing, Experts Predict," *New York Times,* December 16, 2004. See also Sara Corbett, "The Permanent Scars of Iraq," *New York Times Magazine,* February 15, 2004, 34–41, 56–66.

23. Ibid.

24. *The Soldier's Heart,* a *Frontline* film (PBS, WGBH Educational Foundation, Boston, 2005).

25. Chris McGreal, "Horror and Stresses of Iraq Duty," *Guardian,* May 16, 2009.

26. A particularly detailed series of press investigations of the causes and aftermaths of violent crimes by American Iraq War male veterans, several against civilian girlfriends, is Deborah Sontag and Lizette Alvarez, "Across America, Deadly Echoes of Foreign Battles," *New York Times,* January 13, 2008; Deborah Sontag, "An Iraq War Veteran's Descent: A Prosecutor's Hard Choice," *New York Times,* January 20, 2008; Deborah Sontag and Lizette Alvarez, "Combat Trauma Takes the Witness Stand," *New York Times,* January 27, 2008.

27. Rand Corporation, Center for Military Health Policy Research, "Invisible Wounds of War" (Santa Monica, CA, 2008), http://www.rand.org/pubs/mono graphs/2008/RAND_MG720.pdf (accessed March 20, 2008).

28. Joyce Lucey and Kevin Lucey, "Joyce and Kevin Lucey," in Collins, *For Love of a Soldier,* 155–72.

29. These quotes from Joyce and Kevin Lucey are in ibid.

30. Liz Sly, " Suspect in Killing of 5 US Troops Had Weapon Confiscated," *Boston Globe,* May 13, 2009.

31. Timothy Dwyer, "Wounded Soldiers Are Adapting to Altered Lives," *The Washington Post,* August 11, 2004, http://www.washingtonpost.com/wp-dyn/articles/A54883–2004August11 (accessed March 8, 2009).

32. Baum, "The Casualty," 72.

CONCLUSION. *THE LONG WAR*

1. Sudarsan Raghaven, "An End to Baghdad's 'Dark Era,'" *Washington Post,* February 28, 2009.

2. Quoted in ibid.

3. Ibid.

4. Ibid.

5. Hanaa Edwar, quoted in Rod Nordland, "Feeling Secure Enough to Sin, Baghdad Returns to Its Old Ways," *New York Times,* April 19, 2009. For more on Hanaa Edwar's activities as head of the humanitarian and research group Al-Amal, see "Humanitarian Crisis," http://www.ciranda.net/spip/IMG/rtf/Final_IVVM_Conference_Statement_En_Feb_08–1.rtf- (accessed April 25, 2009).

6. Raed Jarrar, "Security Without Empire Conference" (plenary presentation, American University, Washington, DC, February 28, 2009). Raed Jarrar is a specialist on Iraqi peace efforts and civil society organizing for the American Friends Service Committee. The text of the Iraq-United States security agreement is available on the AFSC's Web site, http://www.afsc.org.

7. There is a growing literature on U.S. overseas military bases. The best of this literature analyzes not only the U.S. military doctrine underlying the bases and their operation, but also the local civilian movements responding to those bases. These researchers have revealed that both U.S. overseas military bases and the civilian movements that criticize them rely on particular racialized relationships between women and men: Jana K. Lipman, *Guantánamo: A Working-Class History Between Empire and Revolution* (Berkeley: University of California Press, 2009); Catherine Lutz, ed., *The Bases of Empire: The Global Struggle Against U.S. Military Posts* (New York: New York University Press, 2009); David Vine, *Island of Shame: The Secret History of the U.S. Military Base on Diego Garcia* (Princeton: Princeton University Press, 2009). See also David Vine, "Too Many Overseas Bases," *Foreign Policy in Focus,* February 25, 2009, http://fpif.org/fpiftxt/5903 (accessed February 25, 2009). My first attempt to discover where women were on and near military bases—and why it mattered—was *Bananas, Beaches and Bases: Making Feminist Sense of International Politics,* 2nd ed. (Berkeley: University

of California Press, 2000). I am grateful to Joseph Gerson, a pioneer in tracking the impacts of U.S. overseas military bases and civilian opposition to those bases, as well as to Catherine Lutz and David Vine, for their work in creating an international network of scholars and activists concerned about the continuing multiplication of U.S. military bases worldwide.

8. Sam Dagher, "Defying Hurdles, Thousands of Iraqi Women Vie for Votes and Taste for Power," *New York Times,* January 29, 2009.

9. "4,000 Women Run in Iraq's Provincial Elections: How Significant?" World War 4 Report, February 3, 2009, http://www.ww4report.com/node/6780 (accessed February 20, 2009).

10. Sam Dagher, "A Daughter of Basra," *New York Times,* January 31, 2009.

11. Hadeel al-Shalchi, "Iraqi Women Get Posts, But Want Power and Respect," *Seattle Post-Intelligencer,* February 17, 2009, http://seattlepi.nwsource.com/national/1107ap_ml_iraq_women_in_power.html (accessed February 20, 2009).

12. Sam Dagher, "Tribal Rivalries Persist as Iraqis Seek Local Posts," *New York Times,* January 20, 2009; Ian Fisher, "Iraq Elections Face Crucial Test in Violent Mosul, "*New York Times,* January 30, 2009.

13. Alissa J. Rubin, "Pointing to New Era, U.S. Steps Back as Iraqis Vote," *New York Times,* February 1, 2009; Alissa J. Rubin, "Secular Parties and Premier Ahead in Iraq," *New York Times,* February 2, 2009; Dagher, "Tribal Rivalries Persist"; Dagher, "Daughter of Basra."

14. "The Finance Committee: No Financial Collapse in Iraq," IRAQ directory, February 13, 2009, http://www.iraqdirectory.com/DisplayNews.aspx?id = 8451 (accessed March 13, 2009).

15. Quoted in IRIN, "Iraq: Minister of Women's Affairs Tenders Resignation," February 9, 2009, http://www.alternet.org/theenews/newsdesk/IRIN/d778a3aeb0280de2f90d43ed45b284e5.htm (accessed March 2, 2009).

16. Quoted in ibid.

17. Oxfam International, "In Her Own Words: Iraqi Women Talk About Their Greatest Concerns and Challenges" (Oxford, March 8, 2009), 4, http://www.oxfam.org.uk/resources/policy/conflict_disasters/iraq-in-her-own-words (accessed March 9, 2009).

18. Oxfam, "In Her Own Words," 5.

19. Ibid.

20. Ibid., 9–11.

21. Mark Mazzetti, "U.S. Says C.I.A. Destroyed 92 Tapes of Interrogations," *New York Times,* March 3, 2009.

22. http://www.iraqbodycount.org/database (accessed March 13, 2009). Accord-

ing to Iraq Body Count's Web site, it is "an analytical project, not a news portal. Our procedure is to collect and reconcile every available, distinct report about each incident." Only where possible, was Iraq Body Count able to provide information on the sex of those killed.

23. Timothy Williams and Suadad Al-Salhy, "Fate of Iraqis Gone Missing Haunts Those Left Behind," *New York Times,* May 25, 2009.

24. "Names of the Dead," *New York Times,* January 28, 2009. And by the end of May 2009, the number of American military personnel killed in Iraq had risen to 4,292: "Names of the Dead," *New York Times,* May 25, 2009.

25. Elizabeth Bumiller, "Defense Chief Lifts Ban on Pictures of Coffins," *New York Times,* February 27, 2009.

26. Drew Gilpin Faust, *This Republic of Suffering: Death and the American Civil War* (New York: Alfred A. Knopf, 2008).

27. For a history of the persistent feminization of wartime grieving, see Carol Acton, *Grief in Wartime: Private Pain, Public Discourse* (New York: Palgrave Macmillan, 2007).

BIBLIOGRAPHY

Abood, Lina, Sawsan Al-Barak, Ala Talabani, and Maha Muna. "Women Organizing in Iraq." Conference, Boston Consortium on Gender, Security, and Human Rights, Tufts University, Medford, MA, November 8, 2003.

Abu-Lughod, Lila, ed. *Remaking Women: Feminism and Modernity in the Middle East*. Princeton: Princeton University Press, 1998.

Act Together. Public letter to Patricia Hewitt, British Secretary for Trade and Industry and Minister for Women and Equality. London, September 20, 2003.

Acton, Carol. *Grief in Wartime: Private Pain, Public Discourse*. New York: Palgrave Macmillan, 2007.

Agnew, John. "Commentary: Baghdad Nights: Evaluating the Us Military 'Surge' Using Nighttime Light Signatures." *Environment and Planning A* 40 (2008): 2285–95.

— —. "Satellite Images and 'the Surge'" *AAG Newsletter* 43, no. 11 (2008): 13.

Akallo, Grace, and Faith J.H. McDonnell. *Girl Soldier: A Story of Hope for Northern Uganda's Children*. Grand Rapids, MI: Chosen Books, Baker Publishing Group, 2007.

Al-Ali, Nadje. *Iraqi Women: Untold Stories from 1948 to the Present*. London: Zed Books, 2007.

———. *Secularism, Gender and the State in the Middle East: The Egyptian Women's Movement*. Cambridge: Cambridge University Press, 2000.

———, and Nicola Pratt. *What Kind of Liberation? Women and the Occupation of Iraq*. Berkeley: University of California Press, 2008.

———, eds. *Women and War in the Middle East*. London: Zed Books, 2009.

Albelda, Randy. "Up With Women in the Downturn." *Ms. Magazine*, Spring 2009, 35–37.

Al-Jawaheri, Yasmin Husein. *Women in Iraq: The Gender Impact of International Sanctions.* London: I. B. Tauris, 2008.

Al-Mahadin, Salam. "From Religious Fundamentalism to Pornography?" In *Feminist Interventions in International Communications,* edited by Katharine Sarikakis and Leslie Regan Shade, 146–60. Lanham, MD: Rowman and Littlefield, 2008.

al-Shalchi, Hadeel. "Iraqi Women Get Posts, but Want Power and Respect." *Seattle Post-Intelligencer,* February 17, 2009.

Alva, Donna. *Unofficial Ambassadors: Military Families Overseas and the Cold War.* New York: New York University Press, 2007.

Alvarez, Lizette. "Despite Assurances from Army, An Assault Case Founders." *New York Times,* November 23, 2008.

———. "Home From War, Veterans Say Head Injuries Go Unrecognized." *New York Times,* August 26, 2008.

———. "More Americans Joining the Military as Jobs Dwindle." *New York Times,* January 19, 2009.

Alvarez, Luis. *The Power of the Zoot: Youth Culture and Resistance during World War II.* Berkeley: University of California Press, 2008.

Amnesty International. *Iraq: Decades of Suffering, Now Women Deserve Better.* London, February 22, 2005. http://www.amnesty.org/en/library/info/MDE14/001/2005/en/650b14bf-d359–11 (accessed July 30, 2007).

Anderson, Scott. "When You Can't Quite Find Your Way Home." *New York Times Magazine,* May 28, 2006, 36–56.

Anzaldúa, Gloria. *Borderlands = La Frontera, the New Mestiza.* 3rd ed. San Francisco: Aunt Lute Books, 2007.

Arango, Tim. "Helping War Widows on Road Ahead." *New York Times,* August 25, 2008.

Archibold, Randal C. "Soldiers and Their Families Have Mixed Feelings on Policy that Extends Active Duty." *New York Times,* June 4, 2004.

Arditti, Rita. *Searching for Life: The Grandmothers of the Plaza De Mayo and the Disappeared Children of Argentina.* Berkeley: University of California Press, 1999.

Associated Press. "First Iraqi Women Police Force Set for Work." Gulfnews.com, July 15, 2008.

Azimi, Sharene, and Cyrille Cartier. "Constitutions Give Slow Birth to Female Blocs." *Women's eNews,* October 21, 2005.

Badkhen, Anna. "Rape's Vast Toll in Iraq War Remains Largely Ignored." *Christian Science Monitor,* November 24, 2008. http://www.csmonitor.com/2008/1124/p07s01-wome.html.

———. "Two Portraits of Local Marine Awaiting Trial." *Boston Globe,* July 15, 2007.

Badran, Margot. *Feminists, Islam, and the Nation: Gender and the Making of Modern Egypt*
Princeton: Princeton University Press, 1995.

Bahadur, Gaiutra. "Survival Sex: In Syria, Iraqi Refugees Are Snared in Prostitution." *Ms. Magazine,* Summer 2008, 28–29.

Baldez, Lisa. "The Pros and Cons of Gender Quotas." *Politics and Gender* 2, no. 2
(March 2006): 102–9.

Barreto, Matt A., Luis R. Fraga, Sylvia Manzano, Valerie Martinez-Ebers, and Gary
M. Segura. "'Should They Dance with the One Who Brung 'Em?' Latinos and
the 2008 Presidential Election." *PS: Political Science and Politics* 41, no. 4 (October
2008): 753–60.

Barthe, Elise Fredrikke. *Peace as Disappointment: The Reintegration of Female Soldiers in
Post-Conflict Societies.* Oslo: International Peace Research Organization, 2002.

Baum, Dan. "The Casualty: An American Soldier Comes Home from Iraq." *New
Yorker,* March 8, 2004, 64–73.

Belluck, Pam. "After Duty, New Chance for Old Job." *New York Times,* June 21, 2008.
———. "Far from Home, and Staying There." *New York Times,* October 3, 2003.

Bender, Bryan. "Down Economy Boosts Military." *Boston Globe,* March 1, 2009.

Benedict, Helen. *The Lonely Soldier: The Private War of Women Serving in Iraq.* Boston:
Beacon Press, 2009.

———. "The Scandal of Military Rape." *Ms. Magazine,* Fall 2008, 41–45.

Bergner, Daniel. "The Sergeant Lost Within." *New York Times Magazine,* May 25,
2008, 41–45.

Berkow, Ira. "A Star Athlete, a Soldier, and a Challenge." *New York Times,* June 3, 2004.

Bernazzoli, Richelle M. "Bases and Places: The Cultural Hegemony of Militarism in
American Society." Paper, Association of American Geographers annual meeting, Boston, April 2008.

Blank, Tanya. "The Home Fires Are Burning out." *New York Times,* March 13, 2006.

The Bill Moyers Journal. Public Broadcasting Service (PBS), September 5, 2008. http://
www.pbs.org/moyers/journal/09052008/transcript2,html (accessed September 6,
2008).

Blow, Charles M. "Back to the Future." *New York Times,* November 15, 2008.

Boston Women's Health Book Collective. *Our Bodies, Ourselves for the New Century.*
New York: Simon and Schuster, 1998.

Brocklehurst, Helen. *Who's Afraid of Children? Children in International Relations.* London: Ashgate, 2006.

Broder, John M. "Versions Differ Wildly About Haditha Killings." *International Herald Tribune,* June 17–18, 2006.

Brooke, James. "On Farthest U.S. Shores, Iraq Is a Way to a Dream." *New York Times,* July 31, 2005.

Brown, Elizabeth. "Did Americans Care About Wives of American Servicemen in Vietnam?" *Minerva: Quarterly Report on Women and the Military* 18, no. 1 (Spring 2000): 34–49.

Buckley, Cara. "Iraq Premier Sees Families Returning to Safer Capital." *New York Times,* November 13, 2007.

———. "Refugees Risk Coming Home to an Unready Iraq." *New York Times,* December 20, 2007.

Bumiller, Elizabeth. "Defense Chief Lifts Ban on Pictures of Coffins." *New York Times,* February 27, 2009.

Burns, Ken, and Lynn Novick, dir. and prod. *The War.* PBS, 2007.

Cambanis, Thanassis. "Iraq's Female Candidates Raise Voices before Vote." *Boston Globe,* January 26, 2005.

Canellos, Peter S. "National Perspective: Military Culture Rooted in Geography." *Boston Globe,* May 11, 2005.

Carden-Coyne, Ana. *Reconstructing the Body: Classicism, Modernity and the First World War.* London: Oxford University Press, 2009.

Carey, Benedict. "Stress on Troops Adds to U.S. Hurdles in Iraq." *New York Times,* May 6, 2007.

Castro, Oskar. "Exposing Recruitment Fraud: Youth Counter-Militarism Activism on the Rise." *Resist Newsletter,* May–June 2005, 1–2.

Cave, Damien. "For Army Recruiters, a Day of Rules, and Little Else." *New York Times,* May 21, 2005.

———. "Growing Problem for Military Recruiters: Parents." *New York Times,* June 3, 2005.

———. "Iraqi Premier Stirs Discontent, Yet Hangs On." *New York Times,* August 19, 2007.

———. "San Antonio Proudly Lines up Behind the Military Recruiter." *New York Times,* October 7, 2005.

———. "Shiite's Tale: How Gulf with Sunnis Widened." *New York Times,* August 31, 2007.

Cha, Ariana Eunjung. "The Cost of Liberty." *Washington Post,* June 24, 2004.

Chandrasekaran, Rajiv. *Imperial Life in the Emerald City: Inside Iraq's Green Zone.* New York: Vintage Books, 2006.

Chatterjee, Ayesha, and Sally Whelan. "Motorcycles and Megaphones: The Evolution of Our Bodies, Ourselves." *Our Bodies Ourselves Newsletter,* Fall 2008, 1.

"The Chicana Studies Issue." Special issue, *Feminist Studies* 34, no. 1–2 (Spring–Summer 2008).

Chowdhury, Elora Halim, Leila Farsakh, and Rajini Srikanth, eds. "Feminisms, Religiosites and Self-Determinations." Special issue, *International Feminist Journal of Politics* 10, no. 4 (2008): 439–54.

Cinar, Ozgur Heval, and Coskun Usterci, eds. *Conscientious Objection: Resisting Militarized Society.* London: Zed Books, 2009.

Cockburn, Cynthia. *From Where We Stand: War, Women's Activism and Feminist Analysis.* London: Zed Books, 2007.

———. *The Line: Women, Partition and the Gender Order in Cyprus.* London: Zed Books, 2004.

———. *The Space between Us: Negotiating Gender and National Identities in Conflict.* London: Zed Books, 1998.

Cohn, Carol. "Mainstreaming Gender in Un Security Policy: A Path to Political Transformation?" In *Global Governance: Feminist Perspectives,* edited by Shirin M. Rai and Georgina Waylen, 185–206. London: Palgrave, 2008.

Coleman, Isobel. "Women, Islam and the New Iraq." *Foreign Affairs* 85, no. 1 (January–February 2006): 24–38.

Collins, Jane, ed. *For Love of a Soldier: Interviews with Military Families Taking Action against the Iraq War.* Lanham, MD: Lexington Books, 2008.

Colvin, Marie. "Ticking Bomb of Iraq's Forgotten Refugee Children." *Sunday Times,* March 16, 2008.

Committee for Conscientious Objectors. "Joining the Military Is Hazardous to Your Education Recruitment." http://www.objector.org/before-you-enlist/gi-bill.html (accessed September 18, 2004).

Comstock, Michael. "The Battle for Saydia: An Ongoing Case Study in Militia Based Insurgency." *Small Wars Journal* (2007). http://www.smallwarsjournal.com/mag/docs-tamps/51-comstock.pdf (accessed September 3, 2008).

Cooper, Helene. "Putting Stamp on Afghan War, Obama Will Send 17,000 Troops." *New York Times,* February 18, 2009.

Corbett, Sara. The Permanent Scars of War." *New York Times Magazine,* February 15, 2004, 34–41, 56–66.

———. "The Women's War," *New York Times Magazine,* March 18, 2007, 40–72.

Craig, Jennifer. "How Life Lessons from the Inner City to the Sands of Iraq Shaped an Iraqi Veteran." In *Wounded Warrior Diaries,* January 12, 2009. http://defenselink.mil/home/features/2008/0908_wwd/Green-B (accessed February 2, 2009).

D'Amico, Francine, and Laurie Lee Weinstein, eds. *Gender Camouflage: Women and the U.S. Military.* New York: New York University Press, 1999.

Dagher, Sam. "A Daughter of Basra." *New York Times,* January 31, 2009.

———. "Defying Hurdles, Thousands of Iraqi Women Vie for Votes and Taste of Power." *New York Times,* January 29, 2009.

———. "Gunmen Kill Iraqi Cleric Campaigning for Council." *New York Times,* January 17, 2009.

———. "Tribal Rivalries Persist as Iraqis Seek Local Posts." *New York Times,* January 20, 2009.

———, and Muhammed Al-Obaidi. "5 Bombs Kill 27 in Iraq and Deepen Safety Fears." *New York Times,* September 29, 2008.

Dao, James. "Ex-Soldier Gets Life for Killings in Iraq." *New York Times,* May 22, 2009.

De Leon, Celina R. "For Female Soldiers, Sexual Assault Remains a Danger." *AlterNet,* January 5, 2007. http://www.alternet.com (accessed January 30, 2007).

DeFao, Janine. "Prison Scandal Mars Return for Veterans." *San Francisco Chronicle,* July 25, 2004.

del Castillo, Richard Griswold, ed. *World War II and Mexican American Civil Rights.* Austin: University of Texas Press, 2007.

Diener, Sam. "Countering Military Recruitment in Schools." *Peacework,* September 2008, 15.

———. "Military Recruiting Test Ensnares over 600,000 Students a Year." *Peacework,* February 2007, 24.

Dillow, Gordon. "Dillow in Iraq: Haditha Prospers as 'Massacre' Fades." *Orange Country Register,* September 26, 2008.

Dodge, Toby. *Inventing Iraq: The Failure of Nation Building and a History Denied.* New York: Columbia University Press, 2005.

Domosh, Mona, and Joni Seager. *Putting Women in Place: Feminist Geographers Make Sense of the World.* New York: Guilford Press, 2001.

Drakulic, Slavenka. *The Balkan Express.* New York: Harper Perennial, 1993.

Dwyer, Timothy. "Wounded Soldiers Are Adapting to Altered Lives." *Washington Post,* August 11, 2004. http://www.washingtonpost.com/wp-dyn/articles/A54883–2004August11 (accessed March 8, 2009).

———. "The Wounded." *New York Times Magazine,* March 27, 2005, 26–27.

Edwar, Hanaa. Paper, conference, "Post-election Iraq: What's Next for Women," Middle East Program, Woodrow Wilson International Center for Scholars, Washington, DC, January 19, 2006. http://www.wilsoncenter.org/index.cfm?topic_id=1426 &fuseaction+t (accessed January 6, 2009).

Elass, Rasha. "Iraq Refugee Crisis Engulfs Women Silenced by Rape." *Women's eNews,* April 1, 2007. http://www.womensenews.org/article.cfm/dyn/aid/3116 (accessed August 20, 2008).

El-Khodary, Taghreed. "For War Widows, Hamas Recruits Army of Husbands." *New York Times,* October 31, 2008.

Enloe, Cynthia. *Bananas, Beaches, and Bases: Making Feminist Sense of International Politics.* 2nd ed. Berkeley: University of California Press, 2000.

———. *The Curious Feminist: Searching for Women in a New Age of Empire.* Berkeley: University of California Press, 2004.

———. *Ethnic Soldiers: State Security in Divided Societies.* London: Penguin Books, 1980.

———. "Feminism and War: Stopping Militarism, Critiquing War." In *Feminism and War: Confronting U.S. Imperialism,* edited by Robin L. Riley, Chandra Talpade Mohanty, and Minnie Bruce Pratt, 258–63. London: Zed Books, 2008.

———. *Globalization and Militarism: Feminists Make the Link.* Lanham, MD: Rowman and Littlefield, 2007.

———. *Maneuvers: The International Politics of Militarizing Women's Lives.* Berkeley: University of California Press, 2000.

———. *The Morning After: Sexual Politics at the End of the Cold War.* Berkeley: University of California Press, 1993.

Fagen, Patricia Weiss. *Iraqi Refugees: Seeking Stability in Syria and Jordan.* Washington, DC: Institute for the Study of International Migration and Center for International and Regional Studies, Georgetown University, 2007.

Fainaru, Steve. *Big Boy Rules: America's Mercenaries Fighting in Iraq.* Philadelphia: Da Capo Press, 2008.

Fairfield, Hannah. "Money, Unspent, in Iraq's Pocket." *New York Times,* October 30, 2008.

Fang, Bay. "The Talibanization of Iraq." *Ms. Magazine,* Spring 2007, 46–51.

Fassihi, Farnaz. *Waiting for an Ordinary Day: The Unravelling of Life in Iraq.* New York: Public Affairs, 2008.

Faust, Drew Gilpin. *This Republic of Suffering: Death and the American Civil War.* New York: Alfred A. Knopf, 2008.

Filipovic, Zlata, and Melanie Challenger, eds. *Stolen Voices: Young People's War Diaries, from World War I to Iraq.* New York: Penguin Books, 2006.

Filkins, Dexter. "Afghan Girls, Scarred by Acid, Defy Terror, Embracing School." *New York Times,* January 14, 2009.

Fisher, Ian. "Iraq Elections Face Crucial Test in Violent Mosul." *New York Times,* January 30, 2009.

Franceschet, Susan, and Jennifer M. Piscopo. "Gender Quotas and Women's Substantive Representation: Lessons from Argentina." *Politics and Gender* 4, no. 3 (September 2008): 393–425.

Frank, Dana. *Bananeras: Women Transforming the Banana Unions of Latin America*. Boston: South End Press, 2005.

Frank, Nathaniel. *Unfriendly Fire: How the Gay Ban Undermines the Military and Weakens America*. New York: St. Martin's Press, 2009.

Frustuck, Sabina. *Uneasy Warriors: Gender, Memory, and Popular Culture in the Japanese Army*. Berkeley: University of California Press, 2007.

Garcia-Navarro, Lourdes. "Analysis: Power of Iraqi Women." National Public Radio (NPR), December 20, 2004. http://www.highbeam.com/doc/1P1–103594900.htm (accessed September 13, 2008).

———. "Iraqi Army Eases Militias' Grip on Women in Basra." NPR, May 27, 2008. http://www.npr.org/templates/story/story.php?storyId = 90840993.

———. "Treating Iraqi Children for PTSD." *Morning Edition,* NPR, August 26, 2008. http://www.npr.org/templates/story/story.php?storyId = 93937972.

———. "Widows Face Challenges, Tough Conditions in Iraq." *All Things Considered,* NPR, October 1, 2008. http://nl.mewsbank.com/nl-search/we/Archives?p_action = doc &p_docid = 123934A814 (accessed February 3, 2009).

Geron, Kim. *Latino Political Power: Latinos, Exploring Diversity and Change*. Boulder, CO: Lynne Rienner, 2005.

Gettleman, Jeffrey. "Sectarian Suspicion in Baghdad Fuels a Seller's Market for Guns." *New York Times,* April 3, 2006.

Giles, Wenona, and Jennifer Hyndman, eds. *Sites of Violence: Gender and Conflict Zones*. Berkeley: University of California Press, 2004.

Gillan, Audrey. "Diversity in Forces Slow to Improve." *Guardian,* January 13, 2009.

Gillem, Mark L. *America Town: Building the Outposts of Empire*. Minneapolis: University of Minnesota Press, 2007.

Glantz, Aaron. *The War Comes Home: Washington's Battle Against America's Veterans*. Berkeley: University of California Press, 2009.

Glanz, James. "Some Fear Iraq's Charter Will Erode Women's Rights." *New York Times,* August 8, 2005.

———, and T. Christian Miller. "Official History Spotlights Iraq Rebuilding Blunders." *New York Times,* December 14, 2008.

Golden Oak Montessori. "Charter Founding Members." August 4, 2008. http://www.goldenoackmontessori.org/?p = 111 (accessed February 2, 2009).

Goode, Erica. "War That Traumatizes Iraqis Take Toll on Hospital That Treats Them." *New York Times,* May 20, 2008.

Gordon, Michael R. "For Training Iraq's Police, the Main Problem Was Time." *New York Times,* October 21, 2004.

Gorley, Melissa. "San Antonio Chapter of 'Blue Star Mothers' Gathers Support for Soldiers' Families." *Today's Catholic,* February 16, 2007.

"Graduation Day in Iraq." *Boston Globe,* January 27, 2009.

Grewal, Inderpal. *Transnational American Feminisms, Diasporas, Neoliberalisms.* Durham, NC: Duke University Press, 2007.

Grossman, David. *On Killing: The Psychological Cost of Learning to Kill in War and Society.* New York: Cambridge University Press, 1995.

"Guide to Iraqi Political Parties." BBC News, January 20, 2006. http://news.bbc.co .uk/2/hi/middle_east/4511450.stm (accessed January 7, 2009).

Hall, Nina, and Jacqui True. "Gender Mainstreaming in a Post-Conflict State." In *Gender and Global Politics in the Asia-Pacific,* edited by Bina D'Costa, and Katrina Lee-Koo, 159–74. New York: Palgrave-Macmillan, 2009.

Hamdani, Ali, and Ilana Ozernoy. "No Forwarding Address." *Atlantic,* March 2007.

Hamilton, William. "New Urbanism: It's in the Army Now." *New York Times,* June 8, 2006.

Hammond, Laura C. *This Place Will Become Home: Refugee Repatriation to Ethiopia.* Ithaca: Cornell University Press 2004.

Harman, Jane. "Finally, Some Progress in Combating Rape and Assault in the Military." *Huffington Post,* October 31, 2008.

———. "Rapists in the Ranks." *Los Angeles Times,* April 2, 2008.

Harrison, Deborah, and Lucie LaLiberte. *No Life Like It: Military Wives in Canada.* Toronto: James Lorimer, 1994.

Hassan, Nihal. "50,000 Iraqi Refugees Forced into Prostitution." *Independent,* June 24, 2007.

Hatem, Mervat F. "In the Shadow of the State: Changing Definitions of Arab Women's 'Developmental' Citizenship Rights." *Journal of Middle East Women's Studies* 1, no. 3 (2005): 20–40.

Henderson, Kristen. "Your Money at War." *New York Times,* February 9, 2007.

Henderson, Kristin. *While They're at War: The True Story of American Families on the Homefront.* Boston: Houghton Mifflin, 2006.

Herbert, Bob. "Abusing Iraqi Civilians." *New York Times,* July 10, 2007.

Hickley, Matthew. "He's Back: Mod Launches Own 'Action Man' Range of Toys to Boost Profile of Armed Forces." *Mail Online,* January 14, 2009. http://dailymail .co.uk/news/article-1115462/Hes-MoD-launches-ActionMan (accessed January 14, 2009).

Hillman, Elizabeth. "Front and Center: Sexual Violence in U.S. Military Law." *Politics and Society* 37, no. 1 (2009): 101–29.

Hine, Darlene Clark. *Hine Sight: Black Women and the Re-Construction of American History*. Bloomington: Indiana University Press, 1994.

Hodges, Chris, and Laila Al-Arian. *Collateral Damage: America's War against Iraqi Civilians*. New York: Nation Books, 2008.

Holmes, Georgina. "The Postcolonial Politics of Militarizing Rwandan Women." *Minerva: Journal of Women and War* 2, no. 2 (2008): 44–63.

Horn, Denise M. "Boots and Bedsheets: Constructing the Military Support System in a Time of War." In *Gender, War, and Militarism: Feminist Perspectives*, edited by Laura Sjoberg and Sandra Via. Forthcoming.

Houppert, Karen. *Home Fires Burning: Married to the Military—for Better or Worse*. New York: Ballantine Books, 2005.

———. "I Want You! The 3 R's: Reading, 'Riting, and Recruiting'." In *Security Disarmed: Critical Perspectives on Gender, Race, and Militarization*, edited by Barbara Sutton, Sandra Morgen, and Julie Novkov, 213–22. New Brunswick, NJ: Rutgers University Press, 2008.

Ifill, Gwen. *The Break-Through: Politics and Race in the Age of Obama*. New York: Doubleday, 2009.

Ikeya, Chie. "The Modern Burmese Woman and the Politics of Fashion in Colonial Burma." *Journal of Asian Studies* 67, no. 4 (November 2008): 1277–308.

Institute for Women's Policy Research. "The Gender Wage Gap: 2008." *Fact Sheet*, April 2009.

———. "Women's Vote Clinches Election Victory: 8 Million More Women than Men Voted for Obama." *News*, November 6, 2008.

International Committee of the Red Cross. "Iraq: No Let-up in the Humanitarian Crisis." March 2008. http://www.icrc.org/wb/eng/siteengo.nsf/htmlall/$file/ICRC (accessed September 3, 2008).

International Plan. *Because I Am a Girl*. London, 2007. http://www.plan-international.org/reseources/publications/childrights/becauseiamagirl/ (accessed December 8, 2008).

"Investigating Officer's Report (of Charges Under Article 32 UCMJ 405 Manual for Courts Martial)," [n.d.]. http://64.233.169.132/search?q=cache:1asDBS2Wr6UJ:war chronicle (accessed December 10, 2008).

IRAQ Directory. "The Finance Committee: No Financial Collapse in Iraq." February 13, 2009. http://www.iraqdirectory.com/DisplayNews.aspx?id = 8451.

"Iraqi Governing Council Initiates Shari'a—Iraqi Women Protest." *Peacework*, February 2004, 17.

"Iraqi MP Challenges Speaker of Parliament." http://www.govtube.com/watch ?v+qq1x2kvhp20 (accessed December 30, 2008).

Integrated Regional Information Networks (IRIN). "Iraq: Minister of Women's Affairs Tenders Resignation." 9 February 2009. http://www.alternet.org/theen-ews/newsdesk/IRIN/d778a3aeb0280de2f90d43ed45b284e5.htm (accessed March 2, 2009).

———. "Iraq: Number of Girls Attending School Dropping, Say Analysts." Reuters and *AlterNet,* October 29, 2007. http://www.alternet.org/thenews/newsdesk/ IRIN/378f4f07e8919edb3 (accessed December 26, 2008).

———. "Iraq: Unemployment Forces Female Professionals into Domestic Work." *WLUML Newsheet* 18, no. 3 (November 2006): 22.

———. "Iraq: Women Forced to Give up Their Jobs, Marriages." Reuters and *Alter-Net,* May 30, 2007. http://www.alternet.org/thenews/newsdesk/IRIN/4a66b6c2d 010e2842304ea70ed6e0877.htm (accessed July 6, 2007).

Ito, Ruri. "The 'Modern Girl' Question in the Periphery of Empire." In *The Modern Girl Around the World,* edited by the Modern Girl Around the World Research Group, 240–62. Durham, NC: Duke University Press, 2008.

Jahnkow, Rick. "How Peace Activists Can Win Access to Schools Equal to That of Military Recruiters." *Peacework,* March 2008, 5.

———. "Youth Targets of Military Recruitment: National Counter-Recruitment Movement Enters a New Stage." *Resist Newsletter,* December 2004, 6–7.

Jarrar, Raed. "Security Without Empire Conference." Plenary presentation, American University, Washington, DC, February 28, 2009.

Jaywaradena, Kumari. *Feminism and Nationalism in the Third World.* London: Zed Books, 1986.

Jenning, Kathleen M. "The Political Economy of DDR in Liberia: A Gendered Critique." Paper, International Studies Association annual meeting, San Francisco, March 26–29, 2008.

Johnson, Anna. "Iraqi Women as Police Officers." *Seattle Times,* September 13, 2008.

Jordan, Harold. "Making Student Soldiers: JROTC Academies." *On Watch: Newsletter of the National Lawyers Guild Military Task Force* (San Diego, CA) 16, nos. 2–3 (November 1995): 5.

Joshi, Vijaya. "Building Opportunities: Women's Organizing, Militarism and the United Nations Transitional Administration in East Timor." PhD dissertation, Clark University, Worcester, MA, 2005.

Kamber, Michael. "Wounded Iraqi Forces Say They've Been Abandoned." *New York Times,* July 1, 2008.

Kami, Aseel. "Iraq's Policewomen Struggle to Change Perceptions." Reuters. Reprinted in *Spare Change News,* April 23–May 1, 2009, 6.

Karpinski, Janice. *One Woman's Army: The Commanding General of Abu Ghraib Tells Her Story.* New York: Hyperion, 2005.

Katie Couric Investigates. CBS News, January 28, 2009. http://www.cbsnews.com/blogs/2009/01/28/couricandco/entry4760522.shtml (accessed January 29, 2009).

Kaufman, Leslie. "Enlisting the Aid of Hairstylists as Sentinels for Domestic Abuse." *New York Times,* November 20, 2008.

Kershaw, Sarah. "For Citizen Soldiers, an Unexpected Burden." *New York Times,* September 15, 2003.

Kim, Seung-kyung. *Class Struggle or Family Struggle? The Lives of Women Factory Workers in South Korea.* New York: Cambridge University Press, 1997.

King, Diane E. "The Personal Is Patrilineal: Namus as Sovereignty." *Identities: Global Studies in Culture and Power* 15 (2008): 317–42.

Klein, Naomi. *The Shock Doctrine: The Rise of Disaster Capitalism.* New York: Metropolitan Books / Henry Holt, 2007.

Knickmeyer, Ellen. "Baghdad Neighborhood's Hopes Dimmed by the Trials of War" *Washington Post,* September 27, 2005.

———. "Slowly, Iraq Brings Refugees Home as Security Improves." *Washington Post,* September 8, 2008.

Korac, Maja. *Remaking Home: Reconstructing Life, Place and Identity in Rome and Amsterdam.* [New York]: Berghahn Books, 2009.

Koss, Joshua. "How the VA Abandons Our Vets." *Nation,* September 15, 2008, 15–20.

Kwon, Insook. "'The New Women's Movement' in 1920s Korea." *Gender and History* 10, no. 3 (November 1998): 381–405.

Lasky, Marjorie P. "Iraqi Women under Siege." San Francisco: Code Pink: Women for Peace and Global Exchange, 2006.

Latina Feminist Group. *Telling to Live: Latina Feminist Testimonios (Latin America otherwise).* Durham, NC: Duke University Press, 2001.

Lattu, Kirsti. *To Complain or Not to Complain: Still the Question; Consultations with Humanitarian Aid Beneficiaries on Their Perceptions of Efforts to Prevent and Respond to Sexual Exploitation and Abuse.* Geneva: Humanitarian Accountability Partnership, 2008.

Lewis, Stephen. "Peacekeepers Must Protect Women." AIDS-Free World, May 27, 2008. http://www.aids-freeworld.org/content/view/157/153 (accessed December 19, 2008).

Lipman, Jana K. *Guantánamo: A Working-Class History between Empire and Revolution.* Berkeley: University of California Press, 2009.

Lobasz, Jennifer K. "Women in Peril and the Ruined Woman: Representations of Female Soldiers in the Iraq War." *Journal of Women, Politics and Policy* 29, no. 3 (2008): 305–34.

Lobe, Jim. "Administration Chooses Anti-Feminist Group to Train Iraqi Women." *Commondreams.org,* February 28, 2004. http://www.commondreams.org/headlines04/1005–05.htm (accessed September 14, 2008).

Londono, Ernesto. "Forged by Loss, War Widows Embrace New Roles." *Boston Globe,* April 27, 2008.

Lovato, Roberto. "The War for Latinos." *Nation,* October 3, 2005.

Lown, Judy. *Women and Industrialization: Gender at Work in Nineteenth-Century England.* Minneapolis: University of Minnesota Press, 1990.

Lucey, Joyce, and Kevin Lucey. "Joyce and Kevin Lucey." In *For Love of a Soldier,* ed. Jane Collins, 155–72. Lanham, MD: Lexington Books, 2008.

Luo, Michael. "Soldiers Testify Over Poor Care at Walter Reed." *New York Times,* March 6, 2007.

Lutz, Catherine, *Homefront: A Military City and the American Twentieth Century.* Boston: Beacon Press, 2001.

———. "Living Room Terrorists." In Sutton, Morgen, and Novkov, *Security Disarmed,* 223–27.

———, ed. *The Bases of Empire: The Global Struggle Against U.S. Military Posts.* New York: New York University Press, 2009.

———, and Lesley Bartlett. *Making Soldiers in the Public Schools: An Analysis of the Army ROTC Curriculum.* Philadelphia: American Friends Service Committee, 1995.

MacQuarrie, Brian. "Army Scouting NASCAR Circuit." *Boston Globe,* August 28, 2005.

Macur, Juliet. "Two Women Bound by Sports, War and Injuries." *New York Times,* April 10, 2005.

Mahmoud, Houzan. "Secular Resistance Movement in Iraq." *Peacework,* June 2006, 13.

Manning, Lory. *Women in the Military: Where They Stand.* 3rd–6th eds. Washington, DC: Women's Research and Education Institute, 2000, 2003, 2005, 2008.

Mansbridge, Jane. "Quota Problems: Combating the Dangers of Essentialism." *Politics and Gender* 1, no. 4 (2005): 622–38.

Mariscal, Jorge. "Homeland Security, Militarism, and the Future of Latinos and Latinas in the United States." *Radical History Review* 93 (Fall 2005): 39–52.

Marshall, Carolyn. "On a Marine Base, Disbelief over Charges." *New York Times,* May 30, 2006.

Marshall, Linda. "Yanar Mohammed Talks About the Impact of the U.S. Occupation." *Off Our Backs,* July–August 2004, 14–15.

Martin, Michel. "Shoshana Johnson on Life after Iraq." Interview with Shoshana Johnson, *Tell Me More,* NPR, May 28, 2007.

Mathers, Jennifer G. "Russia's Women Soldiers in the Twenty-First Century." *Minerva: Journal of Women and War* 1, no. 1 (Spring 2007): 8–18.

Mazurana, Dyan, and Khristopher Carlson. "The Girl Child and Armed Conflict: Recognizing and Addressing Grave Violations of Girls' Human Rights." Division for the Advancement of Women, United Nations, New York, September 2006.

———, and Susan McKay. *Where Are the Girls? Girls in Fighting Forces in Northern Uganda, Sierra Leone and Mozambique: Their Lives During and after War.* Montreal: Rights and Democracy; International Centre for Human Rights and Democratic Development, 2004.

Mazzetti, Mark. "U.S. Says C.I.A. Destroyed 92 Tapes of Interrogations." *New York Times,* March 3, 2009.

McGreal, Chris. "Horror and Stresses of Iraq Duty." *Guardian,* May 16, 2009.

Moffeit, Miles. "Rumsfeld Draws Fire on Military Sex Assaults." *Denver Post,* April 16, 2004. http://www.denverpost.com/Stories/0,1413,36~30137~2087145,00.html (accessed May 23, 2004).

———, and Amy Herdy. "Betrayal in the Ranks: Military Response to Rapes, Domestic Abuse Falls Short." *Denver Post,* November 16–18, 2003. http://www.denverpost.com/Stories/0,0.36%257E30137%257E1773329,00.html (accessed May 23, 2004).

———. "Female GIs Report Rapes in Iraq War." *Denver Post,* January 25, 2004. http://www.denverpost.com/Stories/0,1413.36%257E27059%257E1913069,00.html (accessed May 23, 2004).

Mojab, Shahrzad. "No 'Safe Haven' for Women: Violence against Women in Iraqi Kurdistan." In Giles and Hyndman, *Sites of Violence,* 108–33.

Montgomery, David. "After the War, a Struggle for Equality." *Washington Post,* September 22, 2007.

Moon, Katherine. "Military Prostitution and the U.S. Military in Asia." *Asia-Pacific Journal: Japan Focus,* 2009. http://www.japanfocus.org/_Katherine_H_S__Moon -Military_Prostitution_and_the_U.S.__Military_in_Asia (accessed January 19, 2009).

Moore, Brenda. *To Serve My Country, to Serve My Race.* New York: State University of New York Press, 1995.

Mor, Tzili. "WILPF Challenges U.S. Army Central Tactics." *Peace and Freedom,* Spring 2008, 4–5.

Morkert, Michelle. "Securing the Heartland: The Militarization of American Women's Lives in One Small Midwestern Town During the Iraqi and Afghanistan Wars, 2003–2006." Ph.D. dissertation, Clark University, Worcester, MA, 2007.

Musheno, Michael, and Susan M. Ross. *Deployed: How Reservists Bear the Burden of Iraq.* Ann Arbor: University of Michigan Press, 2008.

Myers, Steven Lee. "Woman Held by Iraq Is Accused of Recruiting Suicide Bombers." *New York Times,* February 4, 2009.

———, and Sam Dagher. "After Orderly Elections in Iraq, the Next Big Test Is Acceptance." *New York Times,* February 10, 2009.

Nadelson, Theodore. *Trained to Kill: Soldiers at War.* Baltimore, MD: Johns Hopkins University Press, 2005.

"Names of the Dead." *New York Times,* January 28, 2009.

Newbury, Catherine, and Hannah Baldwin. "Aftermath: Women's Organizations in Postconflict Rwanda." Working paper no. 304, Center for Development Information and Evaluation, U.S. Agency for International Development, Washington, DC, July 2000.

Nordstrom, Carolyn. *Shadows of War: Violence, Power, and International Profiteering in the Twenty-First Century.* Berkeley: University of California Press, 2004.

Nusair, Isis. "Gendered Politics of Location of Three Generations of Palestinian Women in Israel, 1948–1998." Ph.D. dissertation, Clark University, Worcester, MA, 2007.

O'Brien, Suzanne G. "Splitting Hairs: History and the Politics of Daily Life in Nineteenth-Century Japan." *Journal of Asian Studies* 67, no. 4 (November 2008): 1309–39.

Oropeza, Lorena. *¡Raza sí! ¡Guerra no! Chicano Protest and Patriotism During the Viet Nam War Era.* Berkeley: University of California Press, 2005.

Ossman, Susan. *Three Faces of Beauty: Casablanca, Paris, Cairo.* Durham, NC: Duke University Press, 2002.

Oxfam International. "In Her Own Words: Iraqi Women Talk About Their Greatest Concerns and Challenges." Oxford, March 8, 2009. http://www.oxfam.org.uk/resources/policy/conflict_disasters/iraq-in-her-own-words (accessed March 9, 2009).

Oza, Rupal. *The Making of Neoliberal India.* New York: Routledge, 2006.

Pagán, Eduardo Obregón. *Murder at the Sleepy Lagoon: Zoot Suits, Race, and Riot in Wartime L.A.* Chapel Hill: University of North Carolina Press, 2003.

Pao-Tao, Chris-Lin, and Xueliang Wang. "Military Wives in China, 1127–1279." *Minerva: Quarterly Report on Women and the Military* 18, no. 1 (Spring 2000): 7–33.

Parpart, Jane L. and Marysia Zalewski, eds. *Rethinking the Man Question: Sex, Gender and Violence in International Relations.* London: Zed Books, 2008.

Partlow, Joshua. "Widows Strain Welfare System in Iraq." *Washington Post,* July 23, 2006.

Perry, Tony. "Marine to Stand Trial in Haditha Killings." *Los Angeles Times,* January 1, 2008.

Physicians for Human Rights. "Nowhere to Turn: Failure to Protect, Support and

Assure Justice for Darfuri Women." May 2009. http://physiciansforhumanrights
.org/library/report-2009–05–31.html (accessed June 4, 2009).

Pierce, Charles P. "The Forgotten War." *Boston Globe Magazine,* November 2, 2008.

Porter, Eduardo. "Advertising: Army's Hispanic-Recruitment Ads Cater to Mom."
Wall Street Journal, May 24, 2002.

Priest, Dana and Ann Hall. "Soldiers Face Neglect, Frustration at Army's Top Medical Facility." *Washington Post,* February 18, 2007.

Project on the Status and Education of Women. *What Constitutes Equality for Women
in Sport? Federal Law Puts Women in the Running.* Washington, DC: Association of
American Colleges, 1975.

———. *Update on Title IX and Sports, no. 3.* Washington, DC: Association of American
Colleges, 1980.

Puechguirbal, Nadine. "Peacekeeping, Peace Building and Post-conflict Reconstruction." In *Gender Matters,* edited by Laura Shepherd. London: Routledge, 2010.

Pupovic, Jessica. "Silence in the Barracks." *In These Times,* March 2008, 25.

Raddatz, Martha. *The Long Road Home: The Story of War and Family.* New York: Berkeley Books, 2008.

Raghaven, Sudarsan. "An End to Baghdad's 'Dark Era.'" *Washington Post,* February
28, 2009.

Ramirez, Catherine S. *The Woman in the Zoot Suit: Gender, Nationalism, and the Cultural
Politics of Memory.* Durham, NC: Duke University Press, 2009.

Rand Corporation, Center for Military Health Policy Research. *Invisible Wounds of
War.* Santa Monica, CA: Rand Corporation, 2008. http://www.rand.org/pubs/
monographs/2008/RAND_MG720.pdf (accessed March 20, 2008).

Rath, Arun, dir. *Rules of Engagement:* Frontline and Yellow River Productions, PBS,
2008.

Refugees International. "The Iraqi Displacement Crisis." July 18, 2008. http://www
.refugeesinternational.org/content/article/detail/9679 (accessed September 27,
2008).

Relief from Relief. "'Go Tell Your Manager': Sexual Harassment in Aid Agencies."
Humanitarian Relief, February 2, 2009.

Reuters. "Not All Troops Would Report Iraq Abuse, Study Says." *New York Times,*
May 5, 2007.

Riverbend. *Baghdad Burning: Girl Blog from Iraq.* New York: Feminist Press at the City
University of New York, 2005.

———. *Baghdad Burning,* vol. 2, *More Girl Blog from Iraq.* Women Writing the Middle
East. New York: Feminist Press at CUNY, 2006.

Roberts, Sam. "A Generation Away, Minorities May Become the Majority in U.S." *New York Times,* August 14, 2008.

Robertson, Campbell. "New Rules in Iraq Add Police Work to Troops' Jobs." *New York Times,* December 31, 2008.

———, and Stephen Farrell. "Green Zone, Heart of U.S. Occupation, Reverts to Iraqi Control." *New York Times,* January 1, 2009.

Rodriguez, Deborah. *Kabul Beauty School: An American Woman Goes Behind the Veil.* New York: Random House, 2007.

Rubin, Alissa J. "Militants Show a New Boldness in Cities in Iraq." *New York Times,* April 1, 2009.

———. "More Iraqi Dead Last Month, but Fewer Than Last Year." *New York Times,* December 1, 2008.

———. "Pointing to New Era, U.S. Steps Back as Iraqis Vote." *New York Times,* February 1, 2009.

———. "Secular Parties and Premier Ahead in Iraq." *New York Times,* February 2, 2009.

———, and Rod Nordland. "U.S. Military Expresses Concern About Perception of an Iraqi Crackdown on Sunnis." *New York Times,* April 16, 2009.

———, and Sam Dagher. "Election Quotas for Iraqi Women Are Weakened, Provoking Anger as Vote Nears." *New York Times,* January 14, 2009.

Sacchet, Teresa. "Beyond Numbers: The Impact of Gender Quotas in Latin America." *International Feminist Journal of Politics* 10, no. 3 (2008): 369–90.

"Saddam's Execution Brings Satisfaction, Unease." *My SA News, San Antonio Express-News,* December 29, 2006. http://www.mysanantonio.com/news/MYSA123006_11A_saddams_dead (accessed January 10, 2009).

Saint George, Donna. "Limbs Lost to Enemy Fire, Women Forge New Reality." *Washington Post,* April 18, 2006.

Salman, Duraed, and Nasr Khadhim. "Beauty Salons Back in Business." Institute for War and Peace Reporting. http://www.iwpr.net/?p = icr &so = f &o = 345783 &apc_state = henficr345816 (accessed August 20, 2008).

Sanchez, Mark, and Dan Kelly. "San Francisco Votes to Replace JROTC: First City to Eject High School Military Program." *Peacework,* 2006–January 2007, 13.

Santora, Marc. "Rape Accusation Reinforces Fears in a Divided Iraq." *New York Times,* February 21, 2007.

———, and Suadad N. Al-Salhy. "Iraqi Tribes Are Upset by Sentence Given to G.I.," *New York Times,* May 23, 2009.

Schmitt, Eric, and David S. Cloud. "Military Inquiry Is Said to Oppose Account of Raid." *New York Times,* May 31, 2007.

Scranton, Deborah, dir. *The War Tapes*. Senart Films and Scranton/Lacy Films, 2007.

———. *Bad Voodoo's War. Frontline* film. PBS, WGBH Educational Foundation, Boston, 2008.

Seager, Joni. *Penguin Atlas of Women in the World*. 4th ed. New York: Penguin Books, 2008.

———. "The State of Gender-Disaggregated Data on Water and Sanitation: An Overview and Assessment of Major Sources." Paper, Expert Group Meeting on Gender-Disaggregated Data on Water and Sanitation, United Nations, New York, December 2–3, 2008.

———, and Ann Olson. *Women in the World: An International Atlas*. New York: Simon and Schuster, 1986.

Seligman, Melissa. "One Husband, Two Kids, Three Deployments." *New York Times*, May 25, 2009.

Sengupta, Somini. "For Iraqi Girls, Changing Land Narrows Lives." *New York Times*, June 27, 2004.

Servicemembers Legal Defense Network. "Women in Uniform Disproportionately Affected by 'Don't Ask, Don't Tell' Law." June 23, 2008. http://www.sldn.org (accessed July 3, 2008).

Shadid, Anthony. *Night Draws Near: Iraq's People in the Shadow of America's War*. New York: Henry Holt, 2005

Shane, Scott. "A Deluge of Troubled Soldiers Is in the Offing, Experts Predict" *New York Times*, December 16, 2004.

Shanker, Thom. "G.I.s Filling Civilian Gap To Rebuild Afghanistan." *New York Times*, April 23, 2009.

———. "New Lessons for the Army." *New York Times*, February 19, 2009.

———, Eric Schmitt, and Richard Oppel. "Military Expected to Report Marines Killed Iraqi Civilians." *New York Times*, May 26, 2006.

Sheehan, Cindy. Introduction, and "You May Be Killed." In *Ten Reasons Not to Join the Military*, edited by Elizabeth Weill-Greenberg, 1–5, 7–15. New York: New Press, 2006.

Shigematsu, Setsu, with Anuradha Kristina Bhagwati, and Eli Painted Crow. "Women of Color Veterans on War, Militarism and Feminism." In Riley, Mohanty, and Pratt, *Feminism and War*, 93–102.

Sinjab, Lina. "Prostitution Ordeal of Iraqi Girls." BBC News, December 3, 2007. http://www.bbc.co.uk/2/hi/middle_east/7119473.stm (accessed August 30, 2008).

Slatella, Michelle. "Online Shopper: Home Front? Combat? A Mission for Barbie." *New York Times*, October 19, 2001.

Sly, Liz. "Suspect in Killing of 5 US Troops Had Weapon Confiscated." *Boston Globe*, May 13, 2009.

Smith, Suzanne M., and Sam Diener. "Recruiters Target DC, Hawai'i, Rest of Country." *Peacework*, June–July 2005.

Soguel, Dominique. "In Syrian Refuge, Women Find Barest Survival." *Women's eNews*, August 10, 2008. http://www.womensenews.org/article.cfm/dyn/aid (accessed August 20, 2008).

The Soldier's Heart. Frontline film. PBS, WGBH Educational Foundation, Boston, 2005.

Sontag, Deborah. "An Iraq Veteran's Descent; a Prosecutor's Choice." *New York Times*, January 20, 2008.

———, and Lizette Alvarez. "Across America, Deadly Echoes of Foreign Battles," *New York Times*, January 13, 2008.

———. "Combat Trauma Takes the Witness Stand." *New York Times*, January 27, 2008.

Sperling, Valerie. *Organizing Women in Contemporary Russia: Engendering Transition.* Cambridge: Cambridge University Press, 1999.

Staudt, Kathleen. *Violence and Activism at the Border: Gender, Fear and Everyday Life in Ciudad Juárez.* Austin: University of Texas Press, 2008.

Stephen, Lynn. "Los Nuevos Desaparecidos y Muertos: Immigration, Militarization, Death and Disappearance on Mexico's Borders." In Sutton, Morgen, and Novkov, *Security Disarmed*, 79–100.

Sutton, Denise. *Globalizing Ideal Beauty: How the Women Copywriters of J. Walter Thompson Contributed to a Global Concept of Beauty.* New York: Palgrave Macmillan, 2009.

Tai, Hue-Tam Ho. *Radicalism and the Origins of the Vietnamese Revolution.* Cambridge, MA: Harvard University Press, 1992.

Tang, Alisa. "Lives on the Line." *Ms. Magazine*, Winter 2009, 53.

Tanner, Adam. "Soldiers Back in U.S. Tell More of Iraqi Abuses." Reuters, May 7, 2004. http://www.commondreams.org/headlines04/0507–02.htm (accessed March 8, 2009).

Tapscott, Don. "The Girl Effect." *Businessweek*, January 31, 2009. http://www.com/careers/management/archives/2009/01/the_girl_effect.html (accessed February 4, 2009).

Tarabay, Jamie. "Iraq Struggles to Cope with Returning Refugees." Washington, DC: NPR, September 3, 2008.

Tavernise, Sabrina. "Aftereffects: Rights and Tolerance; Iraqi Women Wary of New Upheavals." *New York Times*, May 5, 2003.

———. "Fear Keeps Iraqis out of Their Baghdad Homes." *New York Times*, August 24, 2008.

———. "Iraq Power Shift Widens a Gulf between Sects." *New York Times,* February 18, 2006.

———. "Sectarian Toll Includes Scars to Iraq Psyche." *New York Times,* September 17, 2007.

———. "Shielding Women from a Renewal of Domestic Violence." *New York Times,* October 14, 2004.

———. "The Struggle for Iraq: A Fresh Pattern of Revenge Fuels Increasingly Personal Baghdad Killings." *New York Times,* November 20, 2006.

Taylor, Matthew, and Shane Croucher. "MoD Investigates Race Hate on Web." *Guardian,* January 19, 2009.

Teaiwa, Teresia K., "Globalizing and Gendered Forces: Contemporary Militarization of Pacific/Oceania." In *Gender and Globalization in Asia and the Pacific,* edited by Kathy Ferguson and Monique Mironesco, 318–332. Honolulu: University of Hawaii Press, 2008.

Trustram, Myna. *Women of the Regiment: Marriage and the Victorian Army.* Cambridge: Cambridge University Press, 1984.

Tyson, Ann Scott. "Bid to Limit Women in Combat Withdrawn." *Washington Post,* May 26, 2005.

UNICEF. *A World Fit for Children, Statistical Review, 2007.* New York: United Nations, 2007.

United Nations Educational, Scientific, and Cultural Organization (UNESCO). "UNESCO and Education IRAQ Fact Sheet (28 March 2003)." http://portal. unesco.org/en/ev.php-URL_ID = 11216 &URL_DO = DO (accessed December 21, 2008).

———. "Beyond 20/20 WDS—Report Folders: Time Series Data: Secondary Education/Enrolment." Paris, 2005. http://stats.uis.unesco.org/unesco/ReportFolders/ReportFolders.aspx (accessed December 21, 2008).

United Nations High Commission for Refugees (UNHCR). *Handbook for the Protection of Women and Girls.* March 6, 2008. http://unhcr.org/protect/PROTECTION/47cfae612.html (accessed November 29, 2008).

———."The World of Refugee Women at a Glance." *Refugee Magazine* 126, October 9, 2008. http://unhcr.org/publ/PUBL/3cb6ea290.html (accessed November 30, 2008).

United States Department of Defense. Office of Inspector General. *Tailhook 1991,* pt. 1, *Review of the Navy Investigations.* Washington, DC, 1992.

———. Office of the Under Secretary of Defense, Personnel, and Readiness. *2006 Population Representation in the Military Services.* Washington, DC, January 2008.

Vine, David. *Island of Shame: The Secret History of the U.S. Military Base on Diego Garcia.* Princeton: Princeton University Press, 2009.

———. "Too Many Overseas Bases." *Foreign Policy in Focus,* February 25, 2009.

"Voices of Iraq." September 23, 2007. http://warnewstoday.blogs.pot.com/2007_09_01_ocrdian.html (accessed December 30, 2008).

Von Zielbauer, Paul. "At Least 5 Marines Are Expected to Be Charged in Haditha Deaths." *New York Times,* December 6, 2006.

———. "Case Against U.S. Marine Dismissed." *New York Times,* March 29, 2008.

———. "Forensic Experts Testify That 4 Iraqis Killed by Marines Were Shot from a Few Feet Away." *New York Times,* June 15, 2007.

———. "General and 2 Colonels Censured for Poor Investigation into Haditha Killings." *New York Times,* September 6, 2007.

———. "Killings of Afghan Civilians Recall Haditha." *New York Times,* April 20, 2007.

———. "Lawyers on Haditha Panel Peer into Fog of War." *New York Times,* May 17, 2007.

———. "Marine Says His Staff Misled Him on Killings." *New York Times,* May 11, 2007.

———. "A Marine Tutorial on Media 'Spin.'" *New York Times,* June 24, 2007.

———. "Marines' Trials in Iraq Killings Are Withering." *New York Times,* August 30, 2007.

———. "Military Cites 'Negligence' in Aftermath of Iraq Killings." *New York Times,* April 22, 2007.

———. "Officer Says Civilian Toll in Haditha Was a Shock." *New York Times,* May 9, 2007.

———. "Propaganda Fear Cited in Account of Iraqi Killings." *New York Times,* May 6, 2007.

———. "U.S. Inquiry Backs Charges of Killings by Marines in Iraq." *New York Times,* June 7, 2007.

Vuskovic, Lina, and Zorica Trifunovic, eds. *Women's Side of War.* Belgrade: Women in Black, Belgrade, 2008.

Wajid, Sara. "The Battle against Brutality." *Guardian,* January 28, 2009.

Wall, Tyler. "'School Ownership Is the Goal': Public Schools, Military Recruiting and the Fronts of War." Paper, Association of American Geographers annual meeting, Boston, April 17, 2008.

Welchman, Lynn. *Women and Muslim Family Laws in Arab States: A Comparative Overview of Textual Development and Advocacy.* Amsterdam: Amsterdam University Press, 2007.

Weinstein, Laurie Lee, and Christie C. White, eds. *Wives and Warriors: Women and the Military in the United States and Canada.* Westport: Greenwood Press, 1997.

White, Josh. "Death in Haditha." *Washington Post,* January 6, 2007.

Williams, Joseph, and Kevin Baron. "Military Sees Big Decline in Black Enlistees." *Boston Globe,* October 7, 2007.

Williams, Kristen, and Joyce Kaufman. *Women, the State, and War.* Lanham, MD: Lexington Books, 2007.

Williams, Timothy. "In Dire Need, War's Widows Struggle in Iraq." *New York Times,* February 23, 2009.

——, and Suadad Al-Salhy. "Fate of Iraqis Gone Missing Haunts Those Left Behind." *New York Times,* May 25, 2009.

Winter, Bronwyn. "Preemptive Fridge Magnets and Other Weapons of Masculinist Destruction: The Rhetoric and Reality of 'Safegurading Australia.'" "War and Terror II: Raced-Gendered Logics and Effects Beyond Conflict Zones," edited by Mary Hawkesworth and Karen Alexander. Special issue, *Signs* 33, no. 1 (Autumn 2007): 25–52.

Witchel, Alex. "Confessions of a Military Wife." *New York Times Magazine,* November 6, 2005, 62–68.

Women and Child Rights Project. *Catwalk to the Barracks.* Bangkok: Women and Child Rights Project (southern Burma) in collaboration with Human Rights Foundation of Monland (Burma), 2005.

"Women in National Parliaments." Inter-Parliamentary Union. http://www.ipu.org/wmn-e/world.html (accessed January 5, 2007).

Women Living under Muslim Laws. "Iraq: Women's Rights under Attack—Occupation, Constitution, and Fundamentalisms." London: Act Together, occasional paper 15, December 2006.

Women of Color Resource Center and War Resisters' League. "What Every Girl Should Know About the U.S. Military: Consider This—Before You Enlist." Oakland, CA, 2008.

Women's Initiatives for Gender Justice. "Making a Statement: A Review of Charges and Prosecutions for Gender-Based Crimes before the International Court." The Hague, June 2008.

Women's Rights Watch. "Climate of Fear: Sexual Violence and Abduction of Women and Girls in Baghdad." Human Rights Watch, July 16, 2008. http:www.org/reports/2003/iraq0703/l.htm#_Toc45709960 (accessed September 17, 2008)

——. *Seeking Protection: Addressing Sexual and Domestic Violence in Tanzania's Refugee Camps.* New York: Human Rights Watch, 2000.

——. *Shattered Lives: Sexual Violence During the Rwandan Genocide and Its Aftermath.* New York: Human Rights Watch, 1996.

Wong, Edward. "Draft for New Iraqi Constitution Includes Curbs to Women's Rights." *New York Times,* July 20, 2005.

———. "Iraqi Widow Saves Her Home, but Victory Is Brief." *New York Times,* March 30, 2007.

———. "Job Pinch Trickles up in China as Economy Slumps." *New York Times,* January 25, 2009.

———. "On the Air, On Their Own: Iraqi Women Find a Forum." *New York Times,* September 4, 2005.

World Health Organization and Ministry of Health, Iraq. *Iraq Family Health Survey Report.* Geneva: World Health Organization, 2006–7. http://www.emro.who.int/iraq/pdf/his_report_en.pdf (accessed March 9, 2009).

World War 4 Report. "4,000 Women Run in Iraq's Provincial Elections: How Significant?" February 3, 2009. http://www.ww4report.com/node/6780 (accessed February 20, 2009).

Worth, Robert F. "In Jeans or Vells, Iraqi Women Are Split on New Political Power." *New York Times,* April 13, 2005.

Wright, Ann. "Sexual Assault in the Military: A DoD Cover-Up?" *Truthdig,* August 1, 2008. http://www.truthdig.com/report/item/20080801_sexual_assault_in_the_military (accessed September 25, 2008).

———, and Susan Dixon, eds. *Dissent—Voices of Conscience: Government Insiders Speak Out Against the War in Iraq.* Kihei, HA: Koa Books, 2008.

Wushanley, Ying. *Playing Nice and Losing: The Struggle for Control of Women's Intercollegiate Athletics, 1960–2000.* Syracuse: Syracuse University Press, 2001.

Younes, Kristele. "The World's Fastest Growing Displacement Crisis." Refugees International, March 2007. http://www.refugeesinternational.org/file_iraqreport.pdf (accessed September 27, 2008).

———, and Nir Rosen. "Uprooted and Unstable: Meeting Urgent Humanitarian Needs in Iraq." Refugees International, April 2008. http://refugeesinternational.org/file_unprotectedandunstable.pdf (accessed September 27, 2008).

Youth and Militarism Program. *Is JROTC a Wise Use of Class Time?* Philadelphia: American Friends Service Committee, 1998.

———. "No Child Left Behind Act: Recruiting in the Schools." Philadelphia: American Friends Service Committee, 2003.

Zangana, Haifa. *City of Widows: An Iraqi Woman's Account of War and Resistance.* New York: Seven Stories Press, 2007.

Zoepf, Katherine. "Iraqi Refugees, in Desperation Turn to the Sex Trade in Syria." *New York Times,* May 29, 2007.

INDEX

Text:	10/15 Janson
Display:	Janson
Compositor:	BookMatters, Berkeley
Indexer:	Michael Gossman
Printer and Binder:	Sheridan Books, Inc.